The Diagonal Line

The Diagonal Line

Separation and Reparation in American Literature

August J. Nigro

Selinsgrove: Susquehanna University Press
London and Toronto: Associated University Presses

© 1984 by Associated University Presses, Inc.

Associated University Presses
440 Forsgate Drive
Cranbury, NJ 08512

Associated University Presses
25 Sicilian Avenue
London WC1A 2QH, England

Associated University Presses
2133 Royal Windsor Drive
Unit 1
Mississauga, Ontario
Canada L5J 1K5

Library of Congress Cataloging in Publication Data

Nigro, August J., 1934–
   The diagonal line.

   Bibliography: p.
   Includes index.
   1. American literature—History and criticism.
2. Separation in literature. 3. Reparation in literature.
4. Myth in literature. 5. Fall of man in literature.
I. Title.
PS169.S43N53   1984   810'.9'3   83-50945
ISBN 0-941664-02-3

Printed in the United States of America

For
     my mother and father and Ruth

Here again, as so often, nature delights to put us between extreme antagonisms, and our safety is in the skill with which we keep the diagonal line. Solitude is impracticable, and society fatal. We must keep our heads in the one and our hands in the other. The conditions are met, if we keep our independence, yet do not lose our sympathy. These wonderful horses need to be driven by fine hands.

Ralph Waldo Emerson, *Society and Solitude*

Contents

Acknowledgments

I wish to thank the National Endowment for the Humanities for the opportunity to begin and develop this study during two summer seminars and a fellowship-in-residence, my seminar directors—Albert Friedman, Robert N. Bellah, and R. W. B. Lewis—for their suggestions and encouragement, and my fellow seminarians for their dialogue and support. I am also grateful to Hans Feldmann for his assistance in revising the manuscript and Gloria Heiter for hers in preparing it.

The interpretations of *The Scarlet Letter* and *Light in August* appeared respectively as articles in *The Drew Gateway* (1978) and *Susquehanna University Studies* (1982). Selections from *The Collected Poems of Wallace Stevens* are reprinted by permission of Alfred A. Knopf, copyright 1923, 1931, 1935, 1936, 1937, 1942, 1943, 1944, 1945, 1946, 1947, 1948, 1949, 1950, 1951, 1952, 1954 by Wallace Stevens.

Quotations from *The Complete Poems of Emily Dickinson* edited by Thomas H. Johnson are reprinted with the permission of Little, Brown & Company; poem #1461, copyright 1914 by Martha Dickinson Bianchi, copyright renewed 1942 by Martha Dickinson Bianchi; poems #281, 285, 341, 378, 379, 798, 906, 963, copyright 1929, 1935 by Martha Dickinson Bianchi, copyright © renewed 1957, 1963 by Mary L. Hampson; all other poems are reprinted by permission of the publishers and Trustees of Amherst College from *The Poems of Emily Dickinson* edited by Thomas H. Johnson, Harvard University Press Belknap Press, copyright 1951, 1955, 1979, 1983 by the President and Fellows of Harvard College.

Excerpts from *Collected Poems 1909–1962* by T. S. Eliot are reprinted by permission of Harcourt Brace Jovanovich, Inc. and Faber and Faber, Ltd.; copyright 1936 by Harcourt Brace

The Diagonal Line

1

A Great Fall: Myth and American Literature

Each man does penance for [his] separation from the boundless.

           Anaximander, *Die Fragmente der Vorsokratiker*

In seeking to discover the living and literary tradition out of which
the representative and significant works of American literature
emerge and which these same works reshape and thereby re-create,
many scholars and critics have discerned a national myth that gives
rise to thought that is dialectic. The myth has been variously desig-
nated as an American version of Eden and the Fall; it is implied in
the titles of some of the most important studies of American literature: *Virgin Land, The American Adam, The Quest for Paradise,
An End to Innocence,* and *The Machine in the Garden.* The
dialectic has been read as tension between innocence and experience, perfectibility and fallibility, self and society, the dream of
success and the nightmare of failure, the garden and the wasteland.
Following is a brief, selective review of some interpretations of
American myth and literature, a consideration of the significant
contribution made by these studies to an understanding of the
dialectic in that literature, and a suggestion of how the mythopoeia
of that understanding can be further expanded and the terms of the
dialectic more sharply focused.

    The critical concern with American literature, myth, and
dialectic probably begins with D. H. Lawrence's *Studies in Classic
American Literature* (1922), in which, commenting on Cooper's
Leatherstocking Tales, Lawrence writes, "The Leatherstocking
novels create the myth of this new relation. And they go back-

wards, from old age to golden youth. That is the true myth of America. She starts old, old, wrinkled and writhing in an old skin. And there is a gradual sloughing of the old skin, towards a new youth. It is the myth of America."[1]

Though Lawrence is not primarily concerned with tracing this myth in American literature and though his study reveals as much about Lawrence as it does about American literature, still his interpretation incisively points out elements of a dialectic that later becomes the basis for subsequent interpretations: the dialectic between an Adamic regeneration and an Adamic fall, between America as the Edenic garden and America as the demon-haunted forest, between the American dream of becoming and the contradictory reality of being.

The critical scope of F. O. Matthiessen's *American Renaissance* (1941) encompasses a reference to an American myth—the myth of democracy, of the common man, or, in the words of Walt Whitman, of "man in the open air." It is a myth that gives form and vitality to the comic, and cosmic, celebration of democracy in Emerson, Thoreau, and Whitman and to the tragic dimension of democracy in the fiction of Hawthorne and Melville. Because he concentrates on the literature written during the five years (1850–55) of the American renaissance and because his concern with myth is but a small part of a broad spectrum of aesthetic and social matters, Matthiessen's book, like Lawrence's, is more significant for what it suggests than for what it details about the possibilities of American myth and literature.

The unfolding of the American myth in criticism begins in the decade of the fifties with an exploration of the setting of the myth in Henry Nash Smith's *Virgin Land* (1950) and of the hero in R. W. B. Lewis's *The American Adam* (1955). In his study, Smith contrasts three symbols of the American frontier: the Wild West of romanticism, variously interpreted as a peaceful Eden or a hostile wilderness; a pastoral, agrarian society in which the American yeoman cultivates the garden of the western world; and the new industrial society that replaces the diminishing agrarian culture and closes the frontier. Thus, one of the significant polarities of the American myth is established in Smith's book—America as a peaceful, expansive Garden of Eden and America as a garden, but one wasted and abused by inherent, amoral natural forces and by technological industrialization.

Lewis, acknowledging his debt to Lawrence and Matthiessen, is the first consciously and deliberately to set about defining the myth that underlies the experience in American literature. He focuses his paradigm upon the hero of the ritual, the American as Adam, "an individual emancipated from history, happily bereft of ancestry, untouched and undefiled by the usual inheritances of family and race; an individual standing alone, self-reliant and self-propelling, ready to confront whatever awaited him with the aid of his own unique and inherent forces."[2] The response to this new hero and to this new adventure in the debate and literature of the nineteenth century takes the form of three parties, described by Lewis as the parties of hope, memory, and irony.

The party of hope celebrates the vision of the American Adam, and the key term in its moral vocabulary is innocence. The party of memory emphasizes rather the recurrence in the American experience of the sinfulness of man, and the most significant concept in its dialogue is inherited sin. The ironic temperament, which is characteristic of the best nineteeth-century fiction of Hawthorne, Melville, and James, is described by Lewis as tragic optimism—"a sense of the tragic collisions to which innocence was liable (something unthinkable among the hopeful), and equally by an awareness of the heightened perception and humanity which suffering made possible (something unthinkable among the nostalgic)."[3] Thus, the dialectic between innocence and memory is resolved for Lewis in the ironic initiation of the fallen American Adam into the world.

In the same year that Lewis published *The American Adam*, three other books appeared that supported or reinforced the myth and dialectic revealed in Lewis's study. In *An End to Innocence*, a collection of essays, Leslie Fiedler reiterates the tension between innocence and experience, examines in more detail the great guilt that pervades American literature, a guilt that results from the disillusionment of the American Dream, and, like Lewis, concludes that the "end of the American artist's pilgrimage to Europe is the discovery of America," the discovery that America's ideals are contrary to its practices and consequently that its dream of a utopia becomes a nightmare of an inferno. Frederic Carpenter in *American Literature and the Dream* views the myth of America primarily in political terms—as a dialectic between the dream of ideal democracy and the nightmare of the failure of that dream. In *The Dream of Success*, Kenneth Lynn reinterprets the Western hero in terms of the youth who seeks the realization of his dream in the very city and economy that the earlier Western hero had spurned. The archetypal hero and the basic fable of the new myth are repre-

sented in the Horatio Alger stories: "Alone, unaided, the ragged
boy is plunged into the maelstrom of the city life, but by his own
pluck and luck he capitalizes on one of the myriad opportunities
available to him and rises to the top of the economic heap."[4]

In an article published in 1959, "The American Myth: Paradise
(To Be) Regained," Carpenter, reviewing and synthesizing the
works of Smith, Lewis, Fiedler, Lynn, and himself, concludes that
"there have been two American myths—that of a paradise hope-
lessly lost, and that of a paradise ultimately to be regained. The
two have often been superimposed—the one upon the other—until
they have become confused, and in a sense have become one."[5]
With the advent of the sixties, this interpretation of the American
myth of a paradise to be regained is further developed. In *Radical
Innocence* (1961), Ihab Hassan extends Lewis's analysis of the matter of Adam to an examination of contemporary fiction, in which
he discerns the manifestation of a dialectical interplay between the
ideal and the real in American culture and an encounter between
the individual and the world, in which the individual is either
initiated into the world (confirmation) or victimized by the world
(renunciation).

In the same year, Charles Sanford in *The Quest for Paradise* sees
the discovery of America as the historical event that makes possible
the realization of the old European dream of a millennial return to
Eden. Tracing the roots of that dream from its origins in the personal, psychological desire of an organism to return to its origins
in the womb and in the European social desire to escape the in-
stitutional oppression of civilization to the revolutionary social
and political changes wrought by its relative manifestation in the
new world, Sanford concludes that "moral regeneration became
the collective mission of the American people, who identified their
new country with a restoration of Eden. Associating material
progress with a moral rise, they reconciled themselves to the
change from an agricultural to an industrial nation without a serious wrench." With the revolutionary implications of the dream
achieved, the image of Eden became a more narcissistic symbol of
Eden; and, experiencing the long-range effects of industrial revolution, Americans, according to Sanford, came to feel themselves
"dispossessed of Eden."[6]

In his commentary on *Walden*, Sanford offers an interpretation
of Thoreau that anticipates and is reinforced by the studies of
Americanists Roy Harvey Pearce, A. N. Kaul, and Leo Marx.
According to Sanford, Thoreau suggests that natural man could be

restored to the primal innocence of Adam and Eve by freeing himself of the corrupting institutions of civilizations, not in a back-to-nature movement, but rather in a search for an "integrating mid-point," where he could hold up the mirror of wild nature as an instrument of self-discovery. In Pearce's *The Continuity of American Poetry,* also published in 1961, this search for the middle point takes the form of the twentieth-century poet's attempt to resolve the problem of *communitas:* "that of finding a moral and social order which a man can accept, while remaining sufficiently differentiated from his fellows to be aware that the acceptance yet leaves him a right to be an individual and furnishes him the means to know that he is an individual."[7]

The theme of an integrating midpoint that will not sacrifice individuality to community is the basic American dialectic discerned by Kaul in *The American Vision* (1963) and Marx in *The Machine in the Garden* (1964). For Kaul, the theme is the separation from established society and the searching for ideal community: "While the separation may be voluntary or forced, physical or moral, complete or partial, brought about by the individual's alienation from society or society's rejection of him, by and large it is presented sympathetically. The criticism is of the established order rather than the searching individual." Marx finds that the literature of America evokes a symbolic withdrawal away from the center of civilization toward its opposite, nature, away from sophistication and city toward simplicity and country: "Hence, the pastoral ideal is an embodiment of what Lovejoy calls 'semi-primitivism,' yet in a transcendent relation to the opposing forces of civilization and nature."[8]

The location of the integrating midpoint is transferred from the landscape to the printed page in Tony Tanner's *City of Words* (1971). After reiterating the tension between the abiding American dream of an unpatterned, unconditioned life, in which movement and choice are autonomous and the equally abiding American dread that one is the victim of ubiquitous forces that plot and manipulate one's life, Tanner suggests that the American fear of patterning from without also manifests itself in the form of the American writer's fear that it is an inherited language that patterns most. Thus, there arises throughout American literature and especially in postmodern American fiction, an attempt to create a personal style that is simultaneously free of the restraints of the language of society and the incoherence and formlessness resulting from the rejection of that language. Tanner further suggests that the American's predisposition towards freedom and autonomy leads many American writers to choose "loss of communication rather than loss of private vision."[9]

In his interpretation of American myth and literature, *The Puritan Origins of the American Self* (1975), Sacvan Bercovitch begins by denying that Puritanism is a manifestation of a growing self-consciousness: in the New England way, which is, according to Bercovitch, the basis of the American myth, "self-examination serves not to liberate but to constrict: self-hood appears as a state to be overcome, obliterated." He later recognizes, however, that the agonizing effort of the Puritan to efface himself—to look into the mirror of his soul and discover there not his self, but his Christ—betrays a self-centeredness that is indeed self-conscious and individualistic. Thus, Bercovitch, like the others, acknowledges that the American dialectic involves a tension between individuality and community.[10]

It is as though these many interpretations of the national myth in American literature and culture fuse into a hermeneutic circle whose basic dialectical tension was anticipated a century ago by Orestes Brownson, who wrote: "Community without individuality is tyranny, the fruits of which are oppression, degradation and immobility, the synonym of death. Individuality without community is individualism, the fruits of which are dissolution, isolation, selfishness, disorder, anarchy, confusion, war. . . . What we need then is . . . communalism and individuality harmonized, atoned."[11]

In an essay published in 1971, "The Usable Myth: The Legends of Modern Mythmakers," Albert Friedman draws attention to a puzzling contradiction in American mythography. He asks how a people of a modern state, born in an age of rationalism and science that tends to demythologize, cultivated on a literary rather than an oral tradition, very much aware of myth because only those who do not believe in the literal narrative can discern the symbolic one, how such a people can be said to possess a myth. Friedman goes on to point out that, although it cannot be said that America contains a myth in the strict sense of the word—a body of sacred narratives about divine personae undergoing a ritualistic agon *in illo tempore*—America still contains a rich symbolic tradition that functions as myth insofar as it signifies its charter of belief.

Friedman then sums up the contradiction this way: "How can we reconcile these two conceptions of myth which are related on the plane of function but are otherwise so different? To resolve our problem, we are forced, I think, to hypothesize that the mythology of complex cultures is cryptotypical, that such mythologies are covert systems of assumptions, values, beliefs, personal wishes socialized and social wishes internalized, which reveal themselves only in the images and metaphors in which they get expressed, in syntactical relationships, in the articulation of incidents, in the fleshing out of archetypal personae and situations."[12]

Despite their often-expressed concern with myth, the studies referred to here have in fact been primarily concerned with interpreting and evaluating the images, metaphors, and syntactical relationships of American literary symbolic language and with the dialectical thought that this symbolic language gives rise to. It is as though the American writer, in his reappropriation of the Adamic myth of western tradition, and the American critic, in his interpretation of that reappropriation, are engaged in the process that Paul Ricoeur suggests renews tradition: "A tradition exhausts itself by mythologizing the symbol; a tradition is renewed by interpretation, which reascends the slope from exhausted time to hidden time, that is, by soliciting from mythology the symbol and its store of meaning."[13]

Thus, in such a context, American scholarship and criticism have dealt less with an American myth than with an American mythos—an organic syntax of image, metaphor, and symbol that dialectically evokes the main currents and countercurrents of American thought, belief, and value. Insofar as the several studies reviewed in this chapter have solicited from the myth of Genesis, and to a lesser extent the myth of the Millennium, several symbols and their store of meaning, they have made a provocative and significant contribution to the understanding of the dialectic manifest in classic American literature. It is the thesis of this study, however, that that understanding can be extended and the details of the dialogue more sharply focused by the examination of the symbolic pattern that underlies the Genesis myth and consequently underlies the reappropriation of that myth in American literature: the mythopoeic pattern of separation from and reparation with the boundless.[14]

Genesis begins with a series of separations from the boundless: something is created out of nothing; the earth is separated from the heavens; light is divided from darkness; firmament from firmament; land from sea; day from night. It is a cellular division of the cosmic body, further complicated by the multiplication of flora and fauna and the division of both into male and female. Then, androgynous humanity is created by the separation of its dust from the other dust, and man and woman are created by the rending of that flesh, a separation that is to be repaired as man is commanded to leave his father and mother and ironically cleave unto his wife. Shortly after their creation, man and woman eat the fruit of the Tree of the Knowledge of Good and Evil, and the immediate effect of that act of disobedience is that the world is suddenly divided into good and evil. Adam and Eve discover their nakedness, become conscious of self, and are thereby separated from self and from nature. Moreover, they realize their culpability and feel separated from God; Eve's sorrow in conception is multiplied; Adam's sense of mortality is quickened; and both are exiled from the Garden. The rest of the Judaic and Christian myths is a charter of belief that spells out the way of reparation.

This Fall, upon which so much of the interpretation of the American myth is based, is but a variation of the more universal mythopoeic pattern of separation from and reparation with the boundless. In a physiological sense, man's separation from the boundless occurs in his conception: in the original connection of sperm and egg is the initial separation of the human organism from the plenitude of matter and the cosmos. This separation, however, is not psychically the case for the individual himself; nor is he separated from the boundless through the physical rupture of birth. Of course birth is the original trauma from which man never recovers; postnatal evidence—the recurrence of sleep in a foetal position—suggests an impulse to repair to the womb. Still, there is a more significant severance. Despite the physical rupture of birth, the infant is incapable of distinction, of discerning the me from the not-me, the I from the thou. Within the womb and within the early months of infancy, the foetus-child is part of the boundless, the measureless, is one with mother, with nature, with all. This wholeness is furthered by a mother and a society who, in sheltering and protecting it, create for the infant an environment that is psychically as much a womb as the amniotic one.

At some point in its development, however, the infant is traumatically made aware of itself and its dependence on something outside that self for nourishment. This distinction, this psychic sense of division, is the beginning of knowledge and the end of wholeness, the break in the natural chain. The child's growth, which includes the development of the capacity to discern between things, continues to divide and fragment existence. Just as he learns to distinguish objects in space and thereby loses spacelessness, so he learns to discern objects in time and thereby loses timelessness.

In short, he defines boundaries and separates himself from the boundless.

The ability to bound, however, is paradoxical: it divides, but it also encloses and consequently repairs. In the course of growing, the child establishes surrogate wholes and communities: family, gang, church, school; but he also sharpens the capacity to discern difference within those surrogates and thereby resevers. The adolescent repeats the original separation by becoming narcissistically more self-conscious. In becoming more fully aware of self and in trying to realize that self more completely, he must "kill his parents"—cut them out, and himself, away. That is science: from *scire* (to know) and *scindere* (to cut). That is the other side of the irony in Sophocles' play: in order for Oedipus to know himself, he must "cut out."[15]

Having discovered time and a self separate from the other and from the community, the individual inevitably becomes conscious of his mortality. Thus, consciousness becomes conscience, and as Nicolas Berdyaev writes, "the anguish of every severance in time and place is the experience of death."[16] This anguish is a major part of the penance that each man does for his separation from the boundless, the anxiety that leads to symbolic reparation.

Does phylogeny recapitulate ontogeny: is there a point in evolution, when racial man experiences separation from the boundless? At best, all one can do is infer that there is. One can assume a point in evolution when primitive man does, as Vico suggests, "become all things by not understanding them," a point when he is one with nature. Even Claude Lévi-Strauss's insistence that primitive man's ability to distinguish difference in nature and use it analogically is the leap from animality to humanity implies that animal-man at some point does not discern difference. Thus, one can infer an evolution of the brain and nervous system, in which the holistic dominance by one side of the brain gives way to the analytical dominance by the other side, and the separation from things occurs.[17]

What one cannot take as evidence of primitive man's immersion in nature, however, is the idea of the *participation mystique*, for, as Paul Ricoeur rightly points out, the ritual by which man attempts a oneness with all implies an intention to recover what has already been lost. The primitive man who through myth intends a cosmic wholeness and an undivided plenitude "is already a man of division."[18] That division is his separation from nature and his knowledge of boundaries. Man is the tool-making animal who uses the tool to manipulate nature and create civilization; his dominion costs him his communion. Like his ontogenetic counterpart, racial man falls from the cosmos and the cosmos from him; the means of his reparation is symbolic ritual and myth.

In one of the most oft-cited passages in mythography, Plato, in the *Symposium,* uses the myth of primordial and spherical androgynous creatures, whose severance by Zeus leads to the "ancient desire to reunite our original nature, making one of two and healing the state of man." Both Jungians and Freudians allude to this passage in explaining man's need to repair the split in his psyche and the expression of this need in symbolic language. For the Jungian, separation from the boundless is necessary in order for man to achieve individuation—conscious connection with the archetypal self. Humpty Dumpty's fall is a fortunate fall; it effects the necessary consciousness of separation that impels man to seek dialectical union of the ego and the archetype, a union that manifests itself symbolically in the circular forms of the egg, the *uroborus* or serpent biting its own tail, and the mandala or circle squared. Reparation and consciousness are compatible: the conscious reunion of ego and archetype transcends original wholeness. Heavenly beatitude is greater than Edenic beatitude.[19]

The implication of Freudian psychology, however, is that any *felix culpa* is a rationalization; heaven is an imperfect sublimation of a perfect Eden. Citing the same passage from Plato, Freud suggests that science's explanation of origins—the big bang theory—accounts for the erotic, and subsequently, the thanatotic, impulse of all fragments to couple and become whole. One disciple of Freud extends the suggestion and works out an elaborate psychoanalytical theory in which the act of coitus becomes a symbolic return to the womb, to the aquatic origins of all life, to the "deathlike repose of the inorganic world." Another concludes that all dreams and therefore all myth express this desire to repair to the boundlessness of the womb and infancy. Thus, for the Freudian, the rite of passage is rather a rite of return passage.[20]

In the following quotation from *Themis,* Jane Harrison, in commenting on the meaning of Themis, also comments on the meaning and function of ritual and myth: "She is the force that brings and binds together; she is 'herd instinct,' the collective conscience, the social sanction. She is *fas,* the social imperative."[21] The import of Harrison's words is that ritual and myth bring man together in a community that repairs the sense of alienation and fragmentation effected by the consciousness of separation. Such reparation itself

is doomed, however, by man's continuing evolution of consciousness. The presential oneness of the numen, associated with magic
and myth, is diffused by the abstracting quality of emerging religion and philosophy. The mythic metaphor of spirit—the wind
and "something other"—is rent; only the "something other" is
retained in the word. The religion of the supernatural tends to exalt
the super at the expense of the natural; a dissociation of sensibility
sets in. Philosophy perpetuates the dissociation, and, although
Plato uses myth, he uses it consciously as a tool of discourse—a
participation philosophique, not *mystique*.[21]

The same kind of diffusion is evident in the evolution of drama
from ritual. Ritual originates in the rhythmic, communal dance;
chant is added and the Dionysian rite is born. In the transition to
drama, the initial choral emphasis gives way to the emerging hero
and other dramatis personae, until the chorus is eventually written
out of drama and with it the *participation mystique*. No matter that
the drama retains the mythopoeic in its metaphors and symbols or
that the audience can identify and participate; the immersion in the
ritual of the audience offstage is never as complete as that of the
chorus onstage. The dialectic of separation and reparation evident
in the primitive world is also apparent in the history of Western
civilization.

Medieval civilization is a relatively whole and ordered community of obedience. It is made so by the misconception that the
world is Ptolemy's, by the universal Roman Catholic Church and
its single, international language that evokes the Word, and by the
divine right of monarchy. It is expressed so by the great poem of
the age, in which all community—all that would connect—is
gathered into the white rose of the Godhead, from which the
diabolic, all who would disconnect, are excluded. The symbol of
that communion is also the rose window of the medieval cathedral,
which in turn symbolizes the Lady whose dark womb contains the
Light and for whom a creative and anonymous community builds
the cathedral, establishing a sacred center.

With the Renaissance, that participation in order and wholeness
is split into fragments. Copernicus and Galileo break the circle,
explode the Ptolemaic egg into an infinite number of pieces, which
still have not been put back together again. Henry shatters the rose
window on the Papist cathedral and with it the spiritual and political community. Luther perpetuates the division of the spiritual
community, a division that in time multiplies into a bewildering
number of schisms and sects. The invention of printing effects not

only a dissemination of knowledge, but also an attenuation of the numinous—the oral and illuminated—Word. The community of obedience is replaced by one of will, and division without creates division within. At one moment John Donne can write, "No man is an island, all are part of the main," and in the next, " 'Tis all in pieces, all coherence gone." Still later, the higher criticism will challenge the integrity of the Christian myth; Darwin, by pointing out a connection in the natural world, will ironically effect a disturbance within the psychological one; and Freud will complete the division of the psyche. By the approach of the modern era, Matthew Arnold will lament Thalassal alienation rather than reparation: "In the sea of life enisled . . . We mortal millions live alone."[22]

Complementing the dissolution of community is another dissociation of sensibility. The Reformation purifies the Church of its body: it protests the sensuous use of stained glass, music, and incense; it negates transubstantiation, the mysterious and numinous miracle at the altar; and it denies the claim of sacred contiguity that connects the Pope and Church to Peter and Christ. The scientific insistence on fact—on realism rather than *ur-realism*—sacrifices metaphor to what Philip Wheelwright calls stenolanguage, poetry to prose.[23] The result is an obvious rent in the sensibility that leads to neoclassicism and romanticism. William Blake recognizes the dissociation and tries to repair it in a marriage of heaven and hell; Friedrich Nietzsche's metaphors are Apollo and Dionysius, and his hope for reparation is the superman; and T. S. Eliot labors for himself and his age to restore the unified sensibility through the objective correlative and the mythical method.

The burden falls heavily upon modern man; not only does he inherit the growing consciousness and divisiveness of five centuries, but all around him and within him the fragmentation continues. Rollo May writes that "separation is a split between existence (being whole) and essence (being self)";[24] and the existentialist, who is more precisely an essentialist, urges the acceptance of separation and death and attempts a reparation seemingly from within. Despite the existentialist's claim to choose for all men, that choice seems to be a most private one effected through an equally private act and in defiance of the community. It is an attempt at a very private rite of passage, but all the evidence of anthropology and mythology suggests that rite is communal, not private. Whatever it is the existentialist seeks, it is sought outside community and its efficacy for reparation is doubtful.

The personal existential quest becomes the public existential cause: emerging nations seek selfhood and the result is self-conscious nationalism and divisive revolution. Minorities strive for identity and the result is the splintering of an already fragmented country—a cellular division of the body politic. Each group becomes aware of itself in the narcissistic pool, finds that black (or red or gay or Right or Left or woman) is beautiful, withdraws to realize itself, and the community feels the pain of the withdrawal. Moreover, the withdrawn eventually experiences the full implication of total freedom, and the liberated self becomes the isolated self. The electronic age compounds the fracture with its introduction of high fidelity and television and effects a privation of the communal re-creation in art.

Once more man turns to metaphor and the mythopoeic for reparation: William Butler Yeats, terrified that "things fall apart, the center cannot hold," waits for the tellurian rough beast to slouch toward Bethlehem and begin a new cycle; Robert Frost journeys to the springs of his being, drinks the waters there, and is "made whole again, beyond confusion"; Wallace Stevens orders Tennessee with a jar and Key West with a song and celebrates man's "blessed rage for order"; Dylan Thomas leaps from tomb to womb in the "round/Zion of the water bead"; and Eliot reaches for the "still point of the turning world."[25]

In the turn to metaphor, religion and science join in Teilhard de Chardin's quest for wholeness. For Teilhard, the big bang of the cosmic explosion of gases and sound is the divine explosion of the Light and the Word—an evolution of the cosmos, of all matter and energy—that will resolve itself in the universal, pantheistic Christ, the "Noosphere." Science provides still another metaphor for reparation, one of devolution rather than evolution. According to recent theory, as stars diminish their size, they concentrate and increase their powers of gravity, drawing in all light within their fields. Eventually, their gravity becomes so strong that all light is imploded into a still and perfect sphere—a black hole in the universe. Thus, light and sound are gathered back into the dark and silent void. Transcendence becomes *incendence,* and the *uroboric* circle becomes the big cipher, the nothingness that Heidegger posits is the ground of Being.[26]

If one were to film the fall from a wall of an egg and its shattering and splattering along a deep-blue floor and then darken that room and project that film, first forwards, and then backwards—in slow motion—one would have a metaphor for the mythopoeic pattern outlined here. The original fall and diffusion is man's separation from the boundless; the subsequent ascent and refusion is his symbolic reparation. Boundlessness is the cosmos of matter and energy; it is the preconscious world of womb and nature, in which the primitive and child unconsciously participate, the subsequent ordered and whole community of tribe and society, of which man is a part; it is also the undivided self. Separation is the rupture of the physical wholeness of nature; it is consciousness and the establishment of boundaries, the withdrawal of an emerging ego from the social community, a growing apart from the other; it is the self divided from itself. Such separation is necessary for the growth and development of both the individual and social organism, but that growth is not without pain. Penance, or reparation, is the trauma of separation; it is the anxiety of physical dislocation, the guilt of alienation from the other and "wholly other," the dread of mortality and apocalypse; it is the sense of incompleteness that attends the dissociated self. Reparation, however, is also the attempt to repair—through rite, myth, dream, and art—all division and fragmentation; it is the physical and spiritual reunion of sacrament, the return of the individual to the community, the integration in the design of symbolic language; it is the self reintegrated.

Such is the nature of the mythopoeic pattern of separation from and reparation with the boundless as it is manifest in the genesis and development of ontogenetic and phylogenetic man and in the course of the development of Western civilization. The purpose of this study will be to trace the particular manifestation of that pattern in American history and ideology and in classic American literature. As we shall see, whereas the lived and living tradition presents a dialectic between separation and reparation, between individuality and community, that emphasizes and celebrates individuality and freedom, the literary tradition presents the same dialectic that sometimes confirms individuality—especially in the works of Emerson, Thoreau, and Whitman—but that more often evokes the tragic consequences of individuality and the need for greater community—as in the works of Hawthorne, Melville, James, and Eliot. In the latter case, freedom and individuality often border on chaos and annihilation, and community and communion are the values most sought after.

Just as American literature involves a reappropriation of the universal pattern of separation and reparation, so it also involves a reappropriation of symbols used within that pattern: the circle and the labyrinth, the rite of passage, and the *via negativa*. This study will interpret and evaluate American literature in terms of these symbols as well as the major pattern of separation and reparation. It will differ from prior interpretations of American myth and literature in the following ways: rather than concentrate on the myths of Adam or the Millennium, it will concentrate on the mythopoeic pattern that underlies those myths; rather than examine the general canon of a novelist, it will focus on the particular work of fiction in order to determine how individual design influences the variation of the universal symbol; rather than confine itself to either nineteenth- or twentieth-century literature, fiction or poetry, it will explore works of both centuries and both genres in order to test whether the pattern informs the most representative and significant literature of America.

2

Nomos and the Genesis of America

beauty is a defiance of authority
William Carlos Williams, *Paterson*

In a retrospective essay entitled "Historic Notes of Life and Letters in New England," Ralph Waldo Emerson looks back upon the two decades between 1820 and 1840 as a period in which the New England mind experienced a great awakening that led to a dissociation of sensibility and a division of both the religious and political communities: "It seemed a war between intellect and affection; a crack in Nature, which split every church in Christendom" and "brought new divisions in politics, as the new conscience touching temperance and slavery."[1] What ruptured the society and altered the conscience, according to Emerson, was a "new consciousness" that social prosperity and uniformity are not the "beatitude of man," but rather that "the individual is the world." In alluding to this self-conscious independence, Emerson uses a metaphor that suggests a correspondence between knowledge and separation that leads to alienation: "This perception [that the individual is the world] is a sword such as was never drawn before. It divides and detaches bone and marrow, soul and body, yea, almost the man from himself."

Emerson does not lament the division of self from self; in fact, he rejoices that the young men of the time "were born with knives in their brain, a tendency to introversion, self-dissection, anatomizing of motives." Perhaps only a romantic could find comfort in this surgical self-consciousness; certainly only an American transcendentalist could discover in the separation from the tribe the apotheosis of the self: "It is the age of severance, of dissociation, of freedom, of analysis, of detachment. . . . Instead of the social existence which all shared was now separation. Everyone for himself; driven to find all his resources, hopes, rewards, society and deity within himself." One could not want a more explicit confirmation by a more respected observer that separation plays a significant role in the development of America and the American mythos.

Emerson errs, however, in one important respect; the sword that severs the individual from the tribe, that anatomizes the motives of mind and soul, and that rends the sensibility had been drawn before and drawn in America. The severance in the New England mind between 1820 and 1840 celebrated by Emerson is but one stage of a dialectic between separation and reparation manifest from the very beginning of the American pilgrimage and repeated throughout the American experience. Although this dialectical pattern is, as has been suggested in the previous chapter, a universal one, its manifestation throughout American history, ideology, and literature is made distinctive by the genesis of America at a particular time in the development of Western civilization and in a particular place in the westward expansion of that civilization. What follows is an account of the manifestation in American history and ideology of the mythopoeic pattern of separation from and reparation with the boundless.

What distinguishes the manifestation of that pattern in the American experience is the concurrence of four advanced stages of the evolution of consciousness—the Reformation, the Enlightenment, the Romantic Revolution, and the Industrial Revolution—with the genesis of America and the occurrence of those cultural transformations in a spacious new land with little Western tradition and therefore initially more receptive to change than the traditional societies of Europe. The result of this convergence is the emergence in American ideology and culture of an antinomian and *autonomian* predisposition—a tendency to put the self against and before the law, custom, and usage of society, a tendency toward self-government and self-determination. It is a predisposition that manifests itself overtly in the cause of religious, political, and personal freedom and covertly in the ever-present fault that lies in whatever community Americans have sought or achieved.

The pattern of separation and reparation is apparent in those significant words that characterize the first two and a half centuries of America's beginning, which is also America's past: conversion and covenant, Separatist and Congregationalist, independence and constitution, secession and reconstruction. According to one interpreter of tradition, "a people is constituted when it separates from others and affirms itself with respect to them." The genesis of America is predicated on such separation: the separation of the Protestant churches from the Catholic Church; the separation of the Puritan sects from the mother church of England, still tied, however tenuously, through Canterbury to Rome; the geographical separation of sect and community from England, one that often involved temporary and terminal dissolution of the family and "perpetual banishment from [one's] native soil"; and finally political separation from king and kingdom, father and fatherland. In each instance, separation was an advanced step in an evolution of self, sect, and state identity, a growing discernment of the psychological, religious, and political self and its sovereignty, and a growing willingness to realize the full possibilities of that self.[2]

Protestantism is grounded in Luther's principle of *sola fides*—in the belief that the individual can experience and receive grace and salvation through an inner knowledge of and communion with Christ rather than through charitable good works. Although Luther himself labored to retain the sacramental nature of the mass and the mediating function of the clergy, those who followed and protested more severely renounced ritual and priestly mediation in favor of a purer observance and of a more introspective communion. The Protestant conversion is a "turning away" from the contiguous charisma of papal authority and the homeopathic miracle of transubstantiation to the simpler and more rational form of an inner-worldly asceticism—a turning away from the Word as "traduced" (handed down and altered) by the Church fathers, to the Word as interpreted directly from scripture by the individual. It is interesting to note that the Protestant transformation concurs with a technological innovation—the invention of printing—a fact that led John Foxe to claim that the Lord began to work for the church not with a sword, but with the printed word: "How many printing presses there be in the world, so many block-houses there be against the castle of St. Angelo, so that the Pope must abolish knowledge and printing, or printing at length will shut him out."[3] Thus, one is left to wonder to what extent Protestantism is the result not only of a growing nationalism that led to the translation of scripture into one's native language, but also of a technology that made it possible for every man to confront the Word in the privacy of his own home as well as the privacy of his own soul.

It was in the privacy of his soul that the Puritan had to wrestle with the ultimate questions of election and salvation. Conversion denied the Puritan the attainment of Christian salvation through an imitation of Christ, through good works, and instead forced the converted into a discernment of good and evil without the aid of learned counselors and confessors. The result was great psychological stress—an auto-machia or "agenbite of inwit"—a self-consciousness that became a literary documentation of self-centeredness. As Sacvan Bercovitch points out, "every aspect of [Puritan literary] style betrays a consuming involvement with 'me' and 'mine' that resists disintegration. We cannot help but feel that the Puritans' urge for self-denial stems from the very subjectivism of their outlook, that their humility is coextensive with personal assertion."[4]

This sense of self-centeredness and privacy— this separation of self from society—was seemingly modified in America by a doctrine whose central purpose was the integration and solidarity of the tribe: the doctrine of the covenant. Anyone who reads John Winthrop's "Model of Christian Charity" cannot help but be impressed by the call to community: "For this end, we must be knit together in this work as one man. . . . We must delight in each other, make others' conditions our own, rejoice together, mourn together, labor and suffer together: always having before our eyes our commission and community in the work, our community as members of the same body."[5] Such a covenant, modeled on the Judaic tradition of the Jew's covenant with his God and his brother, held the early settlements and colonies together in the face of great natural hardship and of many sectarian challenges.

However, the Puritan community, like later American communities, was one born of crisis and subsequently one more viable in crisis than in prosperity: one of the major themes of the New England jeremiad was the declension of grace and theocracy in the subsequent generations of American Puritans, generations distracted by the success and security of their calling and enterprise. One's view of the Puritan community (and similar American communities) is more sharply focused when seen in the context of an Old Testament model and a new frontier variation. In his study of the Puritan origins of the American self, Bercovitch reinterprets Cotton Mather's interpretation of the building of New England as the millennial fulfillment and transcendence of the Judaic antitype—Nehemiah's rebuilding of the walls of Jerusalem. In both instances, the rebuilding of walls is seen as the basic symbol of community. What Mather and Bercovitch overlook, however, is that the walls of the new Jerusalem not only brought a people back together, but also kept them together in a time of crisis from without and kept them apart from the defiled tribes and churches around them. (It may be that in the ethnic myth of the Jew all time is a time of crisis from without, a claim that, if true, would partially explain the continuity of the Jewish community and the appeal of such a model to the Puritan in the wilderness.)

Looking ahead of the Puritan community toward the western pilgrimage of the American pioneer, one may recall an image out of countless cinematic westerns: the transformation of a long line of covered wagons into a more unifying and relatively more impregnable circle to protect the rugged and individualistic pioneer from the alien, though indigenous, Indian. That circle—that wall of wagons—in time and in calm and prosperity unwound into the relative diffusion of homesteading and farmsteading on the frontier. Do not these figurative walls of Jerusalem, New England, and the western prairie fuse into the image of a community of crisis whose viability in peace and prosperity is problematical? Is not the Puritan god, like the Hebrew one, a desert god whose numen is attenuated in the lush valley of Baal?

The symbol of the covenant—the sign of God's promise to lead His chosen people out of bondage into the land of milk and honey—was a significant part of the millennial myth that chartered the pilgrimage to America. But, like the Judaic covenant and unlike medieval tradition, the covenant chartered an exclusive community of will, into which each member voluntarily entered and paradoxically was elected. It is the doctrine of election that undermines the community implied in the covenant and explicit in Winthrop's "Model." How is it possible to have an integrated community when some enjoy the grace of an "election and calling sure," while others suffer the disgrace of defection and expulsion from communion? Winthrop himself implies in the "Model" a distinction between the elected brother and the rejected other that undermines the solidarity of the community: "Providence hath so disposed of the condition of mankind" that "some must be rich, some poor; some high and eminent in power and dignity, others mean and in subjection." As Max Weber points out in his interpretation of the spirit of Protestantism, the predestined saints of God in the world were "divided from the eternally damned remainder of humanity by a more impassable and in its invisibility more terrifying gulf, than separated the monk of the Middle Ages from the rest of the world about a him, a gulf which penetrated all social relations with its sharp brutality."[6]

Although the terror of schism may have resided in the invisibility of sainthood, it was visibility that was the cause célèbre that
resulted in the Separatist movement and that became a significant
factor in the colonization of America. As Edmund Morgan points
out in *Visible Saints*, it was a desire to bring the visible church of
Christ on earth closer to the invisible church that prompted the
Separatists to seek for each individual church the discipline to expel
those members whose election was brought into question. In addition, they sought to make knowledge and understanding of scripture a requisite for membership; belief without knowledge and
understanding undermined the willfulness and voluntariness of
membership and consequently amounted to no belief at all. Furthermore, having made guilt a personal and internal matter and
now insisting on visible signs of election—having a need to measure and define election—the Separatists found themselves in their
dissent from the Church of England in the awkward position of
"minimizing faith and emphasizing good works." Thus, a handful
of Separatists engaged in an economical rationalization of a faith
whose raison d'être had been initially a repudiation of good works
on behalf of inner faith. That rationalization was shared by the
nonseparating Congregationalist as well: John Cotton found a
"just reproof of the infidelity found in them that live without a
calling," and later Cotton Mather observed that the righteous was
only more excellent than his neighbor "except he be more excellent
as a neighbor."[7]

The nonseparating Congregationalist shared with the Separatist
more than this rationalization of his faith; to begin with, he shared
the act of separation. Francis Higginson, in defending his church's
attachment to the Church of England, underscores the disconnection: "We do not go to New England as separatists from the
Church of England; *though we cannot but separate from the cor-
ruptions in it;* but we go to practice the positive part of church
reformation and propagate the gospel in America" (italics mine).
An essential part of the positive part of church reformation was, in
Edward Johnson's words, to build "new churches" of a "new
heaven and a new earth" of "such living stones as outwardly appear
saints by calling."[8] The analogy of saints and living stones is an
effective allusion to the dead, stone saints that adorned the papal
churches in Europe as well as an implicit reference to the basic
difference in church membership: that the Protestant church
would be voluntarily entered into by living saints alone.

Such was the nature of covenant and congregation established by the Puritans upon their arrival in the new land; it was without a doubt an attempt at reparation in the form of theocracy—an attempt to build the city of God, a city in which the individual impulse of conversion was held in check by social compact, the covenant. It was an attempt as Winthrop put it "to knit together," and, as Edmund Morgan points out in his biography of the Massachusetts Bay governor, Winthrop's whole life in the new land was dedicated to resisting the separatist impulse and keeping the theocracy intact. But that community, predicated on the values of virtue and commonweal, was mined with a fault from the outset: does not a community brought into existence by schism, by individual and minority rebellion against the dominant and dominating tradition, design a paradigm for future dissent and rupture? Moreover, according to Perry Miller, the contractual theory of the Puritan covenant by inference "denied original sin, proclaimed the competence of human reason, and allowed the autonomous individual a self-interest prior to all moral concerns."[9] Thus, no sooner was the covenant realized in nonseparating Congregationalism, when it was ironically broken by conversion—a turning away from what now appeared to the idealist as an outward covenant of works back to the purer, inner covenant of grace. Just as the first Protestants had sought to reform the Catholic church of its imperfections, so now a few American protesters sought to reform the American congregations of theirs.

Anne Hutchinson's heresy was but an extension of Luther's fideism, purified of the unnecessary sign of visible sanctification. She said, "I seek not for [outward] graces, but for Christ, I seek not for [federal] promises, but for Christ, I seek not for sanctification, but for Christ, tell not me of . . . duties, but tell me of Christ." Hutchinson's experience—persecution in Massachusetts, exile in Rhode Island, violent death in New York—is a prototype of subsequent symbolic expressions of the tragic consequences of an extreme individualism, an exacting antinomianism, in which the chosen self circumvents, rather than have that self circumscribed by, law and custom. Anne Hutchinson had literally made of herself a priestess of true belief and thus established an American prototype for the American churchhood of each true believer, later celebrated in Thomas Jefferson's words, "I am a sect myself," Thomas Paine's words, "my mind is my church," and still later by one interpreter of the American experience in these words: it is "the great work of the divine mission of Protestantism, to place each individual soul in immediate union with Christ and his

Word; to complete in each one the work of redemption, to build in each one a temple of God, a spiritual church, and to unfold and sanctify, all the energies of the individual."[10]

Another American Protestant-turned-protestant, Roger Williams, not only broke with the theocracy in Massachusetts, but in so doing, sought to instruct it of its betrayal of its origins and to prepare the way for what was to become a significant basis for constitutional democracy—the separation of church and state. Williams asserted that the English Parliament had in vain permitted the publication and dissemination of English Bibles amongst the people, if against their "souls' persuasion from the Scripture, they should be forced (as if they lived in *Spain* or *Rome* itself without the sight of a *Bible*) to believe as the Church believes." In that passage from *The Bloody Tenent*, Williams, like Hutchinson, was reconvening—calling back—the Puritans to first principles; elsewhere in the *Tenent*, he defends the right of any church's independence and the toleration of that independence by arguing that a church is like a corporation or company, which in matters of its own society "may dissent, divide, break into *Schisms* and *Factions* . . . yea, wholly break up and dissolve into pieces and nothing" without the general peace of society being impaired.[11]

Roger Williams's controversy with the Massachusetts Bay Colony and his expulsion into the wilderness of Rhode Island form a paradigmatic act in which many symbols of the American experience converge. The paradigm reenacts the Puritan attempt to establish an ideal community that would permit rather than prohibit a wider measure of individual liberty; it anticipates James Madison's claim that "multiplicity is the essence of democracy";[12] it is a plea for religious toleration that clearly reveals that theocracy (the tyranny of the elders) and democracy (the tyranny of the majority) tend toward intolerance. It is also an antitype of Frederick J. Turner's thesis that expansive individualism finds expression and is encouraged by the frontier and that the existence of the frontier invites and accommodates the attrition of sects and churches and thereby promotes cultural pluralism; and finally it dramatizes that, in America, congregations of saints are born of congregations of exiles.

Was not the earliest congregation of saints in Plymouth a congregation of exiles and would not the westward expansion of the continent be in large measure a result of what Richard Niebuhr explains as the tendency of the churches of the disinherited to seek and find on the frontier the emotional, doctrinal, and economic freedom that the established churches prohibited? There is no more recurrent image in the American mythos than this paradoxical conversion of exile into saint, even where congregation is but a company of two as it was for a time in Rhode Island for Williams and his wife. One has only to consider the following, few examples to realize the richness of the motif: the pilgrims at Plymouth, the transcendentalists at Brook Farm, the outcasts of Poker Flat, Natty Bumppo and Chingachgook, Huck Finn and Jim. In the American mythos, antinomianism is literally and dramatically translated into *outlaw*, and the outlaw in his conflict with the prevailing *nomos* is more often celebrated and venerated than condemned. It is a prevalent motif somewhat explained by John Cotton's comment on Williams's exile, that given the immensity of the land, "Banishment in this country, is not counted so much a confinement, as an enlargement," and by Tocqueville's observation that "democracy loosens social ties, but tightens natural ones; it brings kindred more closely together, whilst it throws citizens apart."[13]

Cotton might have viewed Williams's exile as an enlargement, but it was one without the benefit of charisma. Charisma and its attenuation play an important role in the development of New England and of America. Edward Shils holds that the modern state, unlike the traditional state, attenuates charisma from the center of society to the periphery. Luther initiates this attenuation of charisma in the modern world by implicitly redirecting it away from clerical office and dispersing it among the priesthood of all true believers. Calvin stems that dispersal and withdraws it unto the elect—the visible saints and elders of the church, who oversee the religious and political well-being of the theocratic state. The nonseparating Congregationalists in New England started out attenuating charisma away from the center at Canterbury across an ocean into the new periphery of Church and Empire on the New England frontier. With the establishment of the theocracy, however, the Puritan reconcentrated charisma in a tribal brotherhood of elected saints and elders. Thus, Increase Mather could answer Solomon Stoddard's admonishment that the elect made up only a fraction of the population in New England with the retort that that fraction would suffice to effect the millennium in New Jerusalem.[14]

But the theocracy was unable to retain the concentration of charisma. Attenuation took many forms: the halfway covenant, which admitted the second generation to membership in the church (but not to participation in the communion) and also permitted the baptism of their children; Stoddard's distribution of communion among the unregenerate in the hope of effecting their regeneration; John Wise's influential advocation of the democratic basis of the individual church; and perhaps most importantly the success of denominationalism, the development and movement of several sects into the frontiers of the interior. As one interpreter of *Puritanism in Old and New England* puts it, "the fission process, the endless splintering, the Babel of Heresies, or the flowering of sects" that attended the dispersion of denominationalism "demonstrates once again how fundamental the individualism of the Protestant Reformation has proved to be compared with its superficial collectivism."[15]

That attenuation of charisma implicit in American pluralism came to be regarded by many interpreters of the American enterprise as one of its greatest strengths. In his classic definition of "What is an American," Crèvecoeur, citing the country's cultural and religious pluralism, concludes, "Thus all sects are mixed as well as all nations: thus religious indifference is imperceptibly disseminated from one end of the continent to the other; which is at present one of the strongest characteristics of the Americans." A century later, Karl Marx, pointing out that the separation of church and state had altered the essence of religion from *"community"* to *"differentiation,"* cites North America as the political sphere where religion "has been relegated among the numerous private interests and exiled from the life of the community," a relegation that is for Marx the consummation of political emancipation.[16]

In the twentieth century, however, commentators on religion in America, Robert Bellah and Sidney Mead, note that, despite the fragmentation of American religious life through the multiplication of sect and denomination, the American has continued to participate in the greater communality of the civil or national religion. Mead, however, recognizes that the idea of a national religion aggravates the problem of the attenuation of charisma: "It is hard to escape the conclusion that each religious group accepted, by implication, the responsibility to teach that its peculiar doctrines, which made it distinct from other sects and gave it its only reason for separate existence, were either irrelevant for the general welfare of the nation-community, or at most, possessed only an indirect and instrumental value for it."[17] Thus, it was only what was common in the many denominations that participated in a national charisma already diffused by indifference, differentiation, and attenuation.

Samuel Johnson, on a walking tour of the western islands of Scotland in 1773, took notice of the depopulation caused by the immigration of so many Scots to America and made the following observation of those emigrants, an observation that provides us with an image for what we have been calling the attenuation of charisma: "and all that go may be considered as subjects lost to the British crown; for a nation scattered in the boundless regions of America resembles rays diverging from a focus. All the rays remain but the heat is gone. Their power consisted in their concentration; when they are dispersed, they have no effect." Johnson adds the following observation, one that reflects the rootlessness of the Yankee who was in the process of ceasing to be a loyal British subject, but who had not yet become a citizen of an independent America: "It may be thought they are happier by the change; but they are not happy as a nation, for they are a nation no longer. As they contribute not to the prosperity of any community, they must want that security, that dignity, that happiness, whatever it be, which a prosperous community throws back upon individuals."[18]

And in a sense, Johnson was quite right; the colonist's happiness stemmed not so much from his concentration as a nation, but rather from his decentralization into thirteen nations. He enjoyed an expansive life, a new kind of liberty, and the pursuit of private property, because he was the conqueror of a rich, virgin land and because a king and Parliament, three thousand miles away, attended his enterprise and government with salutary neglect. But in the pursuit of liberty and property, he continued to loosen the traditional ties of nationhood. We have already seen how the desire for religious independence affected the religious disintegration of the colonies. Ethnically, the early homogeneity of British settlers was diffused by the Dutch and Germans who poured into the middle colonies and by the black Africans who were poured into the southern plantations. Economically and socially, a significant difference in life-style emerged between the southern aristocracy, which was supported by tobacco, rice, and indigo plantations, and the northern middle class, which made its living from commerce and some manufacturing, as well as farming. The colonist did not yet regard himself as an American, but rather as a Virginian, Pennsylvanian, or New Englander. What all the colonists had in common, however tenuous it might have been, was that they were all loyal subjects of King George. In a few decades, they found themselves no longer bound by that loyalty, but in fact bound by their common grievance against the crown and Parliament, bound by their common crisis.

Looking backward in old age, John Adams believed that the true history of the American revolution could not be recovered for "the revolution was effected before the war commenced. The revolution was in the minds and hearts of the people."[19] In one sense the revolution, whether latent or manifest, had always been in the American psyche; the Puritan conversion had from the beginning intended a form of *autonomianism,* or self-rule. The revivalism of the early eighteenth century not only affected the dismantling of the theocracy and its political formalism, but also reawakened the people to the spiritual inner light that made the self's soul sovereign, a light transformed by the Enlightenment into reason that would make the soul's self sovereign. The distance and disinterestedness of a deistic god concurred with the laissez-faire attitude of the British king and resulted in a Yankee grown accustomed to self-help and self-rule in the pursuit of private property.

When Britain turned its attention and intention toward the colonies and tried to retrieve its attenuated authority and sovereignty, the result was the conclusion of what British loyalty among the many remained and the definition of an American identity and integrity. Alienated by acts of Parliament contrary to economic and political self-interest—acts that would raise revenue through taxation with only virtual representation (Stamp Act, Townsend Act), that would limit the colonies' rights to expand westward (Quebec Act), that would interfere with what had been relative home rule (Writs of Assistance)—the colonies began a series of protests that eventually led to political organization in the form of the congress of the thirteen colonies. What was effected in the colonies by Britain's new intention was something that had not been fully expressed before—a growing sense of Americanness, now objectified, located, and centered in Philadelphia.

Ironically, it was a loyalist who articulated most clearly what was at the heart of the debate between the colonies and Parliament and an alien, an exile, who articulated most movingly for the general reading public in the colonies the resolution of that matter. Thomas Hutchinson was governor of Massachusetts during the Boston Massacre involving British troops and Boston citizens; and in an address before the Massachusetts Assembly, in which he advocated the subjection of local home rule to Parliamentary rule, he defined the conflict: "I know of no line that can be drawn between the supreme authority of Parliament and the total independence of the colonies; it is impossible there should be two independent Legislatures in one and the same state; for although there may be one head, the King, yet the two legislative bodies will make two governments as distinct as the kingdoms of England and Scotland before the Union."[20] Though there were moderates like John Dickinson who hoped for and worked to maintain the British connection while simultaneously defending colonial rights, the American spirit of these controversial times was clearly in favor of "the total independence of the colonies."

Much of the argument in favor of independence is summed up in the following passage from Paine's *Common Sense:* "Whenever a war breaks out between England and any foreign power, the trade of America goes to ruin, *because of her connection with Britain.* . . . Everything that is right or reasonable pleads for separation. . . . Even the distance at which the Almighty hath placed England and America is a strong and natural proof that the authority of the one over the other, was never the design of the heavens. . . . The Reformation was preceded by the discovery of America; as if the Almighty graciously meant to open a sanctuary to the persecuted in future years, when home should afford neither friendship or safety." The latter part of the passage perhaps reflects more of Paine's own personal experience than that of the native American to whom he addressed his propaganda, but nevertheless it does evoke the familiar millennial myth of America as a redeemer nation. But the major argument of course is rationalization that is primarily economical—the same kind of rationalization that led Franklin to translate time into money and that led Weber to cite Franklin as the antitype of the Protestant ethic transformed into the spirit of capitalism.[21]

Seeking to rationalize his claim to political and economic freedom, the Yankee, like his Puritan predecessor, turned to what we might call *antenomianism*—a rejection of the immediate *nomos* or tradition and a return to an antecedent one. The Puritan conversion was really a cultural reversion—a turning away from the immediate tradition of the Anglo-Catholic community and a return to the models of the Hebraic covenant and the simple, pious congregation of primitive Christianity. Thus Cotton Mather could write, "In short, the first age was the golden one; to return unto that will make a man Protestant, and I may add, a Puritan."[22] The American justification of independence involved a comparable antenomianism: a rejection of English constitutional law translated by Parliament into statute law and a return to the earlier forms of customary or common law that was equated somewhat with natural law and that recognized certain unalienable rights. The colonial debaters went back a century and picked up the argument of liberalism as it existed before it had been nullified by later English practice. It was antinomian as well as *antenomian* insofar as it drew upon Rousseau's celebration of natural man living in a state where natural freedom and equality made government unnecessary. Colonists could identify their primary agrarian society with Rousseau's natural model and thereby rationalize their desire for less government.

There is in the antenomianism of the Puritan conversion and Yankee independence a rationalization that somewhat suggests the intention of ritual—a reenactment of the sacred deeds of a sacred time. American independence can indeed be read as such a reenactment; it can be viewed as a variation of what Freud calls the primal deed, from which all acts of liberation and social contract spring. America is not so much the legitimate heir of founding fathers as it is the illegitimate offspring of foundling brothers, who in their exile from the center, from the sacred council of the fathers (king and Parliament), deprived of their full share of motherland (representation) and virgin land (taxation), "knit together" and "convert" against the father (Jefferson's declaration skillfully contrives to lay all grievances upon the head that wears the crown) and succeed in casting off his yoke. Successful, their first order of business is to constitute their newfound strength in a social contract (Constitution) that ironically limits what each had sought— personal and colonial independence. Whether one is receptive to Freudian social theory or writhes when men of letters make it the basis of their interpretation of Western or American traditions, one cannot deny the analogy and therefore must entertain at least the possibility of further motivation in the cause of liberty.[23] The independence of America is after all an act of defiance against a paternal figure by a brethren united in their feeling of natural, political, and economical deprivation that engenders the civil religion and its totems.

The resolution introduced to the Continental Congress by Richard Lee and passed on July 2d is a microcosm of the whole pattern of separation and reparation that unfolds in America between 1763 and 1789. The first part of that resolution is the actual declaration of independence: "That these United Colonies are, and of right ought to be, free and independent states, that they are absolved from all allegiance to the British Crown, and that all political connection between them and the State of Great Britain is, and ought to be, totally dissolved." The second part calls for expedient foreign alliances, and the third part adds that "a plan of confederation be prepared and transmitted to the respective colonies for their consideration and approbation." From that momentous, though less memorable, resolution emerged the two most important documents in the American experience: the Declaration of Independence (which is but a developed rationalization of the "ought to be" of Lee's resolution) and the Constitution of the United States, which replaced the Articles of Confederation in 1789.

Malinowski tells us that the "charters of belief" of primitive and traditional societies reside in numinous rites and myths; in a modern society, where rationalization precludes the viability of myth and where the predisposition to welcome rather than dread change precludes the need for ritual, charisma resides in the charters of belief. Moreover, is it not fitting that its charters of belief should become the numinous center of a state consciously created? The Declaration and the Constitution are as close as this nation comes to a numinous totem that has the power to concentrate and mobilize the energies of all the people. One cannot help but suspect that the need to articulate in detail the "ought to be" of Lee's resolution and the great effort made to reach unanimity in Congress in support of that articulation betray an attempt at reparation as well as separation: united we stand, divided we fall. Thus, with one exception, all members of Congress signed the document that called not for an independence of *a* United States of America, but of "FREE AND INDEPENDENT STATES" that "have full Power to levy War." Great Britain was at war with thirteen independent states allied with one another as well as with France. The Declaration is therefore a document not only of separation but also of fragmentation; it took the Constitution to repair the division effected by the Declaration.

Independence had been sought and achieved in order to secure the natural and unalienable rights of life, liberty, and the pursuit of happiness, a pursuit that included the right to have and protect property. The designers of the Constitution determined that a republican, rather than a democratic, government would best protect property, integrate a pluralistic society, transform self-interest into national virtue, and make the thirteen states one nation. Madison recognized that a "zeal for different opinions . . . divided mankind into parties" and "inflamed them with mutual animosity," and that a fundamental cause of this factiousness was the distribution of property into "landed interest, a manufacturing interest, a mercantile interest," and "many lesser interests." Hamilton agreed and felt that in forming any government *"every man* ought to be supposed a *knave;* and to have no other end, in all his actions, but *private interest."* A republican government was thereby constituted that allowed in Madison's words "a greater number of citizens" and an "extent of territory" that made "it less possible that a majority of the whole will have a common motive to invade the rights of other citizens; or if such a common motive exists, it will be more difficult for all who feel it to discover their strength, and act in unison with each other." Thus, the property interest of the private citizen was protected from the potential tyranny of the *demos,* and the potentially dangerous charisma of the *demos* was attenuated by the expansion of the political sphere. It was for most, and particularly for John Adams, a government of checks and balances, in which the dialectical tension of faction set against faction transformed private interest into national interest.[24]

A similar tension is evident in the juxtaposition of the Declaration and the Constitution—in the separative emphasis of the former and the integrative emphasis of the latter, and consequently one is tempted to suggest that collectively and dialectically they are the charter of belief that is our national totem. But is this the case? How many centennials have celebrated the adoption of the Constitution; how many Americans know the dramatis personae of the drama of constitution as know the heroes of the drama of independence? Even Lincoln in his famous Gettysburg address dates the founding of the country in 1776. Does not this tendency to identify the Declaration rather than the Constitution with our genesis—in the beginning was the deed—suggest once more that the symbol of separation, of the sovereign self, is more intrinsic to the American mythos than the symbol of reparation, the constituted *demos?*

In any event, both documents reveal a failure of integrity and therefore the failure of America to generate itself as one nation. In passing through committee and congressional debate, the grievance against King George for "determining to keep open a market where MEN should be bought and sold" was deleted from the Declaration. In drafting the Constitution, the federal government surrendered to state government the right to determine that the black man was part of the property the Constitution was designed

to preserve. Thus, the Declaration, by omission, violated its assertion that all men were created equal and the Constitution, by
submission, violated its intention to form "a more perfect Union";
and both thereby denied the very basis of their existence—the
virtue, the truth, of natural law. Although having other divisions in
mind, Paine prophetically describes the fault in "that great chain of
the law," which Crèvecoeur was certain "links us all": "Now is the
seedtime of continental union, faith, and honor. The least fracture
now will be like a name engraved with the point of a pin in the
tender rind of a young oak; the wound would enlarge with the
tree, and posterity read it in full grown characters."[25] And so posterity did read it—at Gettysburg and Richmond.

Before reading the full-grown characters of the fracture that
flowered into the Civil War, it is necessary to examine the third
stage in the evolution of consciousness that influences the genesis
of America. That sense of self—that made the Puritan conversion a
matter of inner grace and private judgment, and Yankee independence a matter of "taking liberties"—is also manifest in the Romantic Revolution in America. In a sense, that revolution is one of
several reawakenings to the charismatic. As suggested earlier, the
rationalism of Protestantism that denied the homeopathic magic of
sacramental rite and the contiguous magic of papal authority and
the rationalization of the Enlightenment that removed God as im-
manence and enthroned reason as eminence effected an attenuation
of charisma that not only dispersed charisma throughout the widening circle of empire, but also diffused and repressed its expression from within and its recognition without. The result was a
series of "great awakenings," the first of which might be said to
have occurred in Salem. The viability of a visible sainthood posits
the viability of a visible satanhood; the Salem experience was the
realization of both the cleavage dealt by the doctrine of the elect
and the attenuation of charisma, now reconcentrated and expressed as an embodied defilement—"An Army of Devils . . .
horribly broke in upon the place which is the *Centre*," a stain that
had to be ritualistically and legally exorcised.[26]

The Great Awakening of the 1740s was a reawakening to the
charisma within—a reconcentration within the individual himself
of a religious experience in danger of diffusion by institutionalization and rationalization without. In the words of Jonathan Edwards, it was a recognition that "true religion lies very much in the
affections" and that "no light in the understanding is good, which
does not produce holy affections in the heart." The latter statement

suggests that Edwards's concern was an integration of understanding and affection, a sensibility unified, but the revivalism that affected the masses and outraged its critics was one that emphasized the kindling of a new light that fired passion and ignored reason, that found the authentic religious experience in the phenomenon of eros within rather than in the revelation of logos without. In his polemic against the revival, Charles Chauncy argued that "the plain Truth is, an enlightened mind, not raised Affection, ought always to be the Guide of those who call themselves Men."[27]

Clearly, the American religious sensibility was dissociated: the old lights favored the attenuated fires of reason, the new light, the concentrated fires of affection. The immediate results of the Great Awakening and the collision it wrought were a religious rebirth of the individual, the emergence of the twice-born Christian, and the birth of several denominations, a development that manifested the democratic principle of church sovereignty earlier enunciated by John Wise. Another result was that for the first time, the American Protestant, both revivalist and critic, shifted the ground of religious truth away from the Bible toward the nature of man. That Great Awakening eventually burnt itself out and when it had, the theocracy was dead and the republic conceived.

The awakening that perhaps contributed most to the articulation of an American identity, during the period of greatest self-discovery, the American renaissance, was romanticism. It was primarily as a reaction to Unitarianism, the institutionalization of the rational outlook of the Enlightenment, that romanticism, in the form of American transcendentalism, emerged as a revolt against the displacement of the divine spirit from the physical world and as a celebration of the divine presence in the self and in the landscape. The religion of an abstract and systematic nature gave way to the religion of a sensuous and integrative nature; thus, for Emerson, there is "no disgrace, no calamity . . . which nature cannot repair" and the "best moments of life are these delicious awakenings of the higher powers, and the reverential withdrawings of nature before its God."[28]

In addition, transcendentalism sought to point out that the law of the many—effected by revolution but routinized by constitution and institution—became the tyranny of the majority, a tyranny that needed to be repudiated by the individual whose kingdom was not of the fragmented world of society, but of the integrated world of the imagination. Thus, Emerson could write not only that "society everywhere is in conspiracy against the manhood of everyone of its members," but also that "nothing is at last sacred but the integrity of your own mind," and what Emerson meant by *mind* was not the analysis of rationalism but the integration of symbolism.[29]

Emerson, Thoreau, and Whitman—and subsequent interpreters of nineteenth-century America—came to regard the American as a new Adam, freed from history and tradition, "standing alone, self-reliant and self-propelling," in the spacious Eden of the West: "Why should not we also enjoy an original relation to the universe? Why should we not have a poetry and a philosophy of insight and not of tradition, and a religion by revelation to us, and not the history of theirs?" For many students of the American experience, it was and continues to be the authentic American myth—the myth of a paradise regained. It was a curious borrowing of an antenomian model—the Judaic and Christian archetype—to express what was felt to be an antinomian rejection of tradition and an autonomian regeneration of the individual. Like their Puritan ancestors, nineteenth-century Americans saw themselves as twice-born, but this time not reborn and redeemed in Christ and congregation—"I will have no covenants but proximities"—but reborn and recreated in natural and splendid isolation—"Let me admonish you, first of all, to go alone."[30]

Although Emerson was the primary spokesman for the romanticism of his age, he was echoed by others in the transcendentalist movement and by those passing through and summing up the American phenomenon. Bronson Alcott clearly marked the autonomianism of the day when he wrote, "Church and state are responsible to *me,* not I to them. They cease to deserve our veneration from the moment that they violate our consciences. . . . Why would I employ a church to write my creed or a state to govern me? Why should I not write my own creed? Why not govern myself?" Tocqueville found individualism in America to be a "mature and calm feeling" that led each member "to sever himself" from the community, and drawing "apart with his family and his friends," to form "a little circle of his own." It becomes clear that what had started out as reparation—an attempt to repair the split between reason and emotion—was fast becoming a separation between the individual and the community.[31]

Emerson was not the only one to recognize that it was an "age of severance, of dissociation"; Orestes Brownson discerned it also, but his response to the dissolution was more critical: "The work of destruction, commenced by the Reformation, which had introduced an era of criticism and revolution, had, I thought, been carried far enough. All that was dissoluble had been dissolved. All that was destructible had been destroyed, and it was time to begin the work of reconstruction—a work of reconciliation and love."[32] Brownson was writing in 1857 and, in fact, all that was dissoluble had not yet been dissolved, and his ecumenical exhortation fell upon ears deafened by the roar of continental expansion.

Emerson tried periodically throughout his canon to reconcile the tension between individuality and society. In the essay "Society and Solitude" for example, he recognizes that man has been placed by nature between the "extreme antagonisms" of solitude and society and that "solitude is impracticable, and society fatal." He adds that man must labor to keep "the diagonal line" between the two, "our head in the one, our hands in the other." He then concludes that the "conditions are met, if we keep our independence, yet do not lose our sympathy." Emerson's language betrays his predisposition: solitude is merely "impracticable," while society is "fatal." That same predisposition leads him elsewhere to conclude paradoxically that it is solitude that gives rise to solidarity: "Every thing that tends to insulate the individual,—to surround him with barriers of natural respect, so that each man shall feel the world is his, and man shall treat with man as a sovereign state with a sovereign state,—tends to true union as well as greatness," a sentiment later echoed by Josiah Warren in his treatise on laissez faire economics: "Individuality, division, disconnection, disunion" is "the principle of order, harmony, and progress."[33]

So it must have seemed during the first half of the nineteenth century: given the immense, seemingly boundless American landscape and its potential to redeem, America appeared to be an expanding nation that could absorb individuality, industry, and differentiation and that could virtually annul tradition, annul that which had preceded and that which would succeed. It was as though traditional, tribal charisma in the first modern society could be infinitely attenuated outwardly from the eastern center to an ever-expanding periphery, or, as though America could expand its social framework and institutions to deal with every crisis. But the ability of America to translate crisis into community failed: the rate of expansion—the addition of ten states in the 56 years between 1792 and 1848 compared to the evolution of the original thirteen states in the first 175 years—ran apace with the resiliency of the new and energetic nation. The center could not hold, and things fell apart.

Bearing witness to growing individuality and insularity, Tocqueville concluded that the greatest danger to a democracy was not the despotism of traditional society, but rather the atomism of modern society: "As for the rest of his fellow-citizens, [the individual] is close to them, but he sees them not; he touches them, but he feels them not; he exists but in himself and for himself alone; and if his kindred still remain to him, he may be said at any rate to have lost his country."[34] Secession, the loss of country, was metaphorically the result of diminishing returns. America, by this time, was rent by the weight of too many conversions, too many turns away from obedience to will, from tradition to independence, from community to individuality, from nationalism to regionalism, from commonweal to private interest. Moreover, the country experienced the conclusion of an accommodating expansion—it simply had run out of space that could absorb all difference, and North and South found themselves in direct conflict over the political status of the new western territories. The constitutional dispute between a Hamiltonian, capitalistic republic and a Jeffersonian, agrarian democracy was transformed into regional hostility: the North sought to assert its numerical advantage in Congress, to centralize government further, to continue industrial expansion, and to halt the spread of slavery; and the South, seeking to reverse the trend toward industrialism and needing to revive a cotton industry weakened by the poor use of soil in the East, pursued the expansion of slavery and cotton into the Southwest and the decentralization of government away from Washington and back to the states. That we had lost our country was apparent in Calhoun's rationale for a concurrent majority, the only equitable majority in a "community as made up of different and conflicting interests as far as the action of the government is concerned." Calhoun sought parity and, like most of the country, the avoidance of secession, for he recognized that "many bleeding [pores] must be taken up on passing the knife of separation through a body politic" and that *"it is the most difficult process in the world to make two people of one."*[35]

Of course Calhoun, and the rest of the country, would have learned that from the example of the first American secession, and it was precisely the example of the revolution and the rationale of its declaration of independence, on which South Carolina and subsequently the South modeled its declaration "that the union now subsisting between South Carolina and other States under the name of the 'United States of America' is hereby dissolved." In less than two months, South Carolina was joined by six other states and the Confederacy formed. The parallels between revolution and secession are many, and in light of his devotion to the Declaration of Independence, a devotion Lincoln once exemplified in his pronouncement that "any people anywhere being inclined and having the power have the right to rise up and shake off the existing government, and form a new one that suits them better. . . . Any portion of such people that can may revolutionize and make their own of so much territory as they inhabit," it must have been difficult for Lincoln to reconcile his principle with his great desire to maintain the union.[36]

In the end, a stratagem—forcing South Carolina to fire upon Federal forces at Fort Sumpter—allowed Lincoln to wage a war in defense of the Union rather than in arrest of secession. As John Adams had said of the Revolution, secession and the struggle for domination existed in the heart and mind long before the first shot was fired at Fort Sumpter, and it would continue so, long after Lee surrendered at Appomattox. The Civil War and the three amendments it led to repaired the flaws in the Declaration and Constitution by legally making us more one people and therefore one nation; but it left a great wound in the American social psyche that has persisted down to the present. That an election of a Southerner to the presidency in 1976 should be hailed as a sign that the South has finally risen or that the psychological and regional wound has finally healed bears witness to the persistence of division and to the failure of Reconstruction.

Reconstruction of the Union was beset by two great divisions: one legal, the other economic. In an ironic and self-interested reversal of constitutional positions, the South, which had fought heroically for independence, now claimed that it was never out of the Union, and northern, radical Republicans, who had made every effort to keep the South in the Union, now contended that the Southern states had seceded and thereby had reverted to the subordinate status of federal territories. The result of the dispute was a clash between the moderate reconstruction policies of Presidents Lincoln and Johnson and those of radical Republicans who controlled Congress and the Grant administrations. The legal reunion of the several states was strung out a dozen years and finally was realized in the compromises worked out between Southern Democrats and Hays Republicans that settled the disputed Tilden-Hays election. Abiding by the terms of the compromise, Hays removed federal troops from the statehouse in Columbia and appointed many Southerners to key administrative posts.

Reconstruction, however, was in another sense doomed at the outset by another great division: while statesmen toiled at rebuilding a united nation, another conversion, to technology, given great impetus by the demands of the war, was now in full swing, dividing labor into specialists and alienating the worker from the fruit of his labor, from a part of himself. It was by no means an American revolution, but given the precedent of a Protestant ethic of "calling," an ethic anticipated in the middle-class ways of life of the Puritan Samuel Sewall and the Yankee Benjamin Franklin, given a charter of belief dedicated to making it and making it new, and given a virgin frontier beckoning for westward and industrial expansion, the United States was a nation psychologically and resourcefully receptive to the promise, and the betrayal, of the Industrial Revolution. What had been once a worldly means to an otherworldly end—calling as a sign of election—was increasingly becoming a secular end in itself. American know-how, to know how to control and manipulate nature to enrich its physical well-being, became the American calling, the American vocation.

For Philip Slater in *The Pursuit of Loneliness*, America's secularization of its sense of calling implied a transformation of its god: "Since the technological environment that rules, frustrates, and manipulates us is a materialization of the wishes of our forefathers, it is quite reasonable to say that technology *is* the authoritarian father in our society." Thus, the father (papal and kingly) that we had left behind us in our pursuit of freedom had come back to haunt us in the guise of the ghost in the machine. Emerson put it this way: "Things are in the saddle/And ride mankind," an appropriate metaphor for Emerson, who felt both the burden of things and the burden of authority. For Henry Adams, who was to feel a child of the eighteenth century "suddenly cut apart—separated forever" from the emerging twentieth century, the changing of the godhood was also a conversion of charisma concentrated in the Virgin to charisma concentrated in the dynamo. Moreover, Adams discerned that the change was inward as well as outward; thus, he describes himself and Augustus St.-Gaudens confronting a work of medieval art: "St. Gaudens' art was starved from birth, and Adams' instinct was blighted from babyhood. Each had but half of a nature, and when they came together before the Virgin of Amiens they ought both to have felt in her the force that made them one; but it was not so."[37]   That half a nature of which Adams speaks was the result of an internal division, the dissociation of sensibility, that had been a part of the American experience

from the beginning. That dissociation took many forms: the denial
of the sensuous body of the Church and the self by the reformed
Puritan; the denial of the mystic presence of the divine person and
of the charismatic self by the enlightened Yankee; the denial of
tradition and historical process by the romantic transcendentalist;
and the denial of useless beauty, and the insistence on practical
specialization, by the utilitarian capitalist.

The internal division reinforced what we have seen was a series
of external separations of self and sect from society. Tocqueville,
who spent a scant nine months in America, wrote the following
about the new democratic state in 1835: "Thus, not only does
democracy make every man forget his ancestors, but it hides his
descendants and separates his contemporaries from him; it throws
him back forever upon himself alone, and threatens in the end to
confine him entirely within the solitude of his own heart." Emerson, who had lived all his fifty-four years in America, wrote two
decades later, "But how insular, and pathetically solitary, are all the
people we know."[38] It was in response to the dissociation within
and the separation without that one discontent and alien in
America—the literary artist—began to make catholic protest.

In this respect, the American writer of the early nineteenth century was not unlike his British counterpart. Both witnessed the
disintegrating effects of industrialization; both turned toward art
and culture to stem the modern forces of fragmentation; and both
in the process sought a new language that, in the words of Paul
Ricoeur, "restores to us that participation-in and belonging-to an
order of things that precedes our capacity to oppose ourselves to
things."[39] There the similarity ends, for the American romantic was
dealing with a culture and tradition essentially different from those
of the English romantic and that difference significantly influenced
the manner and method of his reappropriation of symbolic language.

The man of letters in England grew out of and could look to a
tradition that stressed continuity of institutions, mediation between the individual and society, and integration of the community. Continuity manifested itself in both throne and pulpit. Despite the temporary success of Cromwell, the monarchy emerged
with the symbolic, if not political, power to unite the peoples of
the kingdom. Despite the growth of sectarianism, the Anglican
Church remained the dominant and parochial church of the state.
These two institutions, together with a complicated network of
social interrelationship, effected a mediation between the indi-

vidual and society that gave the individual a sense of place in an ordered community.

What tradition the American writer had to look to and draw upon was quite different. The expansive and liberating expression of self—conversion, separatism, and independence—may have yielded in the past to the contracting and concentrated expression of community—convenant, congregation, and constitution—but the force of the former was proving to be greater than that of the latter. The result was an accretion of autonomianism and anti-nomianism, a legacy that posited the self as prior to and in tension with the *nomos,* one that would sacrifice the integrity of the psyche and community on the altar of freedom and individuality. Because his country's past was one so very much determined by the modern forces of rationalization and differentiation, any national heritage the American writer had was as much one of separation as reparation.

Thus, whereas the English romantic poet reached back past the pervading rationalism of the day and reappropriated native, medieval literary prototypes and Renaissance platonism to evoke a transcendent union with a nature and community that were relatively immediate and accessible, the American transcendentalist, believing that he was creating a charter of belief for a nation in its formative years and not having medieval or Renaissance native traditions to draw upon, reached further back to mythological archetypes in his evocation of a sacred communion between nature and the individual in splendid isolation. In addition, whereas the English writer of romance used the Gothic primarily to challenge the utilitarian and pragmatic preoccupation of the day and to reaffirm the presence of the metaphysical, the American writer of romance, faced not only with the fragmentation of industrialization, but also with the individualism implicit in transcendentalism, reappropriated the Gothic to develop a truly new symbolism to evoke modern psychological dislocation and alienation.[40]

With the advent of logical positivism and neoclassicism, life and truth were generally regarded as an external experience that could be known, measured, and expressed by the conscious mind and discursive language. Life was explainable; the dark, mysterious forests had been rooted out, the fields tilled in neat, uniform rows, the earth made plain. Existence thus could be plotted in both field and fiction. With the romantic revolution, however, the conception was challenged by the recognition of the felt life, the tacit dimension that, because of its flux and invisibility, could not be expressed by an analytically-based language. What was needed was a new language or a reappropriation of a more primitive language, a Coleridgean "ensemplastic" language—one that threw together that which was normally and consciously separated.

The evolution of romanticism into modernism involves an evolution of such a language—an aesthetic technique and form best suited to the evocation of the interior life, the psychological condition. As that language evolves, the tensive metaphor—the ironic juxtaposition of disparate experience and heterogeneous ideas—becomes a prevalent characteristic of literature. It is as though the artist were forced to smash up the old order of experience and the old order of words and reassemble them in seemingly irrational juxtaposition to evoke the complexity and ambiguity of felt experience. This is graphically demonstrated in modern art, where dadaism amalgamates disparate media, cubism reassembles, indeed dissembles, human and other anatomies, and surrealism distorts the familiar to evoke not what life looks like, but rather what it feels like, or, as Emily Dickinson would say, to paint "the internal difference, where the meanings are."

In literature, life is no longer plotted; it is orchestrated. For Eliot and Joyce, the Wagnerian leitmotiv—the statement, repetition, and variation of theme—and the contrapuntal movement of point/counterpoint effectively score the dialectical nature of the modern condition. In Faulkner, such orchestration becomes more ironic and perverse, when the conductor is a thirty-three-year-old idiot. Faulkner's narration serves not only to signify the sound and fury of the old South becoming new, but also, through the lapses and fusions of Benjy's unconscious, to collapse time and demonstrate the interdependence of the historical past and present and the synchronicity of psychological time.

In reaching a new form for the expression of the psychological, the twentieth-century writer could draw upon the influences of Frazer, Freud, and Eisenstein and the tensive juxtapositions of myth, dream, and film. Striving for a similar language to express his internal dislocations and needs, the nineteenth-century American writer drew primarily upon the perversity of Gothic fiction. He extended the following Gothic characteristics: the convoluted housescape that turned in upon itself to psychic enclosure; the grotesque persona, encounters with whom disturbed equilibrium; the madman, whose paranoia achieved a double purpose: his behavior beyond *(para)* common knowledge *(nous)* reflected disintegration, while his knowledge beyond common experience evoked forbidden knowledge and hidden taboo that man was loath to acknowledge in his conscious world. Gothic madness is thus a derangement of the quotidian world and an evocation of the buried life, and the Gothic fictive nightmare, an anticipation of the perversity and absurdity of modern literature. Two of the most recurrent and tensive symbols reappropriated in the nineteenth-century American version of that nightmare are the circle and the labyrinth.

3

The Gothic Circle: A Design of Darkness to Appall

A circle is but a dilated point, the center point,
To come from the point is to be born, to go into it
is to die.

Henri-Frédéric Amiel, *La Part du reve*

One of the most universal symbols of original and recovered wholeness of being is the sphere or circle. In the primitive totem of elementary religion—the serpent biting its own tail—that symbol manifests itself as the sacred and androgynous *uroborus,* a completeness in which being has not yet been divided or disclosed in all its binary opposition. In medieval Christianity, it is a more abstract God who is defined as a sphere whose center is everywhere and circumference nowhere—a sphere that, because it encompasses all time as well as infinite space, is without the boundaries of time and space. With the romantic movement, that circle becomes the God-in-man or the man-God, the individual who is in every moment and every place the center of an ever-changing, boundless universe. In all instances, the wholeness associated with the circle is original, and the fall from the sphere or the breaking of the circle is perceived, in time, as traumatic enclosure within the labyrinth.[1]

The myth of the labyrinth is symbolic of man's expulsion from the center of the world and his search for the center through the complexities of consciousness and modern society. In primitive mythology and Greek drama, the labyrinth is a variation on the invisible web of life, the threads of which are manipulated by divinities that would keep profane man in bondage. Such bondage is a knot that must be ritualistically untied—a labyrinth from

55

which the exile must extricate himself in order to return to the
sacred center of an ordered universe. The labyrinth is thus the
penance that each man does for his separation from the boundless;
it is the image of excessive boundaries effected by man's growing
consciousness of the division and fragmentation of the physical
world outside and the psychological one within. The labyrinth is,
however, a symbol not only of the cause and condition of his
expulsion, but also sometimes of the cure: it is the subterranean
cave or womb—the unconscious—through which man must pass
in order to recover wholeness.[2]

The achievement of such a recovery is revealed not always as a
circle, but also as a square within or enclosing a circle, a design that
Jungians identify as a mandala. Although Jung himself emphasized
the quaternity of the mandala—probably because it conformed to
his notion of the fourfold psyche and to his interest in the practices
of alchemy—many of his followers point out that, whereas the
circle is a constant in the mandala, quaternity often gives way to
forms varying from a single triangle to multiples and combinations
of any geometric symmetry.[3] What is appealing symbolically about
the mandala is that it incorporates both circle and labyrinth. It is as
though man integrates his world and himself by ordering the broken lines of the labyrinth and coalescing them with the original
circle in the symmetry of the mandala. The suggestion is that
recovered wholeness is unlike original wholeness, for what falls
between the two and what must be accounted for in any recovery
is the consciousness of boundary. Thus, the circle must be squared.

The American transcendentalist, as one would expect, uses the
circle primarily as a symbol of romantic egocentricity: the individual is the center of a cosmos imagined and projected from
within himself. It is the Emersonian self manifest as a transparent
eyeball, through which the currents of the universal being circu-
late. It is also Walden Pond, "the Earth's eye," looking into which
Thoreau measures the depth of his own nature and recovers the
alienated part of that nature. It is in the poetry of Walt Whitman,
however, that the circle and mandala are richly used as symbols of
the wholeness inherent in and recovered by the true son of God,
the solitary singer.

Throughout his poetry, Whitman celebrates an infinitely expanding universe in which "all goes outward and outward" and
"nothing collapses,"[4] in which "a vast similitude interlocks all"
(261), but also one in which "the converging objects of the universe perpetually flow" (47) to the poet whose "orbit . . . cannot be

swept by a carpenter's compass" (48). Thus, the poet is the center of an infinite, measureless circle; moreover, he is also the source of that expanding circle. Like the noiseless, patient spider, the poet launches forth the filaments that seek out and connect and thereby design the mandalalike, spiderweb cosmos. It is the poet's "insight and power" that "encircles things and the human race" (169).

In "Passage to India," Whitman unites his celebration of the poet as divine encircler with a millennial celebration of the nation's destiny. Perhaps because the poem was written after the cleavage dealt by the Civil War and after the great elegies lamenting separation from nature and the loved one, "Passage" deals with a wholeness that is recovered or one that is original only in the sense that it has not existed yet for man. Whitman sees the progress of the individual and the race as a circumnavigation of the globe, a great chain of technology, whereby "the earth [is] spann'd, connected by network" and the "lands . . . welded together" by the Suez Canal, the transatlantic cable, and the transcontinental railroad. Such a voyage is more than a geographical progression in space; it is also a psychological and spiritual progression in time: it is "a passage indeed O soul to primal thought . . . to realms of budding bibles . . . the voyage of [the] mind's return/To reason's early paradise/Back to wisdom's birth, to innocent intuitions/ Again with fair creation."

Thus, Whitman's passage is a return voyage to an *in illo tempore*—to the eastern garden, to infancy and childhood, to a nature in genesis, and to the intuitive world of the symbol. It is also a realization of Columbus's dream, and Whitman uses the "Genoese" in much the same way that Harte Crane will use him in the next century—as the archetypal American whose dream is transcendental. It is significant that the circumnavigation achieves its penultimate link through the transcontinental railroad, the "bridging" the more than three thousand miles of land travel and "tying the Eastern to the Western Sea/The road between Europe and Asia." For such, Whitman says, were "thou born America/For purpose vast, man's long probation fill'd/Thou rondure of the world at last accomplish'd." Moreover, the navigator of this symbolic voyage shall be the American poet:

> All these separations and gaps shall be taken up and
>   hook'd and link'd together . . .
> Trinitas divine shall be gloriously accomplish'd and
>   compacted by the true son of God, the poet . . .

Nature and Man shall be disjoin'd and diffused no more,
The true son of God shall absolutely fuse them.

The joining effected by the poet as "Trinitas" in "Passage" is rendered as divine quaternity in "Chanting the Square Deific." The first side of this pantheistic square is the paternal God associated with time, law, and authority and identified with Jehovah and Kronos among others; the second is the mediating, "mightier God," associated with love and affection and identified with Jesus, Hermes, and Hercules; the third is the democratic rebel—the "comrade of criminals, brother of slaves"—identified as Satan; and the fourth and most pervasive is the "Sancta Spirita," the unifying general soul and poet, who is also the "life of the great round world." Thus, in the recovery of wholeness in the Whitman canon, the circle becomes the mandala.

For those writers who reacted negatively to American transcendentalism and for whom individuality was a more ambiguous possibility, the circle and the mandala are more ironically developed. Perhaps it was inevitable that the labyrinth should emerge as a dominant motif in the fiction of Poe, Hawthorne, and Melville, a fiction owing much to a Gothic tradition rich in images of hidden panels, trapdoors, haunted corridors, and ruined mansions. What is not expected and therefore ironic is that the circle in American Gothic fiction should manifest itself as that which isolates the self from the other or that the circle should fuse with the images of weight and descent in the symbol of the whirlpool that turns in upon a central point and destroys the self and sometimes the other. Such a fusion suggests that the writers whose power lay in blackness were not as convinced as were the transcendentalists that individuality was necessarily a force for benign reparation. Indeed, individuality, symbolized by both the circle and mandala, carried too far becomes individualism, and individualism turns privacy into privation, regeneration into degeneration, transcendence into death or death-in-life. Such is the nature of the ambiguity that characterizes Poe's use of the labyrinth and mandala.

Kaleidoscope: The Bad Dreams of Edgar Allan Poe

In Edgar Allan Poe's first published short story, "M. S. Found in a Bottle," the narrator, like so many of Poe's subsequent tellers, is an isolate individual—"driven" from his country and "estranged" from his family. He is also a man of positivistic persuasion, whose "education of no common order" has developed in him "a strong relish for physical philosophy" and a tendency "to methodize." The narrator is the straw man of science whom Poe sets up for the shock of phenomenological recognition—the encounter of a "sensation which will admit of no analysis." The encounter between method and mystery is clearly resolved here in favor of mystery, as the Promethean fire of the sun leaves but "a dim silver-like rim, alone," as it rushes down "into the unfathomable sea" and as the hero, "plunging madly within the grasp of the whirlpool," hurries onwards "to some exciting knowledge—some never-to-be-imparted secret, whose attainment is destruction."

In many ways the mise-en-scène is a manifestation of a romantic sensibility that negates method and positive knowledge in favor of feeling and mystery. More particularly and more significantly, it is also evocative of the tension, ambiguity, and dread that attend the imminence of disclosure or reunion that is paradoxically destructive in the fiction of Poe. Characteristically, the symbol that evokes that tension is the recurring one of enclosure within the whirlpool; the Poe hero finds himself turning and turning in a narrowing gyre or, as seen from above, in the whirl of a kaleidoscopic motion that circles in upon a disappearing point. David Halliburton incisively notes that Poe's image of the vortex tensively and paradoxically combines the positive image of the circle—meaning harmony and perfection—with the negative image of descent—meaning annihilation and death.[5]

The tension between the positive and negative connotations associated with the circle and descent is indicative of the basic ambivalence experienced by the heroes in three of Poe's greatest short stories: "Ligeia," "The Fall of the House of Usher," and "William Wilson." In those tales, however, tension and ambiguity are effected not only by the symbol of the vortex, but also by a symbol that fuses the positive associations of the mandala and the negative ones of the labyrinth, one that is perhaps best described by the term *kaleidoscopic mandala.* These tensive metaphors are used to evoke the following central theme in the fiction of Poe: the individual, in his desire to withdraw completely into the spiritual or imaginative or willful self, in order to integrate a particular dimension of his being, ironically comes close to, and sometimes succeeds in, annihilating the whole person.

If the protagonist of "Ligeia" is Ligeia, then the narrative is a rather obvious manifestation of the epigraph of the tale: Ligeia is a woman whose undying strength of will overcomes death and reunites her with her lover—albeit, over and through the dead body of the Lady Rowena. However, if the tale belongs, as it does in most of Poe's stories, to the narrator, then Ligeia and Rowena and their agon with death become symbolic projections of the narrator's experience. Indeed, it is what the narrator wills that is symbolized in the events growing out of the Gothic *ménage à trois* in "Ligeia."

Who is the Lady Ligeia? Whoever she is, she is no ordinary lady, or for that matter, no ordinary wife. She comes and goes as a "shadow"; her voice is all "whisper" and "music"; her hands are "marble," her skin "ivory," her raven hair Homerically "hyacinthine," her chin the fullness and spirituality of "Greek," and her eyes more profound than the "well of Democritus. . . . twin stars of Leda." Taken as a composite image, there is a grotesqueness here that suggests the surrealism of a Salvador Dali, but the grotesqueness is, as in surrealism, no aesthetic lapse. It is a very basic part of the Gothic distortion and incongruity that prepare the reader for the horror of Ligeia's resurrection, while simultaneously evoking the splendor of her being and the meaning of her character.

The learning of Ligeia is immense: not only is she schooled in the modern languages of Europe, but when passionately stirred, she speaks with an appalling "energy of . . . wild words" that suggests the gift of tongues. Her academic acquisitions are "astounding" and "gigantic," and before them the narrator resigns himself with "childlike confidence." Ligeia is the great mother, the goddess muse, who inspires the narrator's education and who, bending over his studies, seduces him away from the outside world towards some inner "wisdom too divinely precious not to be forbidden." Before that seduction can be consummated, however, Ligeia, together with the narrator's youth, is ravished herself by the "Conqueror worm," by the passage of time.

Without Ligeia, the narrator, like a "child groping benighted," turns to the flesh-and-blood Lady Rowena and in a state of "childlike perversity" brings the lady to an arabesque bridal chamber that shortly becomes her death chamber. The bridal room is polymorphously perverse; it is made so not by the grotesque distortions that mark the person of Ligeia, but ironically by the labyrinthine and kaleidoscopic motion of the arabesque. The room's pentagonal angularity is rounded by the huge ebony sarcophagus set in each angle, and the stark gold and ebony of the drapery and walls are complicated by the fretted ceilings, by the parti-colored fires that dance from the Saracen censor suspended from the center of the ceiling, and by the artificial and continual current introduced into the chamber. All this results in a "serpent vitality. . . . a hideous and uneasy animation [of] the whole."

Serpent vitality is especially effective because it extends the metaphor of the conqueror worm of Ligeia's poem and thereby prepares the reader for the intrusion of death upon the bride Rowena. More significantly, it sets in motion the mandalalike symmetry of the arabesque that turns the harmonious and perfect mandala into the kaleidoscopic form of Ligeia's poem—the same hideous animation tracking down the phantom life "through a circle that ever returneth in/To the self-same spot." Thus, the grotesque room of the Gothic abbey becomes claustrophobic as well as phantasmagoric, and it is in such an enclosure that the denouement is spun in.

Who poisons Rowena—the narrator or Ligeia? The answer of course is both. There is no doubt that the spirit of Ligeia, entering as she does early in the tale, as "indefinite shadow of angelic aspect," is responsible for the three or four drops of ruby-colored liquid that murder the Lady Rowena. But the actions of Ligeia and Rowena are but projections of the narrator's will: it is he that wills the death of the mortal Rowena and the rebirth of the immortal Ligeia of his introverted youth and imagination. Daniel Hoffman suggests that the rhythmic failure of Rowena is a manifestation of Poe's identification of sex and death: "What other experience does this description suggest than the repeated, excited violation of the body in successive orgasm?"[6] Such an interpretation is attractive and partially accurate, because it suggests that out of the coital union of the narrator and the Lady Rowena is born the Lady Ligeia, that out of the "serpent vitality" of the bridal chamber does the psyche alter its form, manifest its polymorphous perversity. However, since the spasms of Rowena last the entire night and since Rowena's illness begins in the second month of marriage, it seems more likely that Rowena's spasms are those of labor rather than coitus, and out of that labor is Ligeia reborn. Thus, the ruby-colored drops become the transcendental sperm that conquer the conqueror worm.

Is "Ligeia" then what Halliburton suggests it is: "the strongest testimonial [Poe] ever made, in story form, for the indestructibility of life"?[7] Perhaps, it would be more accurate to call it a testimonial to the indestructibility of the past, more particularly, of childhood. It must be remembered that, if the narrator and Ligeia succeed in conquering death, they do so only at the expense of the death of another, of Rowena. What the narrator wills is deliverance from the real Lady Rowena of the present, from a reality that is doomed to disappoint, from life itself into the spiritual but congenital self that submits with childlike confidence to the recollection or imagination of the gigantic and maternal acquisitions of Ligeia. Though there is a reunion here between the narrator and that past in the form of Ligeia's fantastic resurrection, there is no communion. In fact, in most of Poe's fiction, there is neither communion nor community, because there are no communicants; there is only the introverted self. That is why the euphoria of reunion is almost always mitigated by the horror of isolation and annihilation. Such is the case also in "The Fall of the House of Usher."

Like so many of Poe's arabesques and grotesques, "The Fall of the House of Usher" demands of the reader a bit of ratiocination. The reader asks who is Roderick Usher; what is his relationship with his twin, Madeline; why does he put her "living in the tomb"; why, upon realizing his ghastly deed, does he dare not speak or act, and why, upon realizing that she is climbing the ancestral stairs to avenge herself, does he not try to avert his doom? The reader is told from the outset that Roderick suffers from a "constitutional and family evil," the most apparent symptom of which is a "morbid acuteness of the senses." As the epigraph suggests, "His heart is a suspended lute/ Whenever one touches it, it resounds." Poe has skillfully taken a staple image of the romantic sensibility—the Aeolian harp—and translated it into his own Gothic metaphor of a sensibility so acute that it transforms the ordinary into the extraordinary, the picturesque into the grotesque.

The narration also implies that Roderick's constitutional disease is directly related to another family evil—inbreeding: "the stem of the Usher race . . . had put forth, at no period, any enduring branch . . . the entire family lay in the direct line of descent." Thus, Roderick and Madeline, with "sympathies of a scarcely intelligible nature," live alone and apart from the outside world, incestuously, but spiritually, in touch with one another. That sentient union only becomes physical in Madeline's deathlike, and lovelike, embrace of Roderick at the end of the tale, an embrace that paradoxically destroys the House of Usher.

For Roderick and Madeline, existence has become a death-in-life, in which both share the same emaciated, cadaverous visage, an image that suggests a spiritual introversion that consumes flesh and blood. Roderick's dilemma is expressed in his painting as a clean, well-lighted vault, from which there is no exit. That is why Roderick summons the narrator, for his "cheerful society"; it is a final, but futile, attempt to deliver himself from himself, from the dead-end existence embodied in the personae of his twin sister and his ancestral home. That is why he puts Madeline prematurely in the tomb; that is why he dares not speak nor act, when his sympathies announce to him both his deed and his doom. As much as part of him desires separation from the House of Usher and integration into the external world of society, another part of him desires complete separation from society and union with Madeline, the narcissistic image of himself.

What Poe dramatizes in the Gothic action, he also effectively evokes in the arabesque imagery. The genealogical and psychological House of Usher is the architectural house of Usher: the cadaverous structure, with a "barely perceptible fissure" running down its facade into the tarn that mirrors forth in even more foreboding and "inverted images" the decadence of the House. It is an effective symbol: a fourfold pattern, halved by the fissure and quartered by the tarn's reflection. It is the Usher coat of arms, made more arabesque and grotesque by the order and arrangement of the stones that are overspread with fungi and surrounded by decaying trees.

Once more Poe transforms the arabesque into the kaleidoscope and the static into the dynamic mandala: this time, more subtly and powerfully, without the artificial and obvious censors found in "Ligeia." In an effective contrapuntal movement to the death embrace and collapse of Roderick and Madeline, the house of Usher is rent asunder and, together with its morbid image in the tarn, collapses in a kaleidoscopic implosion into the dark waters, leaving behind the circular, but red-blood, moon. It is once again a symbolic devolution: the House of Usher at last satisfying its perverse desire to turn inward upon itself to the maternal and uroboric womb evoked in the circle of the full moon.

This submergence of the negatively connotative image of the cracked and arabesque house in the positively connotative image of the simple and circular full moon would seem to lend credence to Richard Wilbur's assertion that "The Fall of the House of Usher" is not really a horror story, but rather a "triumphant report by the narrator that it is possible for the poetic soul to shake off the temporal, rational, physical world and escape, if only for a moment, to a realm of unfettered vision." Maurice Beebe concurs with such a reading, for he concludes that Roderick Usher's "most triumphant creation is the obliteration of his suffering, diffused self in a return to that oneness which is nothingness."[8] The problem with such readings is that they seem to ignore the tone of the short story; there is no triumphant celebration here. The narrator has not borne witness to transcendence; on the contrary, he has experienced a revelation of an apocalypse.

It is true that Usher succeeds in shaking off the external world, but only to be destroyed within the introverted world, and though he returns to the oneness that is nothingness—a oneness evoked in the love-death embrace of the twins—it is by no means a triumph. Madeline's embrace of Roderick can be read as a Gothic variation of Plato's myth in the *Symposium:* the two halves of the foetal, androgynous being that was severed in the womb are reunited, but in that reunion the ontogenetic self, the individual person, is lost and its metaphysical counterpart, the phylogenetic House of Usher, is submerged in the womblike tarn that reflects the full, blood-red moon. That the moon is blood-red is significant: once more Poe transforms a traditional romantic symbol into a tensive and ambiguous one. The female moon is not the mother or sister who succors, but rather the one who devours. Madeline is the narcissistic reflection of Roderick, who wastes away in his attraction to the image of himself. What is true for Madeline is also true for Roderick: by his introversion, he has put himself living into the tomb. It is as though Poe as narrator has a nightmare vision of Poe as poet, who would enfold himself into the realm of imagination, into an ever-refined sensibility, that eventually refines the complex, human self out of existence.

Allan Tate sees Poe as the artist whose work reveals a distant, but impressive insight into the modern phenomenon of the disintegrated personality: "Although he was capable of envisaging the unified action of the mind through the three faculties; his own mind acted upon its materials now as intellect, now as feeling, now as will; never as all three together."[9] This is borne out somewhat by Poe himself in his classification of his fiction into tales of ratiocination and tales of the arabesque and grotesque. More importantly, this dissociation of sensibility is also manifest in the typical agon of Poe's fiction, where that dissociation undermines whatever wholeness is evoked. Though there is a manifestation of reunion or reintegration in such works as "Usher," it is rarely, if ever, an integration of the whole person. It is as though there were a part of the hero—consciousness or ego—that hangs back from the spiritual reintegration, because it fears its own annihilation in such a possibility.

In "William Wilson," the divided self is translated into will and conscience rather than imagination and reality. William Wilson, as the name suggests, is the son of his own will. The family curse this time is self-will and an ungovernable passion: thus, "at an age when few children have abandoned their leading strings," Wilson, unlike the narrator of "Ligeia" or the protagonist of "Usher," is completely "left to the guidance of [his] own will" and "becomes the master of [his] own action." But that liberation is soon modified by Wilson's encounter with William Wilson II— "CONSCIENCE GRIM / That spectre in my path." Poe's imp of the perverse, the inner voice that calls attention to its own transgression, takes the form of a twin antagonist; here, however, the twin is not fraternal as in "Usher," but identical. What Wilson discovers when he lowers the lamp in close proximity to the sleeping Wilson II is the narcissistic alter ego, and in a perversion of the myth the response is one of terror rather than rapture.

The complication begins with Wilson's indignation over Wilson II's failure to submit to his will; it winds round to a point where Wilson finds himself on the verge of a "bitterly reluctant submission to [Wilson II's] arbitrary will." What has happened in the meantime is that the narrator has in the course of a reckless youth all but destroyed his willpower and himself. Poe expresses the dissolution of self in a metaphorical variation of the whirlpool symbol: "The vortex of thoughtless folly into which I there so immediately and so recklessly plunged, washed away all but the froth of my past hours, engulfed at once every solid or serious impression, and left to memory only the veriest levities of a former existence."

After the card game accusation, Wilson tries to flee Wilson II, but encounters him later in a cul-de-sac in a Roman palazzo. The final encounter there reveals an imagery that implies the arabesque of "Ligeia" and the reflection of "Usher." Finding it difficult to force his "way through the mazes of the company" in order to engage the young wife of the aged Duke in a compromising seduction, Wilson comes upon Wilson II, dressed in the same masquerade. The idea of a masked ball is a deft touch, for the mask underscores the confusion of identity that dominates the denouement. Wilson drags Wilson II with him, through the maze of company, into an antechamber, where he repeatedly plunges his

sword into his passive twin. Then, Poe plays on the reader's imagination with a fictional sleight of hand.

He has Wilson turn away momentarily to check the entrance of
someone into the chamber. When he returns, he seems to see himself in a mirror that had not been there before, "but with features
all pale and dabbled in blood" and advancing to meet him "with a
feeble and tottering gait." Just as the reader is prepared to conclude
that there is no Wilson II and that Wilson has killed himself in
another perverse moment of remorse, Poe indicates that the mirror
had only "seemed" to be there. For there is Wilson II, "not a line
in all the marked and singular lineaments of his face which was not,
even in the most absolute identity, *mine own!*" Thus, the narrator
himself must be bedecked in blood and gore. Thereby, when Wilson II utters the final pronouncement, Wilson fancies that "I myself was speaking": "*You have conquered, and I yield. Yet, hence-
forward art thou also dead—dead to the World, to Heaven and to
Hope! In me didst thou exist—and in my death, see by this image,
which is thine own, how utterly thou hast murdered thyself.*" Wilson could as easily and rightly have said that of Wilson II as Wilson
II says it of Wilson. It is a brilliant wilderness of mirrors, in which
the hero and the doppelgänger become so intertwined that the
reader is left wondering whether or not the protagonist perishes
with the antagonist. Daniel Hoffman poses the question this way:
"But how can the evil-doing part of the ego survive the murder of
the judging self?"[10] Well, it cannot; however, the willful ego can
and does survive the murder of social conscience. What does not
survive is the person, the whole self; Narcissus does not survive his
severance from Echo.

Henry James Sr. could very well have had in mind the personae
of Poe's fiction, when he wrote in *Society: The Redeemed Form of
Man* that "a man's *proprium*, or private selfhood, is actually his
own particular hell, for by it he communicates with hell." James
believed that it was only through relationship and identification
with others, only through participation in society, that one
achieved authentic selfhood: "Society is the only real or Divine
natural man, and we individual men (falsely so-called) attain to a
real or Divinely recognizeable individuality only in identifying
ourselves with him: that is, *in losing our life in ourselves and
finding it again, resurgent, in society.*" Perhaps nothing more distinguishes the fiction of Poe from that of Hawthorne and Melville
than the relative absence of society; it marks Poe clearly as the
most romantic of the three, rendering his narratives the least fictive

and the most poetic in their evocations of the internal state of the
separate self. Moreover, the ambiguous nature of his fiction suggests that at least a part of Poe shared James's fear of the consequences of extreme isolation from others. Contrastingly, the presence of society and the redemptive effect of society upon the
individual distinguish Hawthorne's *The Scarlet Letter* from the
fiction of Poe and Melville.

The Scarlet Letter: From Maze to Mandala

The dialectic of *The Scarlet Letter* is established in the very first
paragraph of "The Custom House," where Nathaniel Hawthorne,
concerned that a writer may reveal what should only be addressed
"to the one heart and mind of perfect sympathy" or what would
"find out the divided segment of the writer's own nature and complete his own circle of existence by . . . communion with it,"
emphasizes that he should "still keep the inmost Me behind the
veil." Although a comment on the autobiographical aspects of
"The Custom House," the passage introduces the reader to some
of the major polarities of the novel. To begin, it establishes the one
voice that insists on the sovereignty and privacy of the self at all
costs and another voice that suggests that part of the cost may be
purgation and the consequent healing brought about by public
confession. In the tale itself, Dimmesdale becomes the focus of the
argument, for he knows that it would be better to confess publicly
than to "hide a guilty heart through life"; yet, he more than once
reiterates the individual's need and right to keep sin and shame
private.

In addition to this debate over private sin and public confession,
the passage also introduces the reader to the theme of separation
and reparation. In the novel, referring to Dimmesdale, Hawthorne
writes, "the breach which guilt has once made into the human soul
is never, in this mortal state, repaired." Such a remark would seem
to preclude any reconciliation or atonement, but as D. H. Lawrence suggests, trust the tale, not the teller, or, as we suggest, trust
the image, not the narration.[12] To be certain, the romance is filled
with all kinds of separation, of which the primary one is the failure
of each major character to make or sustain a vital human connection. Dimmesdale is only "at ease in some seclusion of his own";
Chillingworth pitches his tent on a wild outskirt of earth, "isolated
from human interests"; Pearl is a "born outcast of the infantile

world"; and Hester is "not merely estranged, but outlawed from society."

In addition to the breach within the guilty heart and the division of self from society, Hawthorne emphasizes the divorcement of one character from another. Hester finds herself in the marketplace thankful for the shame of public exposure, because it maintains a distance between Chillingworth and herself. Hester and Pearl, who once "stood together in the same circle of seclusion from human society," find themselves estranged on opposite sides of a brook that is a "boundary between two worlds." Finally, Hester encounters on Election Day a Dimmesdale so withdrawn unto himself and so concentrated in his unsympathizing purpose, that she despairs of a "real bond betwixt the clergyman and herself."

The basic image of such separation and isolation is the circle of seclusion or exclusion. Hester is in "a sphere by herself," Pearl inhabits an "inviolable circle," there is a "circle of ominous shadow" around Chillingworth, and a "magnetic sphere" around Dimmesdale warns him of the intrusion of others. The circle of exclusion, however, is not the only sphere in *The Scarlet Letter;* there is also the sphere of inclusion—that communion with one's divided nature that completes the circle of one's existence and makes one whole. The most significant of these circles are implied rather than stated and form a more integral part of the symbolic design of the narrative; they will be discussed in detail later. It will suffice for now to refer to those more explicit circles in which one experiences congregation rather than isolation. For Pearl, it is a "wide and various circle of acquaintance" with the denizens of wood and meadow; for Hester and Dimmesdale, it is the "magic circle" of the hour in the forest, where reunion is a discovery of the past and a hope for the future; and for the community it is the "sphere of human charities," where the tribe and the individual are united. It is movement away from the circle of exclusion toward the circle of inclusion, from private agony towards social sympathy, that is the end of the rite of passage in *The Scarlet Letter.*

The fundamental component of all religion and all ritual is *numinosity*—the sacred presence. Hawthorne effectively evokes the numinosity of time, place, and totem in the opening scene of the romance. The occasion of Hester's punishment has all the trappings of a "holiday" or holy day; it is a time outside the profane continuum. In addition, the place of Hester's ignominy is a sacred place: it is the point to which Hester's whole life has tended. The scaffold in the marketplace at the center of the town is, more than the church itself, the altar upon which tribal law and communion are confirmed. It is indeed one of the town's "consecrated places." The sacred presence, however, is felt most strongly, as Emile Durkheim suggests it will be in elementary religion, in the tribal totem, the scarlet letter.[13] The citizens of Boston are never more one as when their unrelenting eyes are "concentred at [Hester's] bosom." Only Dimmesdale's tremulous voice also has the power to effect a communion of the tribe: it vibrated "within all hearts, and brought the listeners into one accord of sympathy." In effecting such concentration and accord, the ritual of public disgrace serves the ancient function of all ritual and confirms the solidarity of the tribe. It also integrates the individual into the tribe.

Emerging from the dark prison house into the "unadulterated sunshine"—the cleansing flame that *un-adulterates*—Hester is the heroine completing her rite of passage from darkness and symbolic death to light and symbolic rebirth. The citizenry behold this transfigured woman as if for the first time: "Those who had before known her, and had expected to behold her dimmed and obscured by a disastrous cloud, were astonished, and even startled, to perceive how her beauty shone out, and made a halo of misfortune and ignominy in which she was enveloped." Hester's fall then is somewhat fortunate: rather than being dimmed (like Dimmesdale) by her experience, she is transformed into a beautifully radiant woman, a mother whose "attire and mien" evoke images of Divine Maternity. Moreover, her first word in the novel, in response to Reverend Wilson's plea that she reveal the father of her child, is a simple "Never," dramatizing a degree of moral independence.

Hester's independence of and integration into the tribe are a key part of the dialectic of self and society. One of the major results of the public ritual of moral exposure is to isolate Hester from the tribe: the "fantastically embroidered and illuminated" letter has the effect "of a spell, taking her out of the ordinary relations with humanity and inclosing her in a sphere by herself." But the same letter also has the effect of establishing extraordinary relations with humanity. Hester's sin strikes roots into the soil, entitles her "to hold intercourse with her fellow creatures," and gives her the power to sympathize. The fortune in Hester's fall is the power of affection—the power not only to feel-with, but also to-do-for:

> The links that united her to the rest of human kind—links of flowers, or silk, or gold . . . had been broken. Here was the iron link of

mutual crime, which neither he nor she could break. Like all other ties, it brought along with it its obligations.

It is an interesting passage, that likens Dimmesdale and Hester to Milton's Adam and Eve; but more significantly it also suggests a foundation for human brotherhood that likens Hawthorne to Freud.

It is a major theme of Hawthorne's that the only viable community or communion is one based on the recognition of communal sin and guilt. That is the same conclusion drawn by Freud in his study of totem and taboo. According to Freud, presocial man becomes social man, when, ambivalent over the deed of having joined with his brothers to kill the horde father and enjoy the horde women, he makes incest and patricide taboo, thereby alleviating his guilt and reinforcing the strength of the new social contract with his brothers. In successive stages, the dead father becomes the totem animal and the totem animal, the apotheosized father, the paternal God.[14] One could theorize that the crime in *The Scarlet Letter* is incest: Dimmesdale is more than once described as filial in his relationship with Hester; Chillingworth is old enough to be the father; and adultery is a rebellion against the law of the elders. More importantly, however, the outcome of crime in both Hawthorne and Freud is the same: sin and guilt lead to social communion. And it is such communion that Hester gains by her ritualistic confession and that Dimmesdale loses by his failure to come down from his high place and stand with her on the scaffold in the center of the tribe.

If Hester's emergence into the unadulterated sunshine of the marketplace is her ritualistic rebirth, then Dimmesdale's midnight vigil is a ritualistic abortion that fails to deliver him from the chaotic darkness. Dimmesdale's plight is obviously different from Hester's. Hester has little choice: her public acknowledgment is a matter of natural necessity. The scarlet letter is the social stigma; the enwombed Pearl is nature's stigma. Hester is forced by nature to acknowledge publicly the violation of a taboo; consequently, she is forced into social disgrace, but also into social integration. Because of Hester's silence, which Dimmesdale recognizes is but a temptation to keep him in sin, and nature's silence, Dimmesdale must initiate his passage from sinner to saint. But despite the fact that the probing Chillingworth has analytically dissolved his soul and set the stage for his rebirth, public humiliation for the professionally public man and the psychologically private man is a greater agony than his own private hell. Thus, Dimmesdale's primordial scream from the scaffold is muffled and his rebirth aborted.

This contrast between Hester's rebirth and Dimmesdale's abortion is further reinforced by the contrast in image and symbol. Contrary to the movement of the first scaffold scene, Hester and Pearl join Dimmesdale on the scaffold and clasp each others' hands in a numinous "electric chain," whose communal energy is discharged into the minister's "half-torpid system." Somewhat revitalized, Dimmesdale stands with his family in the "noon" of the meteoric splendor, "as if it were the light that is to reveal all secrets, and the daybreak that shall unite all who belong to one another." Hawthorne's imagery suggests a sacred moment, a noon not a noon, or to use Eliot's words, "a time not in time's convenant."[15] But it is only "as if" it were the light of redemption; it is but a falling light and there are no tribal witnesses. Thus, the "awful hieroglyphic" in the sky, unlike the awful hieroglyphic on Hester's bosom, fails to purify and redeem, because it has not, like the scarlet letter, the tribal sanction. It is the absence of tribal sanction that also invalidates the apparent renewal in the forest.

In the forest encounter, Hawthorne manages an effective ritualistic counterpoint: he orchestrates on the one hand the movement of renewal and reunion between Hester and Dimmesdale and on the other hand the movement of separation and withdrawal of the couple from society. Hawthorne makes it quite clear that both time and place seem sacred: Dimmesdale feels that he has "risen up all made anew," and Hester finds her "sex, her youth, and the whole richness of her beauty, come back from . . . the irrevocable past." In a moment of *im-puritan* abandonment, Hester sheds the scarlet letter and lets down her dark and luxuriant hair. In that moment, the severity of Puritan law dissolves before the sympathy of nature, and Hester and Dimmesdale experience anew the "consecration" of union.

It is a beautiful tableau of ideal pastoral communion, but communion made possible through withdrawal from community. Moreover, it is Hester's plan that they perpetuate their reunion by withdrawing farther from society into the wood or onto the ocean. This is the real seduction in *The Scarlet Letter:* Hester's attempt to lead Dimmesdale away from the "compass of yonder town," away from the sacred center to the profane perimeter. This seduction of Hester's is a part of Hawthorne's variation of the myth of the Minotaur as much as the myth of the Garden.

In his account of the Minotaur in *Tanglewood Tales,* Hawthorne makes the following observation: "Every human being, who suffers anything evil to get into his nature, or to remain there, is a kind of Minotaur, an enemy of his fellow-creatures, and separated from all good companionship."[16] There is a little of the Minotaur in all the central characters of the novel and more than a little in Chillingworth, one of whose shoulders "rose higher than the other" and one who wears the horns of the cuckold. Hester finds herself in dark labyrinths of "mind," "doubt," and "misery," and Dimmesdale of course is the minister in a maze. Hester tells Chillingworth that "there is no path to guide us out of this dismal maze." Hester, loving well, but not wisely, counsels Dimmesdale, as Ariadne does Theseus, to flee the labyrinth. Dimmesdale, like Theseus, however, discovers that the way out of the maze is through the center.

The tendency in Hawthorne criticism has been to interpret the forest as the site of alteration and redemption. R. W. B. Lewis says that the forest is the scene of reversal and discovery and Roy R. Male concludes that Dimmesdale achieves individuation there.[17] These statements seem inconsistent, however, with the imagery and symbols of the book or at least oversimplifications of the action, for the encounter in the forest at best only initiates the denouement that is realized in the center of the town and not on the outskirts of the wood. The reunion of the forest is, like that upon the midnight scaffold, short-lived and incomplete. The magic circle of the hour is broken by the refusal of Pearl, who is the oneness of Hester and Dimmesdale's being, to enter therein. In addition, Dimmesdale finds himself subsequently in the same moral maze in which Hester has been wandering. It is only after his nightlong vigil in his room and the inspired composition and reading of his Election Day sermon, that one sees "particles of a halo in the dew above his head," a halo heretofore reserved for individuals like Hester and the Reverend Wilson. Furthermore, it is in the Dimmesdale of the procession that Hester truly sees a new man, one whom she feels she does not know.

Having created a forest scene in which Hester and Dimmesdale symbolically reenact withdrawal and initiation, Hawthorne completes the passage by finally returning Dimmesdale to the tribe; and, just as Hester has brought the tribe closer together through its concentration upon the numinous letter, so Dimmesdale effects the same integration through the numinous voice of his calling. Hawthorne's staging of the Election Day sermon is one of the more subtle elements in the romance. With the church walls not only separating Hester and Dimmesdale, but also muffling the sound of the sermon, Hester and the reader are left to respond to the intonations of the breath rather than the denotations of the word. Possessed of the gift of tongues, "the heart's native language," Dimmesdale inspires in the congregation a "symphonious feeling," a "mighty swell of many voices blended into one great voice by the universal impulse which makes likewise one vast heart out of many." Inspiration becomes conspiracy, a breathing together, the same kind of collective rhythms that characterize the chant and dance of ritual. It is the mana of the many that is the elementary form, the sui generis, of the religious life. If Hawthorne seems sometimes attracted to Catholicism and its forms, it is that Catholicism is more than Protestantism an elementary religion, a rite more attuned to the sympathy of body and soul, symbol and object, totem and taboo.

Dimmesdale's return to the tribe, however, is not complete with this gift of inspiration and conspiracy; he must further the bond of brotherhood by acknowledging his guilt. He gathers Hester and Pearl to himself, with their help ascends the scaffold, and tears away the ministerial band from his breast. Once more the eyes of the community are "concentred on the ghastly miracle," and the tribe is one. This time, so are Dimmesdale, Hester, and Pearl. The integration is further completed by the fact that Chillingworth, who had been on the perimeter of the marketplace in the two previous scaffold scenes, kneels besides the dying Dimmesdale and says, "Hadst thou sought the whole earth over . . . there was no place . . . where thou couldst have escaped me,—save on this very scaffold." Chillingworth knows what Dimmesdale has discovered: that the way out of the moral labyrinth is through the center.

By congregating his four principal characters upon the scaffold in the center of the community, Hawthorne transforms the maze into a mandala and the divided self into the individuated self. The individuation is both external and internal. Dimmesdale reconciles himself to his God, his lover, his daughter, and even his tormentor. Hawthorne hints that, in the world beyond, the antipathy of Chillingworth and Dimmesdale shall be transformed into sympathy. More significantly, the convergence of the four symbolic characters upon the scaffold implies the convergence of the many selves—intellectual, spiritual, willful, natural—into the one and whole self. Moreover, the design of that convergence—four characters on a square or rectangular pillory encircled by the community—suggests the mandala, which is the symbol of the four-fold union of animus, anima, shadow, and ego that is achieved in Jungian individuation.[18]

Such is the significance of the larger design of the novel, the choreography around the scaffold; but what is the meaning of the smaller design, the scarlet letter? In a way, it too is a mandala: just as Pearl, who is the scarlet letter "endowed with life," is the oneness of Hester and Dimmesdale's being, so the horizontal bar of the letter *A* sustains and unifies the perpendicular and leaning bars. Moreover, the letter maintains a centricity throughout the novel: its numinosity centrifugally drives others beyond the sphere of the wearer or centripetally draws them to its center. This centricity is well illustrated in Governor Bellingham's Hall, where the exaggerated reflection of the red letter in the brightly burnished, convex breastplate of the Bellingham armor dominates the scene as the centerpiece of the surrounding Bellingham family portraits, and imagistically becomes thereby the center of the whole Puritan tradition. Thus, the image is a subtle foreshadowing of the calligraphy implied in the heraldic wording that ends the novel: "ON A FIELD, SABLE, THE LETTER A, GULES." Into this central image of the scarlet letter, then, much meaning converges.

To begin, the letter *A* obviously stands for adulteress, adulterer, and adultery. The narrative also suggests angel, able, ascension, and the acts of the apostles. It may also be an ironic naming of Arthur and thereby an effective fusing of its totemic nature with what the totem usually signifies, the tribal father. Action and image also suggest that it may indicate the *amor* that conquers all, the affection that softens severity, the atonement that is achieved by the central characters, the art that Hester manifests in her embroidery, and the alpha that is the union of logos and eros in elementary religion, Hawthorne's religion in *The Scarlet Letter.* The letter *A* also signifies adolescence, auto-machia, antinomian, Adamic, and America.

The fall of Hester and Dimmesdale is less an act of adultery than it is an act of adolescence. The fruit of the Edenic encounter in the wood is knowledge of sexuality, of one's physical nature, one's private parts. There is a bit of the fig leaf in the way Dimmesdale is able to keep his shame to himself. But as we have seen, privacy in Hawthorne is cursed: because he keeps so much and so long to himself, Dimmesdale deprives himself of the healing power of the tribal rite, of catharsis, and suffers Puritan auto-machia. It is only after his participation in the rite of aggregation that he assuages his

pain. Thus, the Edenic motif of the romance manifests Hawthorne's vision of the myth of the American Adam: the necessity
and the fortune of the fall from adolescence into adulthood, from
innocence into humanity.

The ritualistic change of life in *The Scarlet Letter* is American in
other ways. America is founded on the privilege of the individual;
throughout Dimmesdale's defense of privacy and Hester's independence of mind and will runs the American antinomian insistence upon the sovereignty of self. Hester counsels separation from
an oppressive society in order to begin a new life; Dimmesdale
feels regenerated in the wild and sympathetic wood. But it is Pearl,
the living scarlet letter, more than any other figure in the book,
who personifies what it is to be and to dream American. Pearl has
"nothing in common with a bygone and buried generation"; she is
"made afresh" through the breaking of a law and has become
thereby "a law unto herself." Returning from a walk by the sea,
where she has adorned herself with seaweed, she is indeed "the
letter A,—but freshly green, instead of scarlet!"

In this suggestive discoloration of his major symbol, Hawthorne
creates another symbol, that of the American dream of the re-
creation of a separate, amoral, and expatriated self; however, it is a
dream that Hawthorne rejects. Pearl's rite of passage is an act of
repatriation: her baptismal kiss upon the scaffold reconciles her to
her father, to prior generations, and subsequently even to Europe.
When she kisses Dimmesdale, a moral spell is broken; she participates in grief, develops her sympathies, and makes possible her
humanity. Pearl's refusal to acknowledge the past, like Dimmesdale's refusal to acknowledge Pearl, denies generation and consequently may be said to be an act of degeneration; and it is the
acknowledgment of each other, of generation, that is the basis of
their regeneration. For Hawthorne then, reparation is possible
only in time and only through the social sanction, and man's humanity is achieved not ideally in sympathy with nature, but really
in community with society.

Hawthorne not only reappropriates the more immediate tradition of his Puritan ancestors, but also the antenomian tradition of a
primitive Christianity that finds atonement through God and tribe
rather than through God and self. Hawthorne aesthetically evokes
what Paul Ricoeur discerns, that "the guilty conscience is shut in
. . . because it is an isolated conscience that breaks the communion
of sinners" and that "to become oneself the tribunal of oneself is to
be alienated." Thus, he calls us back to a more primitive Christian-

ity, where, in the words of Rudolph Bultmann, sin is "not a deficiency or imperfection to be got over by moral endeavor, but guilt in the sight of human society and in the sight of God. That is why man cannot get rid of sin by himself. That must be done by society and God."[19]

Hawthorne's Puritanism is not merely a recovered Puritanism; it is one seen in the context of the greater rationalization of enlightened Unitarianism and the greater self-reliance of romantic transcendentalism. The fictional world of *The Scarlet Letter* is an America that fuses the cultural horizons of Puritan, Unitarian, and transcendentalist America, and the ritual of that world is one designed to assimilate and integrate the changes of its cultural transformations: the shift from a severe life-style that disintegrates man through its conscious rejection of the natural self to those that disintegrate him through their rejections of the charismatic self and the social self. Unitarianism is the rationalization of God and man—the connection between the two takes place within the mind and at the expense of the body and emotion. Transcendentalism is an apotheosis of the natural self—the connection with the oversoul takes place within nature or the individual and often in defiance of society. Hawthorne's work is an attempt to bridge the cultural changes by looking backward, and perhaps forward, beyond change, to a more elementary form of the religious life, in which communion is natural, spiritual, and tribal.

In looking backward, Hawthorne not only rediscovers the more elementary forms of religious life, but also the more symbolic forms of aesthetic life. It is one of the primary theses of Michael Baxandall's *Painting and Experience in Fifteenth-Century Italy* that an artist such as Botticelli could rely on an audience familiar with and sensitive to the *bassa danza*, a geometrized dance popular in Italy then, to respond to and interpret the psychological interplay symbolized in the figural tableaus of painting. Despite the many apologies for the Puritan way of life, most students of Puritanism in America would agree with Max Weber's thesis that ascetic Protestantism is a relatively rational Christianity that tends to reject the choreographical and pictorial arts that are more intrinsic to ritualistic religion such as medieval and Renaissance Catholicism, because they are not useful to salvation and only lead to superstition.[20] In his effective use of tableau and choreography, Hawthorne reappropriates the symbolic pictorial forms, as well as the integrating rite, of a ritualistic culture. The success of that reappropriation is most evident in the symbolic richness of the numinous scarlet letter and the transformation of the maze into the mandala.

Squaring the Circle in *Moby Dick*

In *Moby Dick*, Herman Melville uses the mythos of the primitive cult of Gnosticism to enrich his ironic development of plot, character, and symbol. Like the Gnostic, Ahab believes that nature, the material world of matter, is evil and that malevolent powers conspire to keep from him the purifying light. He is obsessed with the belief that his and the tribe's salvation lies in gnosis—in penetrating the mysterious depths and darknesses that keep secret the redemptive knowledge. His attempt to capture and destroy the White Whale is the supreme quest to overturn that evil conspiracy, but in order to achieve a successful hunt, he must first square the circle—chart and plot the circumnavigation of Moby Dick.

In seizing upon the particular scientific, maritime practice of charting circumnavigational courses, Melville effectively develops concrete variations of the universal symbols of the labyrinth, the circle, and the ancient mathematical quest to square the circle. There is something in the very impossibility of the task that suggests a taboo: man trying to master (square) that to which he ought perhaps submit, nature (circle). Moreover, because the circle squared is a mandala—the image of wholeness and harmony in both nature and man—the design becomes in *Moby Dick* a most polysemous and ironic symbol.

In working out that design, Melville evolves an imagery that is a variation of the very tools employed by the Greeks in their attempt to square the circle: a circle or circumference of a circle, an unmarked straightedge, and a collapsible compass, which in all probability was nothing more than a string. In *Moby Dick*, these tools are manifest as the leitmotivs of circle and line, and with these basic images Melville weaves his narrative of the nineteenth-century transcendentalist personality adrift in an impersonal, naturalistic world. In working out a dialectical contrast between Ahab and Ishmael and their associations with symbols of circle and line, Melville develops a variation of the pattern of separation and reparation, in which separation may be said to be diagnostic and reparation agnostic.

Ahab's charisma stems primarily from a primitive or paranoiac concentration of all his powers upon a single object: his "lunacy

. . . turned all its concentred cannon upon its own mad mark; so that far from having lost his strength . . . [he] did now possess a thousand fold more potency." Like the many mythic heroes with whom he is associated, Ahab directs that concentrated potency toward the penetration of mystery; he will know: "That inscrutable thing is chiefly what I hate, and be the White Whale agent, or be the White Whale principal, I will wreak that hate upon him."[21] It is this confrontation with knowledge that severs Ahab's sensibility, as he himself recognizes: "Gifted with the higher perception, I lack the low, enjoying power."

This internal severance between perception and enjoyment—between the higher logos and the lower eros—is the split symbolized by the two major scars on Ahab's tattered body.[22] The seam that virtually divides the physical self from "crown to sole"—the fissure caused by the numinous lightning—is the incision of knowledge that severs the whole, psychic being. The wound inflicted by the whale effects a similar division: before sailing on this voyage, Ahab suffers an accident in which his "ivory limb having been so violently displaced . . . had stake-wise smitten, and all but pierced his groin." This reinforcement of the actual, or symbolic, castration inflicted by Moby Dick upon Ahab underscores Ahab's concentration of will upon the higher, knowing self at the expense of the lower, feeling self. Such dismemberment also leads to Ahab's external separation from community, nature, and God.

Ahab is the separated, isolated, and alienated man: like a bear "burying himself in the hollow of a tree," he lives "out the winter there, sucking his own paws" and "in his inclement, howling old age, Ahab's soul, shut up in the caved trunk of his body, there fed upon the sullen paws of its gloom." It is a fit metaphor for the hero who broods alone on his wound and the whale that inflicted it. That same brooding concentration upon retribution alienates Ahab from land, hearth, and wife and renders him a "desolate of solitude . . . the mason, walled-town of a Captain's exclusiveness, which admits but small entrance to any sympathy from the green country without." What is soft and sweet and erotic is recessed within Ahab, and what is hard, bitter, and Gnostic is dominant without; he has been enseamed by fire and "dismasted" by the whale.

Ahab's dissociation, isolation, and separation are directly connected to a narcissism that is rendered literally and figuratively as self-centeredness. Ahab is the eccentric or egocentric hero, who is either outside the community of man or who sees himself as the center of the world. Such self-centeredness is evident on the quarterdeck, when the ship's company forms a circle around Ahab as he grasps "the three level, radiating lances at their crossed centre." The tableau is a graphic illustration of the crew's oneness under Ahab's spell-binding leadership, but it is also an illustration of the egocentricity that wills the crew to violate the sacred totem.

This same egocentricity is evident in Ahab's response to the doubloon. His recognition that "this round gold . . . the image of the rounder globe . . . is all Ahab" suggests that Ahab sees himself as the ship's navel, the *axis mundi* of the *Pequod* world. He is also the central cog that fits and turns all the wheels of the *Pequod;* the "close-coiled woe" whose sole tear falling into the Pacific evokes for Starbuck the "measureless sobbing that stole out of the serenity around"; and the "personality" that stands in the midst of the "personified impersonal." It is perhaps one of the most ironic and tragic motifs of the book that Ahab should reappear as the center of so many circles, for it is this very self-centeredness that is his penance. This is symbolically communicated in "Castaway," when one of Ahab's alter egos, Pip, falls overboard, and Ishmael observes his black head at the center of the sea, whose "ringed horizon" begins to expand, and stands in awe of the "intense concentration of self, in the middle of such a heartless immensity." This is the ultimate meaning of Ahab's egocentricity: it estranges him from community, separates him from the boundless, and leaves him awfully alone.

Such is not the case with Ishmael. The contrast between Ishmael and Ahab is dramatized by the juxtaposition of Pip's encounter with the sea and Ishmael's encounter with the sperm in the succeeding chapter. As Ishmael squeezes the whale's sperm and a Dionysian "strange sort of insanity" comes over him, he says, "Come, let us squeeze hands all round; nay let us all squeeze ourselves into each other; let us squeeze ourselves universally into the very milk and sperm of kindness." The image of a tribal circle of whalers squeezing and splicing hands in and round the androgynous milk and sperm of the totemic whale suggests an integration with the totem that contrasts remarkably with Ahab's interrogation and a concentricity that is integrative rather than an egocentricity that is disintegrative.

Immediately after experiencing this *participation mystique,* Ishmael adds that man must eventually lower his conceit of attainable felicity, not placing it in the intellect, but rather in "the wife, the heart, the bed, the table, the saddle, the fire-side, the country." Such warnings are repeated by Ishmael throughout the narrative and are often associated with the image of the circle. For example, after having turned himself around at the tiller, he warns man to "look not too long in the face of the fire," an admonition in keeping with his earlier charge "not to be too fastidious in . . . curiosity touching this Leviathan." In the encounter at the tiller, it is as though Ishmael were Dante, having to turn himself around at the bottom of the inferno, in order to initiate his ascent up purgatory. Elsewhere, Ishmael warns man not to push off from the insular Tahiti of peace and joy within that is "encompassed by all the horrors of the half known life," and points out that the brain of the sperm whale is indeed that "geometrical circle which it is impossible to square."

Perhaps the most sustained sequence of circle imagery associated with Ishmael and in contrast to Ahab's egocentricity is that in "The Grand Armada," where Ishmael finds himself in the "innermost heart of the shoal. . . . that enchanted calm which they say lurks at the heart of every commotion," where he could behold "the tumults of the outer concentric circles." This moment is suggestive of the sacred still point of the turning world, an external center that reminds Ishmael of an internal one, where "amid the tornadoed Atlantic of my being, do I myself still for ever centrally disport in mute calm." Once again, however, from within what seems a design of unity and harmony emerges the foreshadowing image of Ahab's doom—a young cub still tethered within the long coils of the umbilical cord of Madame Leviathan—suggesting to Ishamel one of the "subtlest secrets of the seas divulged to us in this enchanted pond."

In a chapter in *Images and Symbols* called "The 'God Who Binds' and the Symbolism of Knots," Mircea Eliade suggests that patterns of knots and labyrinths in both Eastern and Western mythologies reflect the following beliefs of primitive religions: "In the Cosmos as well as in human life, everything is connected with everything else in an invisible web" and "certain divinities are the mistresses of these 'Threads' which constitute, ultimately, a vast cosmic 'bondage.'" The purpose of the ritualistic initiation into the labyrinth is for the initiate to "undo the labyrinthine knot" and "to rend the veil" of ignorance and thereby liberate the soul from the shackles of existence.[23] In Melville's version of this rich Gnostic symbolism, Ahab, in trying to rend the veil and cut the knot, ironically and tragically weaves the fatal net that destroys him and the *Pequod* world. Ishmael contrastingly redeems himself by submitting to the veil and by tying, rather than untying, the knot.

The symbolic thread or line manifests itself initially in *Moby Dick* as the image of severance; it is most evident in the perpendicular seam struck through Ahab by lightning, in the cracked, split, and jagged-edged crown of Lombardy that batters the brain of Ahab, and in the many wrinkles upon the brows of both the old Captain and the old Whale. Those wrinkles take on added dimension in "The Chart," where "the heavy pewter lamp suspended in chains over his head, continually rocked with the motion of the ship, and for ever threw shifting gleams and shadows of lines upon his wrinkled brow, till it almost seemed that while [Ahab] himself was marking out lines and courses on the wrinkled charts, some invisible pencil was also tracing lines and courses upon the deeply marked chart of his forehead."

The imagery anticipates the metaphor of loom as fate in "Mat-maker" and creates a symbol into which much meaning is compressed. The lines cast by the light on Ahab's brow, a light fueled no doubt by whale oil and shifted by the motion of the sea, reiterate the severing seam and wrinkled brow of Ahab's wounds. Meanwhile, Ahab himself traces and retraces lines, attempting to square the White Whale's circumnavigation of the globe. The concatenation of line imagery—the tension between the lines that sea, fire, and whale cast and those that Ahab casts—suggests that, although Ahab may indeed be the victim of a cosmic bondage, the agents of which are fire, sea, and Moby Dick, Ahab himself participates in weaving the very net in which he feels himself bound. This suggestion that the self-conscious personality unknowingly conspires with the impersonal, naturalistic world to determine his own lot is reinforced later when Ahab twists, plaits, and forges the shaft of his harpoon and joins it to the line of rope that will eventually be the umbilical gallows cord, within which his alter ego, Fedallah, is hanged. Finally, when one considers that Ahab's wrinkled brow is very much like Moby Dick's and that the lines he casts on the charts are very much like those cast upon him, one is left with the conclusion that Ahab's self-serving hunt for the White Whale becomes a self-seeking quest, in which he eventually discovers himself narcissistically tied to Moby Dick.[24]

Ishmael, on the other hand, is identified with seamlessness and connectiveness that make one whole and at one with nature and others. Immediately following the scene in which Perth tells Ahab that he cannot smooth the one seam upon Ahab's brow, Ishmael experiences a serenity of pacified seas that "mixes with your most mystic mind, so that fact and fancy, half-way meeting, interpenetrate, and form one seamless whole." Although the "mingling threads of life . . . woven by warp and woof" dispel that seamless whole, Ishmael at least enjoys the momentary epiphany in which self is repaired to the boundless. Ishmael also experiences splices that connect him with another and consequently with the other, with nature. Ishmael and Queequeg are symbolically "spliced" and he finds in the savage, a father, a "George Washington cannibalistically developed," who effects "a melting within him" that heals and soothes his "splintered heart." Moreover, in being tied to Queequeg by the monkey-rope, Ishmael realizes what Ahab cannot—"that my own individuality was now merged in a joint stock company of two: that my free will had received a mortal wound." In discovering this communion with another, Ishmael discovers himself and his voyage ends in the recovery of self.

In his final words and act, Ahab demonstrates an understanding of his doom and an unending defiance of it: "Sink all coffins and hearses to one common pool! and since neither can be mine, let me then tow to pieces, while still chasing thee, though tied to thee, thou damned whale! *Thus*, I give up the spear!" As he does, the fragments of the *Pequod's* splintered world, including the heavenly sky-hawk, are drawn into the centripetal circling of the whirlpool. It is almost as though Ahab, who consciously sought knowledge and independence of and retribution against the ubiquitous sea— the totem of which is Moby Dick—has unconsciously repaired himself to the eternal round in his annihilation in the navelish vortex. In contrast, Ishmael, who comes dangerously close to completing his circumnavigation in the closing vortex, is delivered from the buttonlike center by the buoyant coffin of Queequeg, upon which is carved the "queer round figure" that had distinguished the intricate tatoo of his body, that "hieroglyphic of the heavens." Thus, Ishmael, through communion with another, emerges from the center reunited to a symbolic mother, the *Rachel.*

Collectively, but dialectically, Ahab and Ishmael are the human psyche. Ahab is the eccentric captain, outside the circle of community, who becomes the egocentric man who wills himself the center of his fragmented world. He is dismembered man: he has lost the eros that connects him to wife, hearth, and tribe—he is estranged from communion and community. Insofar as he is severed and wishes to sever, he is diabolical man, the one who wishes to throw things apart. His penance is both a recognition that he does not know and cannot know all—that he cannot square the circle—and a self-consciousness that drives him to the point of madness. His only reparation ironically is the submergence of self in the boundless sea.

Ishmael is concentric man: he circumambulates the city and circumnavigates the sea, until he loses himself in a *participation mystique* in the still point of a tornadoed world. He does not attempt to make himself the center of that world. He is also remembered man: he begins his rite of passage isolated and alienated, but is eventually reconnected with the other—with man, society, and nature. Unlike Ahab, Ishmael feels no compulsion to penetrate the Gnostic mystery: he can lose self-consciousness atop masts, in spermaceti, and at the still point; and his remembering, his circumscriptive narrative of the voyage of the *Pequod,* implies a healing catharsis of the terror he has witnessed. Finally, he is symbolic man: he submits to an immersion of self in the waters of the boundless and emerges with a reverence for the interpenetration and inscrutability of nature evinced in the totemic Moby Dick. The combined fates of Ahab and Ishmael bear out Eliade's explanation of the symbolism of watery rebirth: "Immersion in the water symbolizes a regression into the pre-formal, reintegration into the undifferentiated mode of pre-existence. Emergence repeats the cosmogonic act of formal manifestation. . . . That is why the symbolism of water includes Death as well as Re-birth."[25]

Thus, *Moby Dick* is a manifestation of the mythopoeic pattern of separation from and reparation with the boundless; it is also a particular American variation of that pattern. Ahab is the dissociated and consequently severe sensibility of early New England. He Gnostically views the natural and corporeal as conspirators against the elevation and salvation of his Puritan soul. He is also the transcendentalist hero who extols personal charisma and individuality at the expense of tradition and community. Rather than join the primitive as brother in a natural and sacred hunt for the hearth-warming oil of the sperm whale, he tends to use him in his unnatural and profane pursuit of the conspiratorial White Whale. Ahab is the American, self-reliant hero whose egocentricity is finally manifest as an awful isolation of the concentrated self in the midst of a heartless immensity.

Ishmael, on the other hand, is the sympathetic exile who discovers brotherhood in the other, in Queequeg, or in what Melville calls and what the Puritan would have called a "joint stock company of two." In addition, by splicing hands with others in the totemic sperm, he not only realizes the knitting together that Winthrop thought necessary to the American experience, but also rediscovers the vital eros that had been relatively repressed by the more severe Puritan. Thus, in contradistinction to Ahab, Ishmael comes to understand his dependence upon concentricity, upon a common center, for survival in the personified, impersonal world. Insofar as he does, Ishmael achieves some harmony with nature and man, a wholeness we might call individuation and one that characteristically takes the form of his emergence from the man-dalalike vortex.[26] Consequently, we may also conclude that in *Moby Dick*, it is more through submission—through a letting go—of the self to nature, rather than through domination of nature, that one successfully, albeit only symbolically, squares the circle.

4

Coming of Age in America

Perhaps to lose a sense of *where* you are implies the danger of losing a sense of *who* you are.

Ralph Ellison, *Invisible Man*

There is a moment in Washington Irving's tale of Rip Van Winkle when the trappings of nineteenth-century romantic fiction seem to slip suddenly away and the terror of modern alienation asserts itself dramatically and most powerfully. Having leaped out of time and over the American Revolution, Rip comes down from the mountain to discover not only his plunge out of history, but also his dislocation in space. The Kaatskill village is no longer his village and he is no longer himself. His home has "gone to decay," the sign of his favorite Dutch inn has been "singularly metamorphosed" from the *King George* to the *George Washington,* and the village folk are speaking "a perfect Babylonish jargon." For Rip, "strange names were over the doors—strange faces at the windows—every thing was strange."

So estranged is Van Winkle that his desolation overcomes all his connubial fears and he calls out to both children and wife, only to be answered by silence. As he encounters the unfamiliar faces of what has become an unfamiliar place, he increasingly begins to feel that, although the eyes of the villagers seem to fix him with a concentrated stare, they also seem to look right through him. Like a twentieth-century counterpart, Rip Van Winkle has become an "invisible man," one who doubts his own identity. On the verge of the kind of madness that possesses one "finding himself thus alone in the world," Rip cries out in despair, "Does nobody here know Rip Van Winkle?" When someone responds affirmatively by ironically pointing to Rip's son leaning lazily against a tree—the very

image and alter ego of his father—and another immediately thereafter questions him as to who he is, Rip, "at his wit's end," responds, "God knows . . . I'm not myself—I'm someone else . . .
everything's changed, and I'm changed, and I can't tell what's my
name, or who I am."

Thereupon, the narrative recovers from its leap into twentieth-
century literature of alienation, and Irving reunites Rip and his
family—conveniently without the presence of Rip's dead, shrew-
ish wife—and all live happily ever after, beyond the yokes of
domineering wives and kings, spinning legends about Rip and his
scored sleep. It is but a brief moment of intense trauma in a canon
of relative bucolic charm and serenity, but it serves well to support
Ralph Ellison's contentions that "to lose a sense of *where* you are
implies the danger of losing a sense of *who* you are" and that the
search for identity is the theme of American literature.[1] In leaping
from history into a new place in order to escape the old self and the
suppression of that self, the American hero risks the loss of his
identity in the quest for freedom. Rip was fortunate to survive that
momentary loss and to be reborn as the virtual son to his protec-
tive daughter, but not all American questers are so blessed.

In *The Hero With a Thousand Faces*, Joseph Campbell defines
the basic agon of the traditional hero of myth and legend in terms
of the symbolic sequence of withdrawal, initiation, and return—a
sequence discerned with little variation in the works of Otto Rank
and Lord Raglan.[2] The hero withdraws from the tribe, undergoes
an initiation that is usually an encounter with a supernatural or
unnatural force, from which he emerges victorious, and then returns to the tribe with a boon wrought from his initiation.

In their interpretations of the American hero, R. W. B. Lewis
and Ihab Hassan discern a similar pattern in the heroic agon of
American fiction, the initiation of which is usually a variation of
the paradigm of the Fall—a fall from amoral innocence into the
knowledge of good and evil and the acquisition of the moral responsibility that attends such knowledge. In the American version
of the heroic formula, there are clear parallels to the withdrawal
and initiation of the archetypal pattern; what is not clear, however,
is whether the American hero always achieves a return to or reparation with society or the tribal community. What occurs often in
American fiction is not so much an initiation into society, but
rather what Lewis calls a *denitiation* from it—a withdrawal or
separation so complete that it precludes the third act of return.[3]

Clearly, the traditional formula is worked out in "Rip Van

Winkle," as well as in the major works of Hawthorne and Melville: Dimmesdale returns from the dark labyrinth of the forest to the well-lighted center of the communal pillory and Ishmael returns to tell society of his encounter with Ahab and Moby Dick. Even the independent Thoreau returns from his two-year sojourn at Walden to Concord. Such a return is not the emphasis, however, of the prototypical fiction of James Fenimore Cooper. *The Pioneers,* for example, finds Natty Bumppo seeking refuge from an encroaching society by moving farther into the wilderness, and, in *The Prairie,* the old leatherstocking rejects the offer to be interred alongside his father and chooses instead burial where he has lived, "beyond the din of the settlements."

Although Natty Bumppo finds communion with the virgin land and community with the native, his movement away from society is the prototype for several heroes of American fiction. Hawthorne's Wakefield, for example, discovers "that by stepping aside [the social institution] for a moment, a man exposes himself to a fearful risk of losing his place [and as Ellison suggests, his self] forever"; thus, Wakefield's reconciliation with his widowed wife and his recovery of self are left in doubt. For Melville's Pierre, the dislocation is internal, and he comes to recognize that it is better for man "to be pushed into material spaces beyond the uttermost orbit of the sun, than once feel himself freely afloat in himself." In a contemporary variation of the same motif, Ellison's hero is shocked by the realization that once you "step outside the narrow borders of what men call reality . . . you step into chaos," and chaos for the invisible man is the estrangement he experiences in an alien Harlem. The result of that alienation is that he literally drops out of society.

It is perhaps one of the major ironies of the American experience that, in a land and literature renowned for its sense of place and the salutary effect of place on person, the American hero should so often be depicted as a displaced person. Self-exiled from the landscape and society of his origins and self-propelled beyond the constrictions, and the continuities, of history and time, he is, as Irving's hero momentarily is, neither at home nor at one in an alien setting seemingly "out of space—out of time." Moreover, his flight from place and history is also a flight from the other, and, if the elder James is right in contending that authentic selfhood is only possible through relationship with others, then, his flight for freedom is also a flight from self.[4] Such is the case with the fantastic figures of Poe, who find themselves trapped and their existence threatened by their suffocating withdrawals within themselves; with the central personae of *The Scarlet Letter,* who, in being cut off from another, are cut off from a part of themselves; and with Ahab, who, in seeking to destroy the wholly other, destroys himself. Thus, the failure to return to society not only precludes a reparation with community, but also precludes a reparation with the divided self. This motif is one of the central variations of the pattern of separation and reparation manifest in four classic American novels: *Huckleberry Finn, The Ambassadors, The Great Gatsby,* and *Light in August.*

The Undiscovered Country in *Huckleberry Finn*

In one sense, Mark Twain's *Adventures of Huckleberry Finn* ends where it begins: Huck informs the reader in the second paragraph that the Widow Douglas "would sivilize" him and concludes his tale by disclosing his aim to light out for the Territory in order to escape Aunt Sally's intention to "adopt and sivilize" him. Huck's response to the initial promise of cultivation, like his response to the final promise, is to withdraw: he lights out, dons his old rags, and resumes his old digs of the sugar hogshead. But Tom Sawyer seeks him out, enlists him in a secret band of robbers, and returns him to the Widow Douglas and society. Given the location of the episode at the very beginning of the novel and its analogous repetition at the end, one is tempted to conclude that Twain presents the reader with a microcosm of the heroic paradigm— withdrawal, initiation, and return—and in so doing describes the symbolic movement of several encounters of the picaresque novel and prescribes the outcome of Huck's final withdrawal.[5]

But is this necessarily the case? Although there are a number of episodes that follow the paradigmatic design of withdrawal, initiation, and return, do all the variations add up to a total pattern that suggests that Huck will return to Aunt Sally and society? Is the Huck of the end of the novel a changed character, a growing young man whose imminent maturity will allow him not only to act out his sympathies in repudiation of society's norms, but also to think out his own moral stance in a society ambivalent to that stance? Or, on the contrary, do design and development of character suggest an altered Huck, but one who will no longer be seduced by the romances of Tom Sawyer, Mary Jane Wilkes, or Aunt Sally into returning to and leveling with society? Is Huck, more hardened against the violence and hypocrisy of society and driven by the failure of real community in society and by the end of ideal communion on the raft, now intent on seeking total freedom in the Territory? Perhaps there is still a third alternative: is it possible that Huck is a relatively unchanged character who is fated to shuttle endlessly across the space that separates a profane civilization from a profane wilderness, at home in neither, in search of the sacred middle estate, and consequently doomed to a life of becoming instead of being—a life in search of identity?

It is the thesis here that Huck Finn is not initiated into the world, that despite the evidence of the part—those instances in which Huck returns reborn to society—the evidence of the whole suggests that Huck will tragically withdraw from a bounded society unto the unbounded Territory, that he is the peregrine picaro forever suspended in the twilight kingdom of becoming. It may seem perverse to read tragedy and despair out of a novel so rich in humor, but if one remembers to search out every man in his own humor and considers that Twain's humor is ultimately melancholic, then the tragic dimension of this comic masterpiece seems less improbable.

The pattern of withdrawal-initiation-return, noted in the incident of Huck's brief escape from the Widow Douglas, is repeated with a significant variation in the first major adventure of the novel. Playing both the role of priest and initiate, Huck ritualistically kills himself by faking a kidnapping and death in order to escape the clutches of Pap. The whole episode takes on a nightmare quality later, when Huck, hiding upon Jackson Island, more or less witnesses his own funeral procession as he watches his whole family—Aunt Polly, Tom Sawyer, the Judge, and Pap—search futilely for his remains. This rite of passage is concluded when Huck reveals his ghostly and resurrected self to the terrified Jim.

Huck's resurrection is not only a manifestation of reparation, but also a part of an ongoing separation, and as such it is a part of a complex, but effective, structure. On the one hand, Huck's resurrection before Jim and his throwing his lot in with Jim are only the beginning of a series of withdrawals from society. On the other hand, Huck has returned reborn to society—albeit, a society of two. And there is little doubt that Huck rejoices at the possibility of community, so much so that he spontaneously and instinctively makes a covenant with Jim not to reveal Jim's whereabouts. Huck and Jim represent the original American pilgrimage: having fled a restrictive society and being fugitives from that society, they transform crisis into community. In a relatively primitive and ambivalent natural environment, they constitute a new covenant in hopes of establishing an ideal community conducive to freedom and the expression of the natural self. It is as though they are the fictional embodiments of Tocqueville's idea that "democracy loosens social ties, but lightens natural ones; it brings kindred more closely together whilst it throws citizens apart."[6]

Huck and Jim are two exiles in the process of forming what Trilling calls a community of saints and what we have called a congregation of saints; Huck will eventually risk the fires of the inferno in order to be faithful to Jim, and Jim will eventually risk slavery in order to be faithful to both Huck and Tom.[7] And for a time there is indeed "no home like a raft, after all. . . . You feel mighty free and easy and comfortable on a raft." You do, provided of course, that the raft is in motion following the benign tide and current and provided that it is only a haven for a compatible couple.

Whenever the raft runs up against other craft or other craftsmen intrude upon the raft, it is no longer a free and easy place. An often overlooked fact about Huck's adventures on the river is that society, in the form of other craftsmen, and nature, in the form of estranging fog and current, can make the raft a mighty uneasy and uncomfortable place. The incident of the fog is the second major variation of separation and reparation—of heroic transformation—and is distinguished from other initiations in the novel by Twain's effective use of symbolic imagery. Elsewhere, Twain uses imagery quite effectively, but primarily to evoke the bucolic splendor and innocence of the river and its environs (chapter 19); in this instance, he uses it to multiply the meaning of Huck and Jim's encounter with nature and with each other. To begin, Huck and Jim are separated from each other when the strong river current tears the line that is connecting them away from the towhead where Huck has tied it. The image of the broken line reminds one of similar umbilical lines in *Moby Dick* and suggests the imminent birth or rebirth of the hero that is to take place. In response to the broken line, Huck jumps into his canoe and tries to paddle away in pursuit of the raft, but he gets nowhere, for he has forgotten to untie his own line. It is an interesting detail: it provides the reader with a bit of slapstick humor, but a black kind of humor, for it has a measure of the terror that ordinarily accompanies those nightmares in which one tries desperately and futilely to move—to be born or reborn. Moreover, it continues a running undercurrent of meaning in the novel by foreshadowing the real distance that Huck manages to put between himself and his oppressors—none.

Having finally freed himself from the towhead, Huck shoots out into "the solid white fog." Having no more idea where he's going "than a dead man," Huck finds himself once more separated from all society, figuratively dead in life. Eventually, the disorientation, effected by the unnatural sounds of voices in a fog, leaves Huck "tangled good," as though quite "turned around." Here, one is reminded of Ishmael's similar disorientation at the wheel of the *Pequod* and of Dimmesdale's confusion in his moral maze, and consequently of the loss of self that must precede the re-creation or regeneration of self. Huck continues to lie in the canoe in a characteristic mood that he evinces throughout the novel, "dismal and lonesome," as though "laying dead still on the water," and he becomes increasingly entangled in "a nest of towheads." This episode is an obvious rite of passage upon the river and its outcome is never in doubt: gradually, he orients himself, discovers the right speck in the river, heads for it, and once again presents his resurrected self to the astonished Jim. Jim's welcome is somewhat ironic, for he rejoices in greeting "the same old Huck."

One would have expected after this rite of passage a changed Huck, but Jim sees the same old Huck. That it is the same old Huck is attested to by the fact that Huck turns the tables on Jim and plays a good joke on him by pointing out that Jim is a "tangled-headed old fool," that he, Huck, has not been gone at all, and that Jim's remembrance of things just past is but a dream. Having turned reality inside out, Huck draws Jim's attention to the leaves and rubbish on the raft; and Jim in turn draws Huck's attention to the insensitivity and cruelty of Huck's lie, makes Huck feel contrite, and inspires Huck to humility before the black man. That Huck is changed is attested to by the fact that Huck can respond to Jim as person and not as Negro, as an other and not as property.

Huck's lie to Jim is a curious one and like most of his lies serves more than one purpose. It is a manifestation of a wit that is oft times cruel, a cruelty that assumes that not only a black man, but any victim of a joke, is not so much a brother but an *it*, to be manipulated and to serve as the butt of one's own narcissistic need. In this respect, Huck's sense of humor is very much like that of Tom Sawyer's. But the joke is also indirectly a comment on the action. In a sense, the separation in the fog was all a dream; certainly, it is rendered so by Twain. Moreover, Huck's attempt to tangle Jim's head is a projection of where he has been physically and where he is headed morally. Though it may appear that he and Jim are floating freely down the river, with every knot he is entering deeper and deeper into a moral maze as labyrinthine as the one in which Dimmesdale finds himself. This moral dilemma is dramatized in the succeeding chapter, when Huck temporarily submits to conscience and sets off on what turns out to be an aborted attempt to turn Jim in.

The identification of Huck's tangledness with Jim's, of Huck's nightmare with Jim's, serves to remind the reader that Jim, who, despite the falling off in the final chapters, is a well-drawn and fully developed character, is nevertheless like others in the novel, a reflection, a shadow, of Huck. Like Jim, Huck is attempting to escape bondage in and by society; like Jim's, Huck's religion is rooted more in magic than in commandment, is predicated more on survival than submission, and is governed more by the expression of the primitive heart's sympathies than by the repression of the puritan head's severities; like Jim, Huck too is in search of family: though he may have severed himself from Pap and the Widow, he shows signs of longing for and having discovered the paternal, the fraternal, and, according to Leslie Fiedler, the maternal in Jim.[8] A different dimension of Huck's character is revealed by two other alter egos—the Duke and the King.

After landing upon the raft, the two flimflam men re-create themselves as the Duke and the King out of the cunning of their own minds. The revelation of their secret births is a reductio ad absurdum of initiation and rebirth and serves to bring into relief a significant aspect of Huck's several disguises and initiations; like the two con artists, Huck is the master of disguise who assumes many identities in order to outwit and outflank society. He is the antihero with many faces; he consciously assumes the identity of, or is accidentally mistaken to be, someone else—Mary Williams, George Jackson, Tom Sawyer, Sarah Mary Williams, George Alexander Peters, and in the raft passage deleted from the published manuscript, Charles William Allbright. When one connects the many masks of Huck Finn with the many initiations into which he symbolically dies and from which he is symbolically reborn, one has the image of a hero who is always in a state of becoming someone else rather than being himself. Now it may be argued that Huck is always in a state of being someone else in order that he might be free to become himself. The novel supports such a reading, but it also supports the former reading, and it is in the dialectical tension between the two that the meaning resides.

Huck is in many ways the hero Proteus—descendant and personification of the very river god whose capacity for change is written in the many disguises and identities Huck assumes and in the very imaginative and flexible shiftiness that precludes his being found out by and committed to society. He can, by deceiving the many mothers who would adopt and civilize him, and by outtricking the many tricksters who would use him, remain free. But that very protean quality brings him dangerously close to his modern descendant—the plastic man of technological and bureaucratic society. If one can shift quickly and continuously enough, one need not be pinned down physically and psychologically and committed to institution. In his flight from institution, the protean, as well as the plastic, hero risks his commitment to human relationship; there is no lasting human relationship because there is no lasting self.

The question of Huck's being and becoming is directly linked to one of the major concerns of the novel and one of the major concerns of Huck: a fascination with death. As Philip Young has pointed out in his study of Twain and Hemingway, Huck confronts thirteen corpses in his voyage from boyhood to manhood,[9] and many of these are the result of killings that climax his encounters with society: the deaths of the three thieves, of Boggs, of Buck and several Grangerfords and Shepherdsons, of Pap. More significant than any or all of these is Huck's awareness of and fascination with death, one that not only makes him effect his figurative death, but also makes him wish for his own literal death. This fascination with death is evident in the very beginning of the novel.

In the first chapter, Huck tells us that "I don't take stock in dead people." Now, this may be nothing more than the young American hero's preoccupation with the present and his subsequent obliviousness to the past, an oblivion that is satirically revealed in Huck's fractured history lesson on Henry VIII to Jim (chapter 23). He may be even protesting too much, trying to bury what is in the process of becoming a serious discovery for an adolescent on the verge of manhood—the discovery of his own mortality. Certainly, his subsequent encounters with death will force him to take stock in dead people. In any case, though he may now not take stock in dead people, he certainly takes stock in death. A few moments after his pronouncement on dead people, Huck finds himself so "lonesome" that he "most" wishes he were "dead," and in the next instance the sounds of the evening take on the presence of death: the owl hoots about somebody that is dead, a whipporwill and dog cry about something about to die, and the wind whispers something to Huck that sends "cold shivers" all over him. The mood is intensified by the ominous spider that crawls over him, by the village clock that tolls out time and mortality, and by the subsequent stillness—"still as death" and "stiller than ever"—that ensues. And then Twain's version of the knocking at the gate—Tom's whistle and summons of Huck to the midnight meeting—dispels the mood.

The significance of this effective evocation of Huck's fascination with death is manifold. One possibility in keeping with the superstitious nature of Huck and the design of heroic adventure is that nature is alerting Huck to his own imminent ritualistic death and Pap's imminent naturalistic death. Another possibility is that Huck is having an intimation of his own mortality, one that comes to him in the sense experience of complete isolation and stillness. That Huck is a young man faced not only with death but with the possibility of his own death is reinforced later on when he witnesses his own death in witnessing the death of his alter ego, Buck: "I wished I hadn't ever come ashore that night, to see such things. I ain't ever going to get shut of them—lots of times I dream about them." Thus, Huck begins to take a great deal more stock in dead people, and thus his initiation is a fall into the knowledge of his own mortality.

A third reading of Huck's initial fascination with death is that Huck does indeed wish he were dead insofar as he wishes he were free. The similarity between the subplots of the two occurrences in the opening chapter suggests a correspondence between freedom and death. Huck does not want to be civilized; he lights out for the hogshead; Tom comes and seeks him out. Huck wishes he were dead; he begins to experience a deathlike stillness; Tom comes and seeks him out. What emerges from the juxtaposition of those incidents is an equation of freedom with death, an equation borne out by the rest of the novel. Huck escapes civilization initially by killing himself, thereby making manifest his desire to be dead. Huck's true escape from society on the island and river, prior to his meeting with Jim, is isolate "dead quiet." The few precious moments of idyllic pleasure on the river for Huck are characterized by the same stillness; it is almost as though Huck and Jim, naked and floating within the tide of the great river, return to the womb as Gemini twins, thereby rejoicing in the stillness, having eliminated the isolation. The final reinforcement of this equation of stillness, freedom, and death occurs just prior to the commencement of the Phelps episode.

Huck, faced with the King's betrayal and the loss of Jim, comes upon the Phelps's plantation and immediately confronts the sounds of lonesomeness that are the sounds of death: he hears the "faint dronings of the bugs and flies" and the "dim hum of a spinning-wheel wailing" and in both instances wishes he were dead, for they are "the lonesomest sound[s] in the world." And once more he is returned from this deathlike experience by Tom Sawyer, but this time there is a significant difference. Tom does not retrieve Huck from this deathlike state, but rather Huck is retrieved from it as Tom. Aunt Sally mistakes Huck for Tom and Huck feels "like being reborn again." But in having Huck be reborn from death as Tom, Twain suggests, as Harold Simonson points out in *The Closed Frontier*, that Huck can only live in society as Tom.[10] The whole Phelps episode is intended as an integral part of the novel, giving the reader an important variation of the dialectic between withdrawal and return. Its failure is not in intention, but rather in execution; it is simply overdone. The fact is that the novel does not end where many critics insist it should end aesthetically—with Huck's tearing up the letter—and that makes *Huckleberry Finn* distinctively different from the novel that would culminate with Huck's heroic act. It also affects significantly the theme of separation and reparation manifest in the novel.

When he is forced back into his own identity, Huck decides to light out, ahead of the rest, and in that decision, his desire for becoming and his fascination with death are most subtly and powerfully fused. The final few paragraphs that lead up to and climax the novel with Huck's memorable pronouncement are important and should be considered closely. It is interesting to note, for example, that whereas the beginning of the novel proceeds from Huck's initial desire to withdraw from society to his subsequent agreement to join Tom's band of robbers, the ending recedes from Huck's initial agreement to accompany Tom and Jim to the Indian Territory to his final decision to light out for the Territory ahead of the rest. This structural retrogression emphasizes withdrawal, not return. It is also meaningful that Huck's initial decision to accompany Tom and Jim and his final decision to leave "ahead of the rest" is separated by Jim's revelation that Pap is dead and has been for some time.

There is no question that Jim's news dramatically halts Huck's narrative; immediately thereafter Huck and Twain conclude their tale. Moreover, the revelation of Pap's death clearly marks and perhaps influences Huck's intention to light out alone. What then is the significance of Jim's revelation and its effect on Huck? One possibility is that the news reveals to Huck a betrayal on the part of Jim. It is easy and right to conclude that Jim did not reveal the identity of the corpse in order to spare Huck, but surely after Huck's subsequent encounters with death it should be clear to Jim that Huck is no stranger to death. Perhaps Jim has other motivation for his silence. One primary reason for Huck's covenant with Jim is that he is a fugitive from Pap. With Pap dead, Huck's crisis, and part of the motivation for his community with Jim, is removed, and he is free to return to the Widow and his fortune, as well as free to turn Jim in. That all or part of this might be the conscious or unconscious suspicion of Jim is borne out by Jim's strong sense of survival, an instinct that he manifests throughout the novel.

Even if we dismiss such a reading—even if we discount the possibility of Huck's sense of betrayal on the part of Jim—the revelation of Pap's death does drive home the fact that the primary cause of Huck and Jim's community upon the raft has been altogether removed. Jim is free of bondage, free to pursue the reunion of his family, if he will; and now Huck is free of paternal bondage, free to return to Aunt Sally, if he will. It seems clear that whatever commitment Huck and Jim enjoyed in crisis fades with the dissolution of the crisis. Thus, Huck is, as Eliot points out, the most solitary of fictional characters; he has just lost the community of "kindship" with Tom and Jim and that of kinship with Pap.[11] He is once again alone, prepared to evade civilization, and Pap has shown him the way. Just as he escaped bondage early in the novel through a feigned death, so now he escapes through a withdrawal that could be said to be a symbolic death.

Huck's decision is to light out not just for the Territory, but for the "Territory ahead of the rest." "Ahead of the rest" could have followed "light out" and the meaning would have been unequivocal: Huck would have been leaving before Tom and Jim. By placing the modifier where he does, Twain allows it to modify either "light out" or "Territory," and that indefiniteness gives "Territory" additional and important meaning.[12] Whether the Territory ahead of the rest is the frontier where the hero can regain paradise in isolate Adamic splendor or a sacred middle estate between a profane civilization and a profane wilderness, a place where he can hover in perpetual becoming or into which he can resolve his protean flesh, it is in Twain's fractured Shakespeare "the undiscovered country from whose bourne no traveler returns" and which "breathes forth contagion to the world."

Huck Finn is often read as the personification and celebration of separation in America, the archetype of American individualism that manifests its sovereign self in violation of the negative norms of society; he is the unconscious, if not conscious, antinomian par excellence: he tears up the letter and risks damnation in order to maintain fidelity with his inner self rather than with the outer *nomos*. He is also seen as the personification of the American desire to retain a viable innocence against the encroachment of the social and restrictive experience: he wards off the evils of civilization by lighting out for the virgin territory. Ironically then, Huck is the hero who is *denitiated* from, not initiated into, society. As Eliot suggests, Huck comes from nowhere and must be bound for nowhere, or as Leslie Fiedler suggests, Huck is only himself insofar as he is always moving and never belonging.[13]

Huck is indeed the hero of the American mythos: he is an orphan, an exile, who denies church, law, and family to seek out an existential autonomy on the frontier. He has no sense of history, takes no stock in dead people, and cares not for what tradition, in the form of the authorities, says. He is a romantic who is drawn to the natural freedom of the river and the equality of brotherhood; he is also the pragmatist who measures experience in terms of how much "profit" there is in it. His imagination is for the most part utilitarian; he uses it to get the job done and denigrates a fancy whose rewards are immaterial. Despite his antinomianism and individualism, he needs the human connection and tries to maintain it. He is betrayed in those attempts, or those attempts come to an abrupt end. Rather than recognize and accept the human frailty implicit in such betrayal, he decides once again to light out. In so deciding, he runs away not only from society, but more importantly, from self. Insofar as he does, the rite of passage ends not with a return that would suggest rebirth, but rather a withdrawal that implies a symbolic death-in-life.

The Education of Lambert Strether

In his preface, Henry James describes *The Ambassadors* as a novel that asks this question of a hero who has "missed too much" in his life: "*Would* there yet perhaps be time for reparation?— reparation, that is, for the injury done his character." James's answer, interestingly enough, is that Lambert Strether "now at all events *sees*" and that the business of his narrative is the "demonstration of this process of vision." The answer seems to beg the question: one has to consider whether seeing is being and thus whether the advent of seeing more is reparation for the event of having lived less, of not having had one's life. Moreover, one must also weigh the intention of the idiomatic "at all events": is that a qualifier, the implication of which is that Strether's reparation has been at least—or at best—the fact that he now sees? The thesis here is that the answer provided by the novel—one consistent with the primary mode of James's narrative strategy and the ambiguity of his moral vision—is an ironic one.

On the one hand, Strether realizes a significant measure of reparation insofar as he comes to see the injury done his character and to avoid further injury of the same kind—something he could not do prior to Paris and something Waymarsh, similarly victimized, still cannot do. In addition, Strether's new consciousness, inspired by Paris, alters the old conscience, conspired by New England, and he, unlike almost all the other emissaries from Woollett, can sympathize with the Old World and break with the New World. On the other hand, there is also a failure of reparation: despite the greater consciousness and the altered conscience, his sympathy is a rather passive one. He is unable to let himself go completely and thereby achieve a fuller dimension of salvation. Because he will not or can not accept the proposals of Madame de Vionnet and Maria Gostrey, he acts out his contention to Little Bilham that "the affair of life . . . [is] at best a thin mould . . . into which, a helpless jelly, one's consciousness is poured." In working out that form of reparation, James also dramatizes that the American rite of passage in Europe is not so much a matter of expatriation as it is of *exmatriation* and that the conversion resulting from that passage confirms once-bornness, not twice-bornness.

The fictional world of *The Ambassadors* is one in which there are no fathers and, consequently, one in which there can be no expatriation. With the possible exceptions of Gloriani, who functions for James as Daedalus did for Joyce—an antitype of the spiritual and aesthetic father—and Chad, who, as we shall see, comes to play surrogate father to the initiate Strether, there is no single paternal figure in the novel—either in Europe or America. Contrastingly, the maternal figures, Mrs. Newsome, Sarah Pocock, Madame de Vionnet, and Maria Gostrey, dominate what action and intercourse there are with the protagonist. Sarah Pocock correctly sums up the agon in the novel when she confronts Strether with these questions: "What is your conduct but an outrage to women like *us*? I mean your acting out as if there can be a doubt—as between us and such another—of his duty?"

Consciousness of the grace, spontaneity, and mystery of Paris and Parisians has already affected Strether's conscience and the result is that he doubts. Indeed, the matter of Strether's reparation evolves as a choice between women. In America there is Mrs. Newsome, who is unchanging, "who doesn't admit surprises," and who is "pure," "austere," "duty," "authority," and "cold thought." There is also Mrs. Newsome's agent, her alter ego, her daughter Sarah Pocock, who, the closer she comes to poor Lambert, the larger-than-life she looms, making Strether feel that much smaller and that much more threatened. In Europe there is Madame de Vionnet, who has "such variety and yet such harmony," who is like "a goddess still partly engaged in a morning cloud or . . . a sea-nymph waist-high in a summer surge." Like Maria Gostrey, she has her abysses, her mysteries, that invite intercourse, because they excite and nurture a sensibility that feeds on "the life of connexions" and "the great nuance." Also, there is Maria Gostrey.

One extended metaphor that confirms Strether's inexperience and innocence is the one that portrays him as an infant to Gostrey's midwifery and their relation as the weaning of the hero. Just after Strether has convinced Chad to stay and buy them both time, Maria tells him that now he can "toddle alone." James extends the metaphor: "The time seemed already far off when he had held out his small thirsty cup to the spout of her pail. Her pail was scarce touched now, and other fountains had flowed for him. . . . it having been but the day before yesterday that he sat at her feet and held on by her garment and was fed by her hand." The reference to "other fountains" implies the maternalness also of de Vionnet in her relation to Strether, and James rounds out the metaphor by suggesting that Gostrey has done for Strether what de Vionnet had done for Chad: "She had decked him out for others."

As James indicates early in the novel, Maria Gostrey is a woman who has before "weaned the expatriated from traditions": in Strether's case, she not only offers Lambert her figurative founts to nurse him through his rite of passage, but she also pledges herself to him "till death" and thereby becomes, in another sense, midwife to him in his movement through the moral maze. Maria is Ariadne to Strether's Theseus; she provides the symbolic thread to Strether's "circumambience" through the "winding passages," the *"alternations of darkness and light,"* in Paris and to his circumspection through the "maze of mystic closed allusions" of Parisian society and intercourse: "without her he had lost himself." With Gostrey's help, things fall into place for Strether, and he comes to see, and it is this "process of vision" that liberates him.

Initially, what Strether sees more than anything else is that Chad Newsome "has been made over." Strether marvels at the "alteration of change," and his awe gradually shifts from the miracle to the woman who has wrought the miracle, and the woman in turn transforms Strether's wonder into devotion and service. It is as a result of this shift in allegiance that Strether, like Chad, is able to realize a measure of exmatriation: the more Strether enters "into relation" with Madame de Vionnet, the more "closely connected" he becomes, the more aware he becomes of the "formation of a split" between himself and Mrs. Newsome, until finally he feels "disinherited beyond appeal." The experience of disinheritance is not new to James's fiction: Catherine Sloper is disinherited both psychologically and financially; Daisy Miller is "cut" off by Winterbourne; and Hyacinth Robinson never does survive his orphanage. Whereas disinheritance is visited upon these agonists as trauma, it is courted by Strether as deliverance. With Gostrey's dialectical help, Strether discovers that the monster of the maze is not the courtesan of Paris, but rather the colossus of Woollett, Mrs. Newsome, the "particularly large iceberg in the cool blue northern sea," Columbia, the gem of the ocean. Thus, when Maria suggests that what one must do with such a magnificence is "make over altogether the woman herself," Strether, realizing the impossibility of such a task with so rigid a presence, responds that "what it comes to . . . is that you've got morally and intellectually to get rid of her." Is this not what Strether has done: his new vision has developed his consciousness and altered his conscience, and he has consequently rid himself of Mrs. Newsome morally and intellectually. Divorcing oneself from one mother to attend another, however, is not to complete one's exmatriation: before that can occur,

Strether must be freed of his French connection, and, in order to do that, he must see more and see differently.

Strether's vision tends to be quixotic: James makes this quite clear when, describing Strether's response to the magic of Madame de Vionnet's rooms, he writes, "It was doubtless half the projection of his mind, but his mind was a thing that . . . he had always needfully to reckon with." That he does not always reckon with it—does not always compensate for his proclivity to see life romantically and therefore does not measure what he sees by how he sees—is evident in his blindness to the true nature of Chad and Madame de Vionnet's "virtuous attachment." Maria Gostrey sums it up this way: "What I see, what I saw . . . is that you dressed up even the virtue." That disclosure of Strether's quixotic vision comes only after James has effectively dramatized it in the subtly rendered tableau within the imagined Lambinet painting.

That scene is but a microcosm of the general excursion of the novel: when Strether steps off the boat in England, he is figuratively stepping into the frame of the Lambinet. Because his mind, like that of Isabel Archer's, is not only an imaginative one sensitive to the impressions of Europe, but also one that both responds to and colors them with projections of its own romantic predispositions, Strether is hardly ever in anyone's Europe but his own. It is as though James were rendering into fictive terms the basic tenets of philosophical hermeneutics:[14] one widens the horizons of one's consciousness through an intercourse between one's presuppositions (subject) and what the world posits (object). When that intercourse is slanted subjectively, one errs in one's interpretations; such is the case with Woollett's understanding of Chad's relationship with Madame de Vionnet. When phenomena in the external world collide with one's faulty presuppositions, the result is the shock of recognition; such is the case with Strether's encounter with an altered Chad. When such phenomena collide with what one believes to be one's revision of reality, but which is in actuality an interpretation as much shaped by one's prevision as one's experience, then, the shock of recognition is perhaps greater and the irony certainly more subtle; such is the case when Chad and Madame de Vionnet intrude upon Strether's Lambinet and force Strether to see the error of his ways of seeing. Thus does James give his circumscriptive narrative—one that circles round and in upon the point of recognition—one more meaningful turn of the screw.

Strether's encounter with the trysting couple suggests what psychoanalysts call the primal scene. Strether is the infant, boyish, and adolescent hero who not only feeds off the maternal sustenance of Madame de Vionnet, but also looks to an older, grayer, and more gentlemanly Chad as a surrogate father he would most like to be. He makes of the attachment of these surrogate parents what most innocents make of the attachment of their parents: idealized virtue. She is the beloved one, belladonna, *notre dame;* he is courtly lover and attendant. Strether has been "framed" this time by the imagination, not by New England conscience; when the shock of recognition comes, it is not so much the trauma that accompanies the disclosure of their sexual connection, but rather the shame and disappointment attached to the revelation that Madame de Vionnet is not the madonna he thought she was, but a mere "maidservant crying for her young man," a woman "visibly less exempt from the touch of time," and one afraid for her life. Quixotic Strether has discovered that the virtue expressed by Dulcinea is but a human virtue, and, though to his credit he does not lose sight of that virtue, his connection to Madame de Vionnet is severed and his reparation ironically circumscribed.

When Strether arrives in Paris, he "feels launched into something of which the sense would be quite disconnected from the sense of the past and which was beginning there and then." In other words, Strether feels himself reborn or twice-born; indeed, later on, Maria Gostrey will refer to his shift of allegiance, his attempt to keep Chad in Paris, as his "conversion." Strether's sense of beginning anew is reinforced by his sense of Chad's alteration; the very rupture of Chad's identity concurs with the disconnectedness of Strether's experience. It seems that James is anticipating brother William's conclusion that religions like Protestantism that insist upon conversion, upon twice-bornness, as a necessary step to salvation also insist upon historical discontinuity—a crisis in the life of the individual that implies a rupture with the past and with tradition.[15] It is as though James were reversing the American pilgrimage and sending the American *exmatriate* to Europe to slough off his fallen American self and begin anew. Such, however, is not the case, nor could it be the case, for a writer like James, for whom a sense of the past is always present and viable.

Chad is still his mother's son: like her, he has a lack of imagination that makes others feel he is magnificent. He is also his father's son: Chad is industrially able and now that he has sown his wild oats—he has committed fornication with a wench in a foreign country—he is to return to America and the sober business of selling. Despite the real influence of Paris and de Vionnet upon him—he has been decked out for Woollett to enjoy—his new identity is not a rupture with the old. Neither is Strether's. Strether has undergone a rite of passage, but it is still the old Strether who sees and feels anew. Do the expansion of consciousness and the alteration of conscience constitute reparation for the affront to one's character? What it finally comes down to is what is the significance of Strether's rejection of Maria Gostrey's offer?

One might say that Strether rejects Maria, because, devoted to and fascinated by Madame de Vionnet, he cannot bring himself to compromise himself and Maria by accepting Maria's offer of marriage; consequently, he gives her the gentlemanly lie about his not wanting to get anything for himself out of his ambassadorship. Thus, one might say that he rejects Maria because he does not love her. One might also say that he ought not to love her or to surrender himself to her. To do that would be to give up his newfound freedom and to *rematriate* himself. Perhaps this is the real significance of Strether's pronouncement to Maria, "It's you who would make me wrong." It may be that Strether's decision also makes it possible for him to return and repatriate himself to the America of his fathers; whatever that might be, however, it is not spelled out in the novel. Nevertheless, Maria is once again an agent for repatriation.

On the other hand, Strether's gentlemanly lie may be no lie at all, but the truth, the New England truth. Is not Strether's refusal a residual of the old New England conscience still manifest in a somewhat altered exmatriate? He has not returned Chad to America and he has betrayed Mrs. Newsome; he has not earned anything for himself and he cannot freely accept Europe and nature's bounty. That part of Lambert holds back from the spontaneity of Europe and from what James calls its "circumjacent charm" is evident in the guilt he confides to Little Bilham: "I feel as if my hands were embued with the blood of monstrous alien altars—of another faith altogether." Moreover, the old New England conscience and the growing self-consciousness will not permit him to let himself go all the way; thus, when de Vionnet credits him with knowing how to let himself go, he responds that "Oh, I've not let myself go very far." Strether has discovered that "if to deal with [women] was to walk on water, what wonder that the water rose?" To have given himself up to Maria Gostrey, or for that matter, to any woman, would be to submerge one's consciousness and oneself, to plunge into the abyss of woman, of the other, and that the *exmatriated* and autonomous, self-conscious modern American cannot do.

There is still another reason why Strether rejects Maria's offer—for the same reason that he would have liked Madame de Vionnet to accompany the American party of tourists to Switzerland—for the "symmetry" of it. It is easy of course to see how Strether's refusal rounds off the hourglass symmetry of the novel for James: *The Ambassadors* begins with the implicit arrival of Strether in England and the ensuing meeting with Maria Gostrey, and it ends with his farewell to Maria and his imminent departure from Europe. As it proceeds initially with Strether's exmatriation from the *femme du dynamo,* so it recedes with his exmatriation from the *femmes du monde.* In short, it manifests the fictive claim of James in the preface that "one's work should have composition, because composition alone is positive beauty."

Indeed, composition alone is positive beauty, not only for James, but also for Strether. That is why the Jamesian hero of the later fiction can love only the dead—Densher, his Milly; Marcher, his May; and Stransom, his saints—because the dead belong to the hero in his imagination in a way that they never could in reality. Lambert Strether has just seen how the real woman suffers in comparison to the imagined one and how the real Parisian suburb suffers in comparison to the Lambinet. He would rather pursue, Theseus-like, without Ariadne, the circumjacent charm of the figure in the aesthetic carpet than risk the unconsciousness of the conjugal connection. Strether, like Waymarsh, has a sacred rage, but Strether, in reaction to the rigidity of Waymarsh's New England conscience, has translated his to a rage for an organic, unwinding aesthetic order. That is why he dresses up even virtue, why his sojourn in Europe is an excursion through a Lambinet, why he responds to Parisians as "types," "specimens," and "cases," why he is accused by Chad of too much imagination, and why he refuses the offer of Maria Gostrey. Strether is the modern, self-conscious hero, the man of vision and revision, who dares not eat a peach and who prefers to hear the mermaids singing. His rejection of Maria is his "tribute to the ideal"; one can say of that rejection what E. M. Forster has said of James's narrative technique: "It is for the sake of a particular aesthetic effect, which is certainly gained, but at this heavy price."[16]

If, as T. S. Eliot suggests, the real hero in James's fiction is the social entity, then, what is the significance of Strether's farewell to

Gostrey, which is his final farewell to all the society of *The Ambassadors?* James in his prospectus to the novel sums up Strether's rejection this way: "He *can't* accept or assent. He won't. He doesn't. It's too late. . . . He has come so far through his total little experience that he has come out on the other side—on the other side, even, of a union with Miss Gostrey."[17] Strether had started out in search of, among other things, intercourse with society, participation in the maze of mystic closed allusions that is society, and now he has come out of the maze, on the other side, more alone than he has ever been in this fictional world. His freedom, isolation, and imminent departure at the end of the novel are part of an interesting and revealing correspondence between his case and Huckleberry Finn's.

Mark Twain describes his novel as "a book of mine where a sound heart and a deformed conscience come into collision and conscience suffers defeat."[18] James in his preface similarly describes his hero as one "primed with a moral scheme of the most approved patterns which was yet framed to break down on any approach of visual facts." Though that conscience, Puritan and American, suffers defeat in both instances, there is an important variation. Huck's conscience does not significantly alter; he still accepts the code of slavery and he consequently believes that his act of befriending Jim will send him to hell; he acts in defiance of conscience. Strether, contrastingly, has altered his conscience—his judgment of Europe is softened—but still he cannot let himself go: his failure to act is in defiance of an extended consciousness. Huck Finn and Lambert Strether share one other common fate: both heroes are free and very much alone at the conclusion of their rites of initiation and both are on the threshold of another passage. For Huck it is a journey to the Territory ahead of the rest. For Strether, it is a return passage to America, but to what society? He has disconnected himself from all the society in the novel. What then is the real destination of his return trip to America?

If "The Beast in the Jungle" and "The Jolly Corner" are any indication of the direction of Strether's journey—and insofar as both short stories extend the theme of too-lateness in images that reflect those of the novel, they are—then Strether's journey shall turn from an exploration of the maze of social connection to an exploration of the labyrinth of self. Strether-Marcher-Brydon will come to see that reparation lies not in keeping vigils for the self that will be, the beast in the jungle, or in stalking the self that might have been, the monster round the jolly corner, lies not in narcissistic self-consciousness and the supreme fiction, but rather in self-surrender to the other, to May Bartram and Alice Staverton and implicitly Maria Gostrey. Though Lambert Strether has widened the horizon of his consciousness, he fails to see or "at all events" fails to act upon his knowledge that reparation lies not only in severance but also in connection. Thus, as James himself says, the "last note" of *The Ambassadors,* is not one of reparation, but an ironic one of a "lingering, ripe, separation."[19]

The Lost Generation of Jay Gatsby

Perhaps no modern American writer has commented on "the disintegration of one's personality" as directly and intensely as F. Scott Fitzgerald has in the series of articles that constitute the core of *The Crack-up.* In that series, Fitzgerald portrays himself as one "prematurely cracked"—a broken, fragmented sensibility, who finds it necessary to divorce the self that is from the self that seeks to become: "The man I had persistently tried to be became such a burden that I have 'cut him loose.' " Apparently, the internal divisions that marked the breakdown of Fitzgerald's personality had their origins as early as his marriage to Zelda; in a letter to his daughter, Fitzgerald acknowledges that "I lived with a dream. . . . Then the dream divided one day, when I decided to marry your mother. . . . I was a man divided—she wanted me to work too much for her and not enough for my dream." In his notebook, Fitzgerald discloses that the division initiated with his marriage suffered a further irrevocable rift just prior to the publication of *The Great Gatsby.* Commenting again on his marital state, Fitzgerald writes, "That September 1924 I knew something had happened that could never be repaired."[20]

The purpose of introducing these autobiographical passages is not to chronicle a parallel between Fitzgerald's life and Gatsby's agon, but rather to suggest that just as irreparable division was an explicit dimension of Fitzgerald's psyche and sensibility, so it is in the design of *The Great Gatsby.* Dislocation and fragmentation are quite visible in the novel: for Nick, the Midwest shifts significantly from center to periphery: "instead of being the warm center of the world, the Middle West now seemed like the ragged edge of the universe." Tom feels that civilization is "going to pieces" and both he and Daisy participate in the disintegration by being the couple who "smash up things and creatures." The most meaningful separation in the novel of course is Jay Gatsby's from Daisy Fay; his attempt to repair that separation, to repeat the past, is the primary agon, and that agon is enhanced by Fitzgerald's use of myth.

In developing his plot and characters, Fitzgerald employs what Eliot calls the mythical method to give order to the chaos and fragmentation of contemporary life. Nowhere is that method more evident than in the development of Gatsby's character. Fitzgerald deliberately casts Gatsby in the "blurred and patchy" strokes of the traditional hero of romance in order subsequently to demythologize that figure and render him human in terms of his dreams and the frustration of those dreams. Initially, Jay Gatsby is, in the words of Tom Buchanan, "Mr. Nobody from Nowhere," the solitary host who appears suddenly on the social scene with a charismatic glow that attracts the social butterflies of the islands. His origins are unknown and consequently countless legends grow up around him: he is related to the Kaiser; he is an Oxford man; he is a spy and bootlegger; he has killed a man. Eventually, the mystery is cleared up as Carraway recounts the confessions of Gatsby's father and of Gatsby himself; Jay Gatsby is only Jimmy Gatz, decked out by success and the dream of further success.

Just as interpreters like Rudolph Bultmann demythologize the Christian myth in hopes of recovering the viable symbol from the dying myth,[21] so Fitzgerald demythologizes the romantic, American hero in order to recover from the myth a deeper symbolic truth, into whose expression many traditional symbols converge and are converted. The most obvious and most sustained of these is the recurrent identification of Gatsby with images of light. Carraway tells us that enroute to the city, Gatsby, "with fenders spread like wings . . . scattered light through half Astoria" and that from the lofty steps of his mansion, he "dispensed starlight to casual moths" in the hope of attracting the spritish Daisy to his home, a house that "catches the light," is found "blazing with light," and, until Daisy disapproves of the spectacle, "glowed with light." When he is not dispensing light by motor or mansion, Gatsby is himself literally radiating light.

Carraway finds that after the momentary boyish awkwardness of the early moments of his reunion with Daisy, Gatsby is once again confidently brilliant: "He literally glowed; without word or a gesture of exultation, a new well-being radiated from him and filled the little room." Later, with "twinkle bells of sunshine [now] in the room," Carraway views Gatsby as "an ecstatic patron of recurrent light." And even greater than the external glow that radiates from this dreamer is the internal one that fires his dream: "No amount of fire or freshness can challenge what a man will store up in his ghostly heart." It is as though Gatsby, in his platonic conception of himself, and Fitzgerald, in his mythical conception of his hero, conceive Gatsby in the guise of the most ancient of heroes, an Apollo or Helius, or better yet, a young Phaeton. Like Phaeton, who, when he convinced his father Helius to allow him to drive the sun-chariot across the skies, could not control the fiery horses and drove the sun-chariot too far from earth and froze its inhabitants or too close and scorched its fields and consequently was struck dead by Zeus, so Gatsby, "a true son of God," sets about to do his father's business—the dispensation of light—only to find himself incapable of moderate dispensation and therefore the victim of pomp and circumstance.

As Gatsby is the god-hero of light, so Daisy is the mortal incarnation and reflection of that light. She is constantly described in terms of whiteness: back in Louisville, when Gatsby and she consummated their mutual attraction, she dressed in white, she drove a white roadster, and her porch was radiant with "the bought luxury of star-light." On the memorable night when Gatsby kissed her and "she blossomed for him like a flower," completing the incarnation of Gatsby's platonically conceived self, "the sidewalk was white with moonlight" and it made a Jacob's ladder that reached to the heavens. All of the glitter associated with Daisy is appropriate to her role as the uroboric half with whom Gatsby seeks reunion and completion. Thus, it is also appropriate that in his eyes she blossom like a flower—like a daisy—or *day's eye*—like the sun itself.

This symbolic relationship between Gatsby and Daisy is manifest in the novel in at least two other ways. There is the homonymic balance of their very names—Jay Gatsby/Daisy Fay—which suggests that Daisy is but an Echo to Gatsby's Narcissus. In addition, East Egg, the home of Daisy and the green light, is from the vantage point of the sky the mirror image of West Egg, the home of the hero who yearns to be one with Daisy, the green light, and East Egg. It is almost as though Fitzgerald were, like Yeats, attempting to "alter Plato's parable" and to suggest that Gatsby's attempt to repeat the past were but an attempt to unite Daisy and himself "into the yolk and white of one shell."[22]

When Gatsby utters his memorable response to Nick about Daisy and Tom's marriage—"In any case . . . it was just personal"—he reveals a great deal more than what is generally regarded by Nick and the critics as the magnificent dimensions of his dream; he also reveals its human limitations. For Gatsby, apparently, what is personal in others is relatively trivial; his love and desire for Daisy is impersonal. He does not love Daisy for what she intrinsically is as a person, but rather for what she embodies as a reflection. Daisy is primarily the narcissistic image: her whiteness reflects Gatsby's lightness; her voice, full of money and therefore full of promise, echoes Gatsby's dream of money and success. She does indeed complete the incarnation.

Daisy is but one of many characters who act as foils to Jay Gatsby, as reflections of his dreams as well as of the dust that floats in the wake of those dreams. Both Nick and Tom share with Jay his desire to recover the past, or at least some semblance of order out of the past, in a present disordered by the loss of innocence. Returning home from the East and "the riotous excursions with privileged glimpses into the human heart," Nick wants "the world to be in uniform and at a sort of moral attention forever." Tom, feeling that "civilization's going to pieces," longs for the rule-controlled "turbulence of some irrecoverable football game." Even Jordan Baker, in her relocation of the lie of the golf ball, shares with Gatsby the notoriety of using infamous means to gain famous ends. The least obvious of the many foils to Gatsby, but one of the most meaningful, is George Wilson.

Just as the valley of ashes, in its bleak yellow, gray, and black landscape, reveals the sterility of the moral landscape that lies beneath the gaudy glitter of island society, so George Wilson in his "colorless ways" reflects the grotesque nightmare that lies behind Gatsby's dream. Both characters are blond and blue-eyed, but in Fitzgerald's descriptions, Gatsby's golden charisma is transformed into Wilson's anemic jaundice, Gatsby's white suits into the "white ashen dust" that veils Wilson (and everything else in the valley), and Gatsby's Daisy, elfish emblem of the sun, into Wilson's Myrtle, erotic emblem of Venus. When Fitzgerald tells the reader that George Wilson is a ghost, it is Jay Gatsby of whom he is the ghost.

Both Gatsby and Wilson are absolutely friendless men; both suffer the loss of their women to Tom Buchanan; both women suffer the pain of Tom's brutality; and, though both men are made physically ill and are psychologically destroyed by their knowledge of the connection of their women to Tom, both men continue to hope that they can deliver their women and recover the past. The correspondence between the characters of Gatsby and Wilson sheds light on the manner and significance of Gatsby's death and thereby on the meaning of his dream.

At one point in the novel, just after Nick has advised Gatsby not to expect too much from Daisy, since one cannot repeat the past, and Gatsby responds that of course one can, Fitzgerald describes Gatsby in this fashion: "He looked around him wildly, as if the past were lurking here in the shadow of his house, just out of reach of his hand." In the context of the novel up to this point, the past that lurks there would seem to be the moment of incarnation in Louisville. By the end of the novel, however, after Fitzgerald adds the following passage, the context grows wider and the meaning more ironic. As Gatsby waits in vain for Daisy to call, Fitzgerald describes his disillusionment this way: "A new world, material without being real, where poor ghosts, breathing dreams like air, drifted fortuitously about . . . like that ashen, fantastic figure gliding toward him through the amorphous trees." The figure is Wilson bent on retribution, but perhaps the fantastic figure, breathing dreams like air, is also Jimmy Gatz.

Part of the mystique of Jay Gatsby is that he has the look of a man who has killed someone; however literally true or untrue that might be, it is certainly figuratively true. In platonically conceiving Jay Gatsby, he murdered Jimmy Gatz. The past that lurks in the shadow of Gatsby's house includes the moment of self-destruction as well as the moment of self-apotheosis. Thus, George Wilson is the ghost of Jimmy Gatz as well as Jay Gatsby, and, when he exacts vengeance upon Gatsby, it is as though Jimmy Gatz—the past lurking in the shadow—exacts vengeance too. Gatsby in his "overwhelming self-absorption" is finally overwhelmed by that self-absorption, and in that moment he ironically succeeds in repeating the past. Such is the nightmarish outcome of an American dream that denies history by seeking to reject and repeat the past. Nick is wrong when he refers to Gatsby's "incorruptible dream"; any dream that denies history by denying time is corrupt to begin with.

In dreaming their dreams, both Gatsby and the Dutch sailors try to deny the past, to deny history. Gatsby denies the past in at least two instances; he rejects his patrimony in denying his parentage and denying what he has been, Jimmy Gatz, and he rejects Daisy's matrimony in denying what she has become, both wife and mother. Daisy (and America) has become one who wants her life shaped not in the future and according to some ineffable promise, but "now, immediately—and the decision must be made by some force—of love, of money, of unquestionable practicality—that was close at hand," and Tom Buchanan is the brute reality close at hand. Gatsby would deny the marriage of America to practicality and in so doing would alter time. Unlike Meyer Wolfsheim, who merely tries to fix the World Series, Gatsby tries "to fix everything the way it was before," to fix time. Of course he is doomed and just as he has to struggle against the falling mantlepiece clock while trying to collect himself before Daisy, so, while "a universe of ineffable gaudiness spun itself out in his brain," a "clock ticked on the washstand" for Jimmy Gatz.

Interestingly enough, the only deliverance from time seems to occur when Jay and Daisy experience a momentary ecstasy during their reunion at Nick's, a repetition of the past, which is played out to the accompaniment of a lyric of the day: "In the meantime/ In between time/ [Ain't we got fun]." It is only "between time" that Gatsby recovers a trace of the past, but that moment, like the reunion of Hester and Dimmesdale in the New England wood, is as fleeting as time itself. What Gatsby does not realize and what Fitzgerald, implicitly, and Eliot in "Burnt Norton," explicitly, came to realize is that "only through time time is conquered." In paradoxically trying to both recover the past—recapture the moment in Louisville—and deny the past—reject his heritage and his self—Gatsby, like Van Winkle before him, is responsible for a lost generation.

The Dissociation of Sensibility in *Light in August*

In Plato's parable of the severed androgynous creature, the emphasis falls on the desire of each half to find its other half and reunite; that is the end of love and implicitly the end of life. Such an emphasis is apparent in Fitzgerald's fictive variation of the mythopoeic pattern: Gatsby's quest is to find Daisy Fay, reunite himself with her, and thereby repeat the past. In William Faulkner's version of the pattern, *Light in August,* the emphasis shifts from reunion to dissociation, to the forces that drive men away from women, whites away from blacks, individuals away from themselves and from the other.

In that novel, the three, central, alienated characters seek a purity of being that necessitates a denial of aspects of their personae and a separation from nature and the community. Gail Hightower unconsciously divorces himself from his wife and parish and also strives to suppress his sympathy; Joanna Burden does not know how to be a woman and isolates herself from the white community in her absurd ministrations to the black community; Joe Christmas not only rejects the numerous females about him and suppresses the female softness within, but also attempts at various stages in his life to purge himself of his whiteness as well as his assumed blackness.

Now, it is true that these unnatural, Gothic portraits of the dissociated self are framed by the natural conjunctions of Lena Grove with the community and Byron Bunch, and thus we can conclude that Faulkner's version of the mythopoeia includes reparation as well as separation. Indeed, that Faulkner chooses to open the novel with the communion of Lena and the community and close it with the imminent union of Lena and Byron is indicative of his ultimate hope for man. That hope, however, does not blind him to the present human condition, and thus his narrative stresses the dissociation of the modern psyche and suggests that, in Yoknapatawpha County, such dissociation is the outcome of a tradition obsessed with the purification of a tainted body and the recovery of a glorious past.

Calvinistic Protestantism is a significant part of a social heritage bequeathed to the otherwise disinherited alien in *Light in August,* and an important characteristic of that puritanical Christianity is that it tends to dissociate the sensibility—to extol a cold, hard, logical, and male austerity at the expense of a warm, soft, emotional, and female sympathy. Although Joe Christmas will not accept the name and catechism of his foster father, he nevertheless adopts the very life-style fashioned by that faith. When Calvin McEachern tries to force Joe to learn his catechism, Faulkner describes their kinship of stubbornness as a "rigid abnegation of all compromise." McEachern, whose words are not human, but "cold, implacable, like written or printed words," is described as sadomasochistically experiencing homosexual pleasure in whipping the boy: "The boy's body might have been wood or stone, a post or a tower upon which the sentient part of [McEachern] mused like a hermit, contemplative and remote with ecstasy and self-crucifixion." Faulkner adds, however, that as McEachern methodically whips Joe, "it would have been hard to say which face was the more rapt, more calm, more convinced."

McEachern's Protestantism is above all the negation of compromise: for him, there is no *co-promise,* no mutual concession or submission. He is the one whose life is cold, hard, rocklike, impersonal, implacable, and pure; but, as Faulkner has Jason Compson

tell his son Quentin in *The Sound and the Fury,* "Purity is a negative state and therefore contrary to nature" and therefore contrary
to the implied morality of Faulkner's grotesque pastoral. It is the
concentration on purity and austerity—the obsession with but one
of the several Christian truths—that renders the Protestantism of
Light in August aesthetically grotesque in the terms set forth by
Sherwood Anderson in his prologue to *Winesburg, Ohio.*[23] Like
the Puritans of Boston, the Presbyterian of Yoknapatawpha has
eschewed sympathy in his obsession with severity. Even Byron
Bunch has to fall in love with Lena Grove contrary to a tradition
that demands in the object "physical inviolability."

It is this very physical inviolability that so desensitizes McEachern and Christmas that the only rapture of their lives occurs in self-
crucifixion—through the rigid abnegation of mutual submission.
Thus, Hightower speaks somewhat for Faulkner when he recognizes that people who cannot bear too much pleasure will escape it
through violence, through a religion that drives them to a
"crucifixion of themselves and one another." And thus does Faulkner reflect that Protestant music has a stern and implacable quality
that asks not for love, but for death, "as though death were the
boon."

In developing his theme, Faulkner reappropriates the symbols of
Plato's parable and dramatizes the dissociation of sensibility as a
division between maleness and femaleness. Joe Christmas's rejection of women and of the food they proffer and Joanna Burden's
suppression of her own femininity are the two central manifestations of Protestantism's denial of eros and its affirmation of logos
and thanatos. Joe has unconsciously learned from his grandfather
and the orphanage nurse about the bitchery and vagary of woman.
Moreover, that early initiation has been confirmed by the indoctri-
nations of McEachern, upon whose logical and inescapable rule
and retribution he has learned to count, and by the seductions of
Mrs. McEachern, who conspires to feed him and make him feel,
make him cry, and thereby proves to him once again that woman
was the unpredictable "soft kindness which he believed himself
doomed to be the victim of."

Joe Christmas, however, is not so much the victim of women,
but rather the victim of a dissociated sensibility that rejects the
experience personified by women. Even Joanna Burden is a victim
who does not know how to be a woman, because she has been
"mantrained" of a "thinking born of a [New England] heritage and
environment" that has made her sexual release "hard, untearful and

unselfpitying and almost manlike." Thus, when she and Christmas copulate, "it was as if he struggled physically with another man for an object of no actual value to either, and for which they struggled on principle alone," just as he had once struggled homosexually with his adopted father. Whatever else it bequeathes its heirs, the grotesque Protestantism of *Light in August* leaves them, like the hair at the back of Joanna's neck, "screwed" up.

In describing the relationship of Mrs. McEachern to Joe Christmas, Faulkner associates the female with conspiracy; what else is conspiracy but a breathing together, a feeling together, the give and take of mutual submission? Since such submission would compromise the implacable self, it, and the females that personify it, must be abhorred and avoided. That is why, when Christmas enters Burden's house through the window, he is described as a shadow returning "to the allmother of obscurity and darkness" and why, when he wanders into Freedman Town and feels that he has "returned to the lightless hot wet primogenitive Female," he shudders at the prospect and is relieved to find his way out of "the black, impenetrable . . . abyss" and breathe "the cold hard air of white people."

Faulkner uses the conflict of the races in the same way that he uses the battle of the sexes—as metaphor. The several variations of the folk fear of black blood is less significant as an overt part of the social conflict than as a symbol of the dissociated psyche: despite the fact that he is believed to be a black man who has raped and killed a white spinster, Christmas is not lynched by any mob. In *Light in August,* self-crucifixion is a "palpitant chiaroscuro," in one example of which Joanna Burden envisions generations of white babies with a "black shadow in the shape of a cross . . . falling upon them" and "beneath them . . . as if they were nailed to the cross," a crucifixion, which her father describes as the curse of the white man that the white man can never escape.

The truth of Nathaniel Burden's gospel is dramatized in the life of Joe Christmas. His curse is not so much not knowing for certain whether he is black and/or white, but rather not being able to accept whatever he is and consequently striving for a purity of being that denies either his black self or his white self. Plato's androgynous figure has become Faulkner's *chiaroscuric* self, and the crucifixion of that self is evident in the scene where, lying with a black woman, Christmas tries to breathe in "the dark and inscrutable thinking and being of Negroes" only to have his nostrils ironically "whiten and tauten, his whole body writhe and strain with physical outrage and spiritual denial."

It is only after he murders the symbolic projection of his dissociated self—a Joanna Burden who, having experienced menopause and the end of her grotesque womanhood, has once again become the manlike, praying, spiritual self—that Christmas is able to don the black woman's shoes and feel "the black tide creeping up his legs, moving from his feet upward as death moves." Ironically, the black envelopment from without prepares Christmas for the release of the blackness within. Just as he had symbolically murdered a part of himself in slaying Joanna Burden, so a part of himself—in the guise of the alienated and fascistlike Percy Grimm—murders Joe Christmas and releases "from out the slashed garments about his hips and loins the pent black blood [that] seemed to rush like a released breath . . . out of his pale body." And as Faulkner tells us, "upon that black blast the man seemed to rise soaring into their memories forever and ever."

Those who read the death of Joe Christmas as an evocation of Christ's crucifixion and therefore as an extension of the Christian analogy implicit throughout the narrative are justified in their reading:[24] one cannot avoid the suggestion of Calvary in the slashed garments about the loins, nor the metaphorical linking of the release of black blood with the release and ascent of the holy spirit, nor the perpetuation of a martyrdom in the minds of those who have borne witness. Faulkner's crucifixion, however, is grotesque; it is a black crucifixion, because it is the self-crucifixion of the dissociated Calvinistic self who finally achieves a purity of being in the release of the warm and wet black blood from the cold and dry pale body. Thus, the parallels between Joe Christmas and Jesus Christ work ironically and reveal Christmas as an antihero who is also an anti-Christ: contrary to Christ, who had to withdraw from a pure spiritual being in order to incarnate himself and become impurely natural, Christmas has renounced the femaleness and blackness of the body in order to become unnaturally pure.

The symbolic polarities of male and female and black and white do not play as prominent a role in the self-crucifixion and dissociation of Gail Hightower as they do in that of Joe Christmas and Joanna Burden. It is true, however, that Hightower has felt betrayed by the flesh and blood reality of the female. Upon entering the seminary, he saw his future intact and characteristically "inviolable. . . . like a classic and serene vase." Indeed, he married the daughter of a minister there, thinking that their marriage would not be a physical communion, but rather "a dead state carried over into and existing still among the living like two shadows chained together with the shadow of a chain." In other words, he saw his marriage as an extension of his ghostly commitment to his dead grandfather. Consequently, when his wife demanded release from that physical inviolability, from the unholy ghosts with whom he lived, he must have felt that his vase, like Christmas's, had cracked and turned foul. Because he has experienced the female violation of the closed circle of his ghostly existence, Hightower later implores Lena Grove to leave Byron Bunch to himself and thus to his peace.

Despite the intrusion of the female and the black Christmas into his life, Hightower's dissociation is more a matter of a division from and within time. He has withdrawn himself from all mechanized time as well as all cyclical time, and in so doing he has rejected the continuum of diachronic time or history. Instead, he has sought the still point of synchronic time that transcends history: the recurrence of that moment when the power and the glory of the South blossomed in the absurd, and therefore grand, futility of a grandfather shot to death stealing chickens. In the presentation of Hightower's vigil for the revision of that moment, it is as though Faulkner were presenting another variation of his theme of a grotesque Protestantism: a shepherd who seeks a fold in order that he may gather the wool of its ghostly past.

Hightower believes that with his loss of wife and parish and the consequent indignity to his person, he has bought immunity from the present, from the community, from the other; but he comes to discover that the price he has paid has been not only his own life, but also another's life. Like the very people he recognizes are driven to the crucifixion of self and others because they cannot bear very much pleasure, he has been so driven because he cannot bear very much reality. His cross is not that of the black shadow; rather it is that of the golden and ghostly past. As he approaches the realization of his culpability in his wife's death—the knowledge that he became the instrument of her despair and death by making her the means of his own selfishness—his thinking "slows like a wheel beginning to run into sand." Once he experiences the shock of recognition, however, "the wheel whirls on . . . freed now of its burden . . . fading, without progress as though turned by that final flood which had rushed out of him."

The similarity of language here with that used in Christmas's death, as well as the progression of the entire scene, suggest another apotheosis, but again it is a grotesque one. Despite his momentary participation in the blood, in the generation of Lena Grove's son, and despite his self-awareness, Hightower succeeds in ridding himself of continuum and community in recovering the still point where then and now are one. But that too is a condition contrary to nature and it is nature in Faulkner's novel that emerges as the comic affirmation in an otherwise grotesque negation.

Clearly, Lena Grove is the personification of nature in *Light in August*, and she is presented as the counterforce to the dissociation experienced by the other central characters; equally clear is the contrast of the stasis experienced by her and that by Hightower. As the novel opens, Faulkner describes the progression of the wagon and progression of Lena in comparable terms: Lena's past is a succession of "peaceful and undeviating changes . . . through which she advanced in identical and anonymous and deliberate wagons . . . like something moving forever and without progress across an urn." The metaphor is almost misleading, for it would have the reader think of Lena's movement in association with the still movement on a work of art—on a Grecian urn—but it is only like that of an urn. Indeed, the urn in its evocation of stasis may be said to be imitating life, the very stasis of a real wagon that according to Faulkner, "seems to hang suspended in a middle distance forever and forever, so infinitesimal is its progress."

Does not the earth (and perhaps implicitly the earth mother) move in a progression so infinitesimal to the naked and natural eye that it seems to be at rest? Thus, even when Lena feels her first labor spasm, Faulkner notes that contrary to the seeming, the "wagon has not stopped; time has not stopped." This is the vital stasis of *Light in August*—the seeming stillness of generation and the natural progression of the earth—and not Hightower's vision that seeks to arrest time and halt generation.

One of the most suggestive and revealing passages in the novel ironically takes the form of an infrequent reflection of Lena Grove. As she listens to the sound of the wagon coming toward her, a wagon that she can hear before she can see, she muses: *"Then it will be as if I were riding for a half mile before I even get into the wagon, before the wagon even got to where I was waiting; and that when the wagon is empty of me again it will go for a half mile with me still in it."* This reflection, together with the identification of the wagon with natural progression, with linear time, implies Lena's participation in generation and tradition, implies a continuity of existence that lives not only in the present or, like so

many of Faulkner's characters, arrested in the past, but also and
most importantly in the future.

That is what the Faulknerian grotesque has been dissociated
from—a sense of tradition that in the words of T. S. Eliot is not
only a "piety towards the dead, however obscure," but also, "a
solicitude for the unborn, however remote."[25] Insofar as Hightower emerges from the past to assist Lena in her delivery, he is
momentarily involved in that solicitude and consequently delivered from the past; that he retreats back into his piety for the past
implies the fleetingness of his salvation. Insofar as Byron Bunch
chooses to mate his life with that natural, still-moving progression
that is Lena and the earth, he moves toward a greater solicitude for
the other—for the unborn, the future—toward the female flux and
unpredictability that others have repulsed.

Prior to his decision to try to force Lucas Burch to return to
Lena, Bunch faces an interesting metaphorical dilemma. He is riding away from Lena and Lucas and approaching the crest of a hill,
when he thinks the crest "is like the edge of nothing. Like once I
passed it I would just ride off into nothing. . . . And Byron Bunch
he wouldn't have to be or not be Byron Bunch." He decides,
however, not to murder the suffering Bunch; he does not, like
Burch, "grasp the iron ladder at the end of the [railroad] car and
leap upward and vanish from sight as though sucked into a
vacuum" or like Joe Christmas, "run headfirst and laughing into
something that was obliterating him like a picture in chalk being
erased from a blackboard."

Unlike Burch or Christmas, Byron Bunch chooses to be himself
rather than to become; he chooses to engage the continuity of
generation and tradition rather than be twice-born in another
American peregrine pilgrimage away from the community, the
other, and the self. In making that choice, he moves closer toward
a unified sensibility that is for Faulkner, as well as for Eliot, the
equivalent of moral salvation.

5

The *Via Negativa:* An American Pilgrimage

... having nothing, and yet possessing all things.
St. Paul, *II Corinthians*

Walden opens with Thoreau's account of the crisis that underlies the quiet desperation of the mass of men; he says they go about "doing penance in a thousand remarkable ways . . . that the twelve labors of Hercules were trifle in comparison with those which my neighbors have undertaken." Moreover, they "have no friend Iolus to burn with a hot iron the root of the Hydra's head, but as soon as one head is crushed, two spring up" in its place. Thoreau further suggests that this multiplication and division of labors is both the punishment and the crime, for man has resigned the pleasure of home construction to the carpenter and the architect, and consequently it is not only the tailor who is "the ninth part of a man." Thoreau had read Emerson carefully and had learned that the integrated enterprise of the whole man, "this original unit, this fountain of power, has been so distributed to multitudes, has been so minutely subdivided and peddled out, that it is spilled into drops and cannot be gathered."[1] Thus, Thoreau laments that "our life is frittered away with detail" and wonders "where is this division of labor to end?"

His answer of course is that it will end with himself—with his withdrawal from Concord and his sojourn at Walden—where he will gather in those scattered drops from the fountain of power by contracting and concentrating his own life into its original and pure simplicity. This intention, as well as the whole direction of *Walden*, is beautifully summed up in the following passage from

119

his *Journal* of 1857, in which Thoreau seems to respond to a critique of his espousal of poverty:

> By poverty, i. e. simplicity of life and fewness of incidents, I am solidified and crystallized, as a vapor of liquid by cold. It is a singular concentration, of strength and energy and flavor. Chastity is perceptual acquaintance with the All. My diffuse and vaporous life becomes as the first leaves and spiculae radiant as gems on the weeds and stubble in a winter morning. You think that I am impoverishing myself by withdrawing from man, but in my solitude I have woven for myself a silken web or *chrysalis,* and nymph-like shall ere long burst forth a more perfect creature, fitted for a higher society. By simplicity, commonly called poverty, my life is concentrated and so becomes organized, or a κόσμος, which before was inorganic and lumpish.[2]

In *Walden,* the regeneration of the pond by nature takes the form of winter freeze and spring thaw. Through the icy solidification of its surface, the pond concentrates itself just as Thoreau in the *Journal* transforms his diffuse self into a radiant crystal shining on a winter morning. The thaw, with the torrents of spring running into the pond, effects the crisis or molting of both pond and man, as one is rid of its old coat and the other of his old self. The mazelike silken web that Thoreau weaves for himself in his impoverishment in the *Journal* becomes in *Walden* the many "concentric layers of woodedness in the dead dry life of society," from which a beautiful winged life emerges "to enjoy its summer life at last." Thus, the Daedalian hero, who is at the beginning of the book surrounded by the social labyrinth of a multiplicity of labors and distractions, is now liberated into a more chaste communion with nature through the wings of his own devising. Such artifice, however, is one derived from simplicity, poverty, and concentration, and both the *Journal* passage and *Walden* suggest that Thoreau's renewal is one effected by the *via negativa.*

In Western Christendom, there have been two basic approaches to an experience and understanding of God: the *via positiva* and the *via negativa.* The former ascribes to the creator the perfect manifestations of those virtues found in creatures and the creation. The difference between God and man is thereby primarily a quantitative, and not a qualitative, one. Thus, God is faith, hope, love, light, majesty, beauty, mystery, all made perfect. Such a view is subject to the criticism that it tends to create God in the image of man; its defense is the biblical one that man is, after all, created in the image of God. The latter view of the *via negativa* denies in

God the manifestation of any human or earthly virtue. God is the wholly other who is completely detached from and independent of creation. Moreover, he cannot be known by the finite modes of human intellect or understanding.[3]

Because God is like no thing man knows, he can be said to be no thing or nothingness itself. In order for man to have an experience of God in this life, he must become like God—detached and nothing himself. Man prepares himself to receive God through the threefold way of purgation, illumination, and union. He must strip away the things and affections of this world, rendering himself naked and poor in earthly terms. Renouncing the ordinary modes of perception and memory, he must seek a forgetting of things done and undone and enter a "cloud of unknowing," where he feelingly sees the wretched self he has been. In this paradoxical state where the bitterness of dread is transformed into the sweetness of grace, the soul is made ready for a "great one-ing" with Christ. The *via negativa* of the medieval mystic is then a transcendent union made possible by negation. As such, it bears a striking similarity to the antimetaphysical philosophy of Martin Heidegger.[4]

What the ontology of Heidegger has in common with the theology of the medieval mystic is that both see transcendence of the quotidian world largely in terms of a phenomenological encounter with nothingness. For Heidegger, man is thrown out of nothing into existence, into being-in-the-world; he is separated from Being (the totality of what-is) in the form of being (whatever-is-in-totality). Such existence, however, is not authentic, for man is caught up in calculation and calculation uses up whatever it calculates. In order for man to establish an authentic self, he must experience dread.

In dread, the whatever-is-in-totality withdraws and man feels oppressed by the resulting emptiness. Furthermore, man as existent slips away and has the uncanny feeling that it is another "one" that experiences the anxiety of dread. In the trepidation of this encounter, where the whatever-is-in-totality and the "I" have withdrawn, one is left with nothing to hold on to. That nothing, however, is the ground of Being, because dread, in encountering no-thing-ness, has an intimation of the original what-is or pure Being. The one that intuits Being is what Heidegger calls pure *Dasein*, the authentic self, that transcends the boundaries of the quotidian whatever-is-in-totality: "The projection into Nothing on the basis of hidden dread is the overcoming of what-is-in-totality: Transcendence." The primary difference between the *via negativa* of the mystic and that of the existentialist is that the former is a nothingness that leads to a metaphysical Supreme Being who transcends time and history, while the latter is a nothingness that leads to a physical pure Being that is contained within time and history.[5]

In both cases, however, the *via negativa* is the progression toward a wholly other reality by way of negation, and as such the term *via negativa* will serve to signify a symbolic variation of the pattern of separation and reparation manifest in American literature. For example, one could suggest that the Puritan pilgrimage is a *via negativa*, an unlayering of centuries of Catholic accretion of dogma and ritual in an attempt to recover the original Christian *kerygma* of primitive Christianity, the simple message that Jesus is the Christ. Thoreau's withdrawal to Walden is partially a *via negativa*, in which simplicity, poverty, and concentration lead to communion; Thoreau, however, transfers from the *via negativa* to the *via positiva*, when, like his fellow transcendentalists, he celebrates a pantheistic nature or creation that is also God. For Emily Dickinson, T. S. Eliot, and Wallace Stevens, the *via negativa* is respectively and variously the mode of reparation with the boundless, with Christ, and with Being.

Emily Dickinson: An Imp of the Perverse

Like her literary ancestors—the Gothic writers of nineteenth-century America—and her literary descendants—the modern symbolists of twentieth-century America, Emily Dickinson assumes that in order to reveal the internal, as well as the external, reality—in order to tell the whole truth—one has to tell it slant, to be ironically and tensively circumlocutive. In evoking the felt life, not only does success lie in circuit, but also does circumference, the expansion of understanding, lie in circumscription. In addition, she realizes that "had we the first intimation of the definition of life, the calmest of us would be lunatics"; therefore, for Dickinson, divinest sense lies in much madness.[6] In both the slantedness and "madness" of Dickinson's poetry, a strong element of the perverse—of surprise, excitement, shock, terror, and affront—issues from ironic and paradoxical juxtaposition and from a departure from norms and expectation.

Sometimes the perversity is quite obvious. Technically, her lines are cast in a peculiar prosody: she excites and affronts with the archaic word, the perplexing ellipsis, distorted syntax, and unusual and enigmatic punctuation. She uses figures of speech that amalgamate the abstract and concrete, i.e., "Hour of Lead," and oxymorons that yoke together disparate experiences, i.e., "sumptuous destitution."[7] Finally, this child of Puritan and Yankee traditions chooses among her master metaphors the symbols of Catholic nunnery and European royalty for the wedding of the self to the other and the soul to God.

Thematically, this imp of the perverse damns God with feint contrition: "Heavenly Father . . . We are Dust—/We apologize to thee/For thine own Duplicity" (1461); she measures love by the infinity of pain: "Time is a Test of Trouble/But not a Remedy/If such it prove, it prove too/There was no Malady" (686); she enjoys suffering: "We will not drop the Dirk/Because We love the Wound" (379); she nurtures what hurt she has: "Agony is frugal./Puts itself severe away/For its own perusal" (1243); and maintains consistently that "Delight—becomes pictorial—/When viewed through Pain" (572).

The austerity and severity evident in all of this is attributable somewhat to a Puritan heritage that can be, as we have seen, a dissociation of sensibility. This dissociation tends to make Dickinson pledge her fidelity to the soul at the expense of the body, to the distant at the expense of the near, to death (and death-in-life and life-in-death) at the expense of life itself. This predisposition is glimpsed in a letter in which she confesses that "I do not care for the body, I love the timid soul, shrinking soul" (L, 1:103). In another letter, she links this preference for the spirit with her ideas on friendship and love: writing to the Norcross sisters, she says, "I wish you were with me, not precisely here, but in the sweet mansions the mind likes to suppose" (L, 2:510). Emily Dickinson prefers some distance between herself and her friends and family and the communication of an epistle to the communion of the flesh, for she writes, "A letter always seemed to me like Immortality, for is it not the Mind alone without corporeal friend" (L, 3:752).

Elsewhere in her epistles is the suggestion of a transcendentalist influence that freed the impish Dickinson into speculating not only on deific duplicity, but also on deific discontent: "To be human is more than to be divine, for when Christ was divine, he was uncontented till he had been human" (L, 2:592). Indeed, the friction between an inherited Puritan conscience and a newly acquired transcendentalist consciousness accounts in part for the tensive nature of Dickinson's poetry.[8] Thus, she writes, "I felt a Cleaving in my Mind/As if my Brain had split—/I tried to match it—Seam by Seam—/But could not make them fit" (937). That cleavage led to perversity, and that perversity, apparent in her unusual prosody and her explicit poetic and epistolary avowals, is rendered more implicit and therefore more effective in the poetry that deals with estrangement from nature.

In "I dreaded that first Robin so," Dickinson affronts the reader with the paradox that April is the cruelest month, because its visual and musical celebration—its surrealistic piano in the woods, spear-wielding daffodils, and unthinking drums—persecute the already mourning queen of calvary. Here, nature as festival is indifferent to the sorrows of the persona, and consequently the separation felt in widowhood is intensified. In "Further in Summer than the Birds" and "There's a certain Slant of light," estrangement is compounded by the persona's feelings of exclusion from a sacred presence. In the former, Dickinson employs the language of Catholic ritual to evoke an epiphany in nature, a phenomenon that enhances nature but enlarges human loneliness, because the persona is outside the "Druidic Difference," the primitive numinosity. In the existential landscape of the latter, Dickinson again uses religious language to evoke psychic dread; this time, however, the figure of speech is even more tensive, for, like the modern symbolist, she uses a paradoxical image of music, "the Heft/Of Cathedral Tunes," which simultaneously lifts and oppresses the spirit, to capture the impression left by a certain slant of winter afternoon light that yields little illumination and even less warmth. In addition, her conclusion linking the passing of that light to the "Distance/On the look of Death," like symbolist imagery, is linguistically indefinite, but emotionally precise in its intensification of the estrangement.

In the jolly corner poems, "One need not be a Chamber—to be Haunted—" and "I Years had been from Home," it is the alienation of a self divided from itself that concerns Dickinson. Like Poe before her and James after, Dickinson recognizes that one need not be a house to be haunted. Because of the cleavage in the mind, the "Brain has Corridors," around which one encounters the specter superior to the external ghost, the "More" that is the hidden self behind the surface self. It is such encounters that make the solitudes of space, sea, and death seem like society when compared to the "polar privacy" of a "soul admitted to itself" (1695).

In "I Years had been from Home," Dickinson drops the more

obvious trappings of the Gothic haunted house and in so doing moves further from Poe and closer to James. It matters not from where the persona has returned: it may be from the Catskills with Rip Van Winkle—indeed, the poem can be viewed as a psychological internalization of the kind of dread Rip experiences upon his return home—or it may be from the grave, with Emily Webb in Wilder's *Our Town.* What is important is the powerful sense of alienation felt by one on the threshold of two worlds, a sense achieved by the relatively restrained extended metaphor of the house haunted by one's former self, by the metaphysical conjunctions of "leaned upon the Awe" and "lingered with Before," by the telescoping of a traumatic second in time into an eternal ocean's roll, and by the suggestion of a Munch-like image of an angst-ridden persona holding her hands to her ears, trying to muffle the shriek of a second's oceanic roll and fleeing what was once a familiar home, but is now a strange house. The poem is a distinctive variation of a recurrent theme of Dickinson: the retreat from a figurative, and in this case literal, threshold that leaves the persona estranged.

Estrangement for Dickinson is a result not only of the threshold experience, but also of the brooding that attends and follows such experience. So much of Dickinson's poetry is evocative of the "agenbite of inwit." For example, in "After great pain, a formal feeling comes," it is not so much the pain as it is the "Hour of Lead" that follows, not so much the experience of snow as it is the recollection of the snow, that effects despair, the "Chill—then Stupor—then the letting go." Throughout the canon of Dickinson recurs the evocation of Puritan auto-machia, a terrible self-consciousness whose stress cannot be assuaged: "Narcotics cannot still the Tooth/That nibbles at the soul" (501).

Although self-consciousness brings the Dickinson persona an emotional poverty—an isolation, alienation, and estrangement—it is that very impoverished existence that also extends the horizons of her understanding. For Dickinson, it is the consciousness of death that is the mother of beauty; more than any other nineteenth-century American writer, she anticipates the existential claim that only the recognition of and encounter with mortality give meaning to life and essence to self. Thus, she writes that "The Admirations—and Contempts—of time—/Show justest—through an Open Tomb—"; the awareness of death alters consciousness and we cease to see what has distracted and begin to see what has been hidden. It is "Compound Vision . . . Back—toward Time—/

And forward—/Toward the God of Him—" (906). These passages serve well as a gloss on so many of Dickinson's death poems and particularly on "I heard a Fly buzz when I died" and "I felt a Funeral in my Brain."

Both poems look at life through an open tomb and both conclude with compound vision, by which the persona alters her consciousness. In "I heard a Fly buzz," the interposition of the blue buzz between the persona and the light evokes an insight into the something other, while it simultaneously closes the windows of the quotidian world; thus, the persona can "not see to see." "I felt a Funeral in my Brain" suggests the following scenario. The persona is one who has died literally as well as figuratively at sea. While she lies in state aboard ship, she feels her own funeral in her brain. The double fiction tensively evokes the anguish of death and the greater anguish of consciousness of death. In the penultimate stanza, the death knell isolates the persona more completely and terribly by telescoping her isolation from the enclosure of the mind to the spaciousness of the universe. In the final stanza, the plank supporting her coffin and her reason breaks, and both she and her consciousness fall into the sea, into death, but also into the death of knowing death. Not only does migrainous self-consciousness conclude, but with her plunge into the sea, she hits a new world. Rational knowing gives way to intuitive unknowing, and thus is death once more the mother of beauty. The beauty that unfolds from such phenomena is that of circumference.

Dickinson writes in two letters that "The Bible dealt with the Centre not with Circumference" (L, 3:850) and that "My Business is Circumference" (L, 2:412). Once again the imp of Amherst seems to set herself against tradition; her poetry, however, deals with the center as well as with circumference. Whatever else it is in Dickinson's poetry, circumference is an expansion of consciousness away from a phenomenological center towards a boundless infinity and eternity. The voyage of death, for example, is an uncharted progress towards infinity: in a letter to her sister-in-law, Dickinson attempts consolation for the death of her nephew with this observation: "Moving on in the Dark, like loaded Boats at Night, though there is no Course, there is Boundlessness" (L, 3:800). The experience of love is a similar journey: in the ecstatic moment of "Wild Nights," the passionate persona abandons "Compass" and "Chart" for what we can infer is a voyage toward boundlessness that requires no instruments of navigation. Throughout many poems, eternity is the wheeling of cycles in a centrifugal direction towards circumference; thus, the bound-lessness associated with love and death is elsewhere the circumference that transcends the limitations of the temporal.[9]

In "I saw no Way—The Heavens were stitched—," the earth reverses its hemispheres and the speaker soars "out upon Circumference [eternity]—/Beyond the Dip of Bell [time]—," and in "She staked her feathers—Gained an Arc—," the bird of the poem rises "beyond the estimate/Of Envy, or of Men . . . Among Circumference." For Dickinson, the "God of Width" (1231) extends over a centrifugal universe whose circumference will be full at the Resurrection (515). It is only with the cessation of time, either through epiphany or the intimation of death, that one has an intimation of immortality: "When Cogs—stop—that's Circumference—/The Ultimate of Wheels" (633). Clearly, circumference is the movement from the temporal towards the eternal, from limited knowledge towards expansive understanding.

Such a conclusion is borne out by the recurrence of a symbol in both a letter and a poem. In the letter, Dickinson writes, "These sudden intimacies with immortality; are expanse—not Peace—as Lightning at our feet, instills a foreign landscape" (L, 3:661). Thus, the phenomenological experience, the lightning at the center, instills a foreign landscape, a wider horizon of insight and understanding that was not there before, and thereby is "Circumference [the] Bride of Awe" (1620). The greater understanding that is circumference is manifest not only in the poet, but also in the poem and the reading of the poem. Though the poets in "The Poets light but Lamps" are themselves extinguished before their poems, "the wicks they stimulate/If vital light—/Inhere as do the Suns—/ Each age a lens—/Disseminating their Circumference." For Dickinson, then, there is a reciprocity of understanding between the object—the Dickinson poem—and the subject—the reader of that poem; the result of that reciprocity is the widening of the horizons of understanding. Finally, in a variation of the image of the central light that irradiates a circumference of greater understanding, Dickinson anticipates Wallace Stevens's belief in the need for a supreme fiction: "The abdication of Belief/Makes the Behavior small—/Better an *ignis fatuus*/Than no illume at all" (1551).

To repeat, Dickinson's circumference of vision and revision is a *via negativa*, a direction by which "inwit" is sharpened by "agenbite": it is "Affliction ranges Boundlessness" (963). Like Thoreau in the simplicity and solitude of *Walden*, Dickinson achieves a concentration of the spirit through a poverty of existence that illuminates the undiscovered country of circumference. Dickinson's understanding is born of "A homelier maturing—/A process in the Bur—/That teeth of Frosts alone disclose/In far October air" (332), and like her Gentian, "The Frosts were [Dickinson's] condition—/The Tyrian would not come/Until the North—invoke it—" (442). In such images of an impoverished existence that stimulates the imagination, Dickinson not only reflects Thoreau's poverty, but also anticipates Stevens's proclivity to find the imagination stirred more by the bleak snowscapes of the North than the lush landscapes of the South.

Like Thoreau and Stevens, Dickinson sees "New Englandly" (285), and to see that way is to see through crumb rather than banquet, pain rather than pleasure, intimations of mortality rather than immortality, and consequently dying rather than living. If, as Dickinson suggests, "Looking at death, is dying" (281), then, as her poetry clearly reveals, Emily Dickinson, in her retreat into the world upstairs—in her detachment from society and her fellow creatures—looked a great deal more at death than at life and therefore did a great deal more dying than living. It must be noted that the stress in the poetry is really on death-in-life and not death, for Dickinson points out that in the anguish of repeated separations, death appears as a respite from the despair of death-in-life: "Parting is one of the exactions of a Mortal life. It is bleak—like dying, but it occurs more times. To escape the former, some invite the last" (L, 2:514).

Dickinson is not one of those "some," for surrender to the supple suitor death is too easy and therefore too great a compromise of love: to die for love "is a trifle, past,/But living this include/The dying multifold" (1013). To love New Englandly is to suffer as much as to enjoy; in what would seem an inversion of Emerson's law of compensation, Dickinson writes, "for each ecstatic instant/We must an anguish pay/In keen and quivering ratio/To the ecstasy" (125). The wounded deer "leaps highest" in the "ecstasy of death," and the dirk is not dropped, because it "Remind us that we died" (379). Dickinson's metaphorical connection of the consummation of love with dying is no mere borrowing from the Elizabethan lexicon, but again a manifestation of a perversity that renounces the nearness-to for the distance-from the loved one, for "It was the Distance—/Was Savory" (439). The Dickinson lover cannot give up her fidelity to the distant or the dead for the mere pleasure of the corporeal present: "Ours be the Cargo—unladen—here/Rather than the 'spicy isles—'/And thou—not there—" (368). It is as though Dickinson has given her bounty to the dead or kept it to herself, "unladen," lest the manifestation of it in the physically near diminish the sanctity of her fidelity to the absent.

The perversity manifest in Dickinson's letters and poetry curiously is not unlike that manifest in Faulkner's "A Rose for Emily." Writing to her sister-in-law visiting in Geneva, New York, Dickinson alludes to the cost of Susan's absence and vows "I will never sell you for a piece of silver. I'll buy you back with red drops, when you go away. I'll keep you in a casket. I'll bury you in a garden—and keep a bird to watch the spot" (L, 2:340). Elsewhere she writes that "Essential Oils" like the attar of the rose are not evolved by the sun alone, but are the "gift of Screws," a gift that will "Make Summer" long after the lady lies "In Ceaseless Rosemary—" (675).

Faulkner's Gothic fiction can be read as an interpretation of the Dickinson persona. Do not both Emilys (we will call the Dickinson persona Emily) give their bounty to the dead; do not both demonstrate different, yet similar kinds of necrophilia—a fascination with the dead; do not their attachments to the dead estrange them physically and psychologically from the living, from society and community; and are not both evoked as the rose, the image of an unladened love tied to the past and a testimony to the independent identity achieved by that connection? Of course, the comparison, as far as it goes, serves nicely to confirm the interpretation of Dickinson as an imp of the perverse, but it needs to go further. No essential oils are wrung from Faulkner's rose and no winter made summer.

If Emily Dickinson is an imp of the perverse, she is more impish than perverse. As a noun, *imp* of course means mischievous child or small demon; as a verb it means to graft feathers in order to enhance flight. Dickinson's dual heritage of Calvinistic severity and transcendentalist independence, her dedication to telling the whole truth, but telling it slant, are the grafting, the divinest sense in her seeming madness, that enhances the flight of her imagination. It is a flight that, in a canon that concentrates on separation, brings Dickinson an occasional reparation, a "nearness to her sundered Things" (607). In addition, it is a flight that is not only outwards, toward the widening circumference of the transcendental cosmos, but also inwards, toward the widening circumference of the human psyche, in the direction of the modern sensibility.

T. S. Eliot: The Right Order's Restoration

Hans-Georg Gadamer writes, "The right order has no history. History is always a history of disintegration, and, sometimes the right order's restoration." The work of T. S. Eliot reflects a similar view of history and a distinctive literary credo deriving from that view. Eliot's aim as a man of letters is to reveal the disintegration that is history and in so doing to achieve the restoration of the right order, "to recover what has been lost."[10]

Eliot recognizes that the psychic condition of modern man is one of isolation and fragmentation in a time grown quite out of joint. His work is dedicated to redeeming the time, and the basic means of redemption is integration, the integration of the self, sensibility, culture, and cosmos. For Eliot, the master metaphor of contemporary disintegration is the wasteland—a Heraclitean flux without pattern; the metaphor for integration is the still point—an Eliadic center that effects a still pattern throughout a moving world. Eliot's work and life are a continuous movement from the wasteland to the still point by way of the rose garden—a journey from the profane to the sacred, from separation to reparation, along the *via negativa.*

Separation is evoked in the poetry and plays primarily in three ways: in images of the divisiveness of a fragmented world, in dramatizations of the isolation and estrangement of the individual in such a world, and in the mutability of a self divided from itself. Disintegration permeates the early poetry: Prufrock is suspended in a world of "decisions and revisions/Which a moment will reverse"; Gerontion, "with a thousand small deliberations," multiplies variety in "a wilderness of mirrors" and laments those whirling "beyond the circuit of the shuddering Bear/In fractured atoms." The major evocation of the fragmented world of course is *The Waste Land,* a poem whose structure suggests the disintegration of a profane world and whose theme is summed up in the words, "I can connect/Nothing with nothing" (CP, 46).

In such a world there are no communicants, for there is neither communion nor communication. The international set in "Gerontion" partakes of the host, but its devotion is elsewhere—in the arts or the black arts. Gerontion himself has lost the power of his senses and cannot manage a "closer contact"; Prufrock finds it impossible to "say just what I mean"; the young man in "Portrait of a Lady" remains "self-possessed," while the lady herself laments her "buried life" and their imminent separation. Finally, the personae of *The Waste Land* are variations on the theme of profane love: they touch but do not unite; their physical connection is without spiritual communion.

This estrangement of the individual is perhaps the single most significant conflict in all of Eliot's drama. Like the persona of the poems, the central character in the plays finds himself within the closed circle of his own experience;[11] however, the protagonist manages to find a way out of that circle toward the other—either by way of martyrdom or resignation. In either case, as Sir Reilly tells Celia, "each way means loneliness—and communion" (CP, 365). Becket is the one who is "always isolated" (CP, 179); Harry confesses to a "sense of separation/Of isolation, unredeemable, irrevocable" and to the fact that "all this year, I could not fit myself together" (CP, 272). For Edward and Celia, hell is being alone, being trapped inside oneself, having "a feeling of emptiness, of failure/Towards someone, or something outside of myself" (CP, 362). This narcissistic isolation becomes even more unbearable when it is combined with Heraclitean fluidity, and selfhood becomes transient, elusive, and haunting.

Like Prufrock, the Eliot dramatic hero has to prepare a face to meet the faces that he meets; he is without consistent identity. Sir Reilly informs Edward that his psychological and spiritual problem is that he has lost contact with the self he thought he was. Both Sir Claude and Colly Simpkins acknowledge that they live "in two worlds. . . . that have nothing to do with each other" (CC, 50, 64). Gomez tells Lord Calverton, "You're not isolated—merely insulated./It's only when you come to see that you have lost *yourself*/That you are quite done" (ES, 30).

Eliot compounds the pain of the divided self, when, applying the lesson of Henry James, he confronts the present self with the ghost of the past self. Thus, Agatha says to Harry,

> The man who returns will have to meet
> The boy who left . . . round the corner
> Of the new wing, he will have to face him—
> And it will not be a very jolly corner
> When the loop in time comes . . .
> The hidden is revealed, and the spectre shows itself.
>
> [CP, 229]

Thus, in Eliot's drama the hero must do penance not only for his separation from the boundless, but also for his separation from self. Like Spencer Brydon in James's "Jolly Corner," the circular journey through the loop in time effects "the rending pain of re-enactment/Of all that you have done, and been; the shame/Of motives late revealed, and the awareness/Of things ill done and done to others' harm" (CP, 142). The circular journey, however, results in guilt and suffering that are purgative and therefore redemptive. In Eliot's drama, redemption is a matter of discipline—the austere discipline of the martyrdoms and pilgrimages of Becket, Harry, and Celia—and the more commonplace discipline of the resignation of Edward and Lavinia, who patch things up and make the best of a bad job.

The reparation implied in the drama is more explicit in the criticism. The impulse toward integration shapes Eliot's views on tradition and the individual talent, the mythical method, and the poetic sensibility, unified in the seventeenth century and dissociated in the modern world. In "Tradition and the Individual Talent," indeed, in almost all his prose on the subject, Eliot urges a catholicity on the part of the poet and the critic: the poet who will progress into artistic maturity must acquire a historical sense of the existing and organic body of Western literature; this helps shape the new poem and in turn is redefined by the new work. Such a poet will "be aware that the mind of Europe . . . is a mind more important than his own mind." Eliot's regard for the mind of Europe reflects an insistence on tribal and cultural unity at the expense of personality and individual freedom: Eliot writes, "the progress of an artist is a continual self-sacrifice, a continual extinction of personality."[12]

It is their power to integrate that attracts Eliot to myth and the metaphysical conceit. Myth—that of Ulysses in Joyce's novel or the Fisher King in Eliot's poem—is a general structural device that "is simply a way of controlling, of ordering, of giving a shape and a significance to the immense panorama of futility and anarchy which is contemporary history."[13] The metaphysical conceit is a more particular poetic structure that symbolically implodes what has been discursively exploded. Through ironic, tensive juxtaposition, the poet is able to amalgamate disparate experience, to feel idea and think emotion. In a sense, the metaphysical conceit is a still point that reconciles the fragments of a turning world. For Eliot, the seventeenth-century metaphysical poetry of Shakespeare, Donne, and Jacobean dramatists is the supreme English manifestation of the unified sensibility.

The early seventeenth century in England is not only a period of aesthetic integration for Eliot, but also one of cultural integration.

Prior to the civil war that rends the nation as well as the sensibility, church and state are integrated in a state church, and industrial specialization, which Eliot equates with cultural disintegration, has not yet become a way of life.[14] The crown, symbolic of tradition and order, has not yet toppled and Separatists have not quite set sail for America. Eliot's poetic evocation of this cultural unity occurs in the parish integrity of East Coker village life, where the "association of man and woman" is a "necessarye coniunction . . . whiche betokeneth concorde" (CP, 124).

It is interesting to note that Eliot's ancestor, Andrew Eliot, departed from East Coker as part of a pilgrimage that subsequently became a division of family, church, and nation or in other words the disintegration of a culture. Moreover, Eliot in a subsequent quartet celebrates another seventeenth-century site, Little Gidding, as a place where the dead are "united in the strife which divided them," where all "accept the constitution of silence/And are folded in a single party" (CP, 143). This not only reflects Eliot's commitment to seventeenth-century England as the manifestation of cultural unity, but also implies his contention that cultural unity is an organic phenomenon that allows and needs friction within. But what culture does not need and cannot afford is division.[15] The genesis of America implies such cultural division: the American separates himself and ultimately his society from the tribe that is Europe. Thus, for Eliot, the American pilgrimage is one ironically away from, not toward, the sacred place. Eliot felt compelled to reverse the direction of that pilgrimage and journey back to East Coker.

Thus, when Eliot writes that "the past experience revived in the meaning/Is not the experience of one life only/But of many generations" (CP, 133), he means, among other things, that the return to East Coker is a "further union, a deeper communion" (CP, 129) with the tribe of his grandfathers. The poet's vision of and participation in the village dance symbolize a reintegration into parish communal life, from which his ancestors had divorced themselves. Eliot had to expatriate himself from the relatively splintered and provincial society of America in order to repatriate himself to the relatively whole and catholic society of Britain. Family for Eliot is a "bond which embraces a larger period of time" than the lifetime of a single family unit; it is "a piety towards the dead, however obscure, and a solicitude for the unborn, however remote."[16] The goal of Eliot's cultural exploration is to end where it began, at East Coker, "and know the place for the first time" (CP, 145).

The tribal reparation of East Coker village life is but one variation of the major theme of reparation in *Four Quartets.* Just as *The
Waste Land,* which concerns itself with separation, is primarily an
evocation of the profane, so the *Quartets,* which concerns itself
with reparation, is primarily an evocation of the sacred. There are
five kinds of sacredness in *Quartets:* the "unattended/Moment,"
which is a moment both "in and out of time" (CP, 136); the austere
and disciplined occupation of the saint, which is "to apprehend/
The point of intersection of the timeless/With time" (CP, 136); the
poetic achievement, "where every word is at home" (CP, 144); the
Incarnation, where the "impossible union/Of spheres of existence
is actual" (CP, 136); and what may be called the reincarnation,
"When the tongues of flame are in-folded/Into the crowned knot
of fire/And the fire and rose are one" (CP, 145).

The unattended moment recurs throughout the *Quartets:* "in
the arbour where the rain beat" (CP, 119) and "the draughty
church at smokefall" (CP, 120), but the most significant moments
are the four associated with the sacred places of the titles. We have
already seen how the Germelshausen moment of East Coker celebrates tribal sacredness. The rose garden of "Burnt Norton" is a
sacred place and moment, where a former experience is revived in a
present meaning. It is another jolly corner around which the self
that has been encounters the self that might have been. Although
the encounter is a reality that humankind finds difficult to bear, it
is one that implies an integration of the self. Moreover, here the
past and future of the collective life point to one end that is the
perfect present, the still point. The moment in the rose garden is a
backward look toward the beginning and man's incarnation in the
garden of innocence and a forward look toward the end and his
reincarnation in the garden of permanence. The light in "Burnt
Norton" that casts the shadows of children that might have been
becomes the creative light of "Little Gidding," into which the
shadowy children and all other creation are ingathered.

The seascape of "Dry Salvages" is another variation of the intersection of time and the timeless. There is a tendency to read the
river as a symbol of time and the ocean as one of timelessness; such
a reading seems somewhat inaccurate for both river and sea are
images of Heraclitean flux and thereby images of time. It is the sea
after all that "tosses/Its [evolutionary] hints of earlier and other
creation" (CP, 130). However, here, as well as in the other quartets, the eternal intersects with the temporal, as from out of the
varied sea voices "the tolling bell/Measures time not our time, rung

by the unhurried/Ground swell" (CP, 131). As we learn later in the
poem, the clanging bell is a "perpetual Angelus" (CP, 135) that
reiterates the Annunciation of a Christ, who, unlike the worried
women anxiously lying awake counting time, can "unweave, un-
wind, unravel/And piece together the past and future" (CP, 131).

Eliot's development of these unattended moments in the *Quartets* is a progression through the elements of air ("Burnt Norton"),
earth ("East Coker"), water ("Dry Salvages"), and fire ("Little
Gidding") to the still point where all elements and all sacredness
converge. The experience of midwinter spring at Little Gidding
blends the unattended moment with the saint's pilgrimage along
the *via negativa,* for here the Heraclitean senses are dissolved in a
purgatorial fire that refines but does not singe. In this time out of
time, "the brief sun flames the ice" and causes a "blindness." Thus,
the eye cannot see; nor can the ear hear, for there is a noticeable
absence of the sounds and voices that permeate "Dry Salvages."
Moreover, there is nothing for the numb body to feel, for the cold
is "windless," and nothing for the nose to sense: "no earth smell/
Or smell of living thing" (CP, 138)—gone is the odor of rank
ailanthus in the nursery. It is as though Eliot comes to Little Gidding as a Dantean penitent, to hide himself in the pentecostal fire
that refines the spirit and defines the word.

The word as an intimation of the Word is a major consideration
of the poem, and again there is a definite progression from "Burnt
Norton," where the meaning and movement of words evoke a
Heraclitean flux,

> Words strain,
> Crack and sometimes break, under the burden,
> Under the tension, slip, slide, perish,
> Decay with imprecision, will not stay in place,
> Will not stay still.
>
> [CP, 12]

to "Little Gidding," where "every word is at home . . . the complete consort dancing together" (CP, 144). Thus, form integrates
the dance of words and the words and the dance become "still
moving" (CP, 129).

Moreover, at Little Gidding, the "communication/Of the dead is
tongued with fire beyond the language of the living" (CP, 139).
The communication of the dead, in one sense, is the directive of
the Dantean soul, with whom the speaker walks "in a dead patrol"

(CP, 141). It is also the voice of the dead who have come to Little Gidding for sanctuary and who speak to the poet through the numinosity of place. In another sense, the communication of the dead that extends beyond the language of the living is that corpus of Western literature before which Eliot feels the poet ought to extinguish himself. Eliot here suggests that the traditional word is tongued with fire, and to the degree that that fire manifests itself in the work of the modern poet will the poet's words evoke the Word.

And so it is in "Little Gidding," as the words of Dame Juliana and Dante manifest themselves most beautifully in the final image of the *Quartets*. Dante writes,

> In that abyss I saw how love held bound
> Into one volume all the leaves whose flight
> Is scattered through the universe around;
>
> How substance, accident, and mode unite
> Fused, so to speak, together, in such wise
> That this I tell of is one simple light.[17]

And Eliot writes,

> And all shall be well
> All manner of thing shall be well
> When the tongues of flame are in-folded
> Into the crowned knot of fire
> And the fire and rose are one.

[CP, 145]

The symbol of fire suggests the ultimate reparation: the still point that is Incarnation. The pentecostal annunciations—the tongues of flame—are folded into the foetal and infant Christ, the crowned knot of fire; and Christ and Mary, the fire and rose, are one. Thus, the still point is the literal Incarnation. But, crowned knot of fire also suggests crown of thorns, the crucifixion, which is a kind of reincarnation, since resurrection implies an in-folding of the natural Corpus Christi into the supernatural Godhead. Incarnation is mythopoeically the way down—the intersection of a descending spirit with nature, metalunar timelessness with sublunar time. Reincarnation is mythopoeically the way up—the intersection of an ascending nature with God, time with eternity. Both are the still point. Furthermore, the crowned knot of fire is the briared rose—the eternally crucified Christ-child, which gathers into itself both the Heraclitean elements of the cosmos and the words of prophet and poet. The creator in-folds the creation, and creator and creation are one. Reparation is the act of becoming: God becoming man and man becoming God in the "still-born" Christ.

Eliot's symbolic fire lights up and refines, but does it warm; it is clearly a manifestation of the logos, but does it neglect eros? Does all of Eliot's poetry in fact concentrate too severely upon the word at the expense of the body and consequently fail to achieve a unified sensibility? Does Eliot, despite his efforts to the contrary, remain subject to the influence of Puritan American society, a society that presents Eliot with the experiences and materials necessary for an effective evocation of separation, but that does not instill in him those necessary for an equally effective evocation of reparation? Perhaps Eliot himself suggests the answers to these questions when he writes the following in *After Strange Gods*: "To be converted, in any case, while it is sufficient for entertaining the hope of individual salvation, is not going to do for a man, as a writer, what his ancestry and his country for some generations have failed to do."[18]

What his native country had failed to do was provide Eliot with a mythos necessary for the kind of poetic reparation he sought. The celebration of the self as the single artificer of the world within whom all things are reconciled is the dominant tradition in American poetry as exemplified in the egocentric poetry of Walt Whitman and Wallace Stevens.[19] Eliot, throughout his poetry, criticism, and drama, runs counter to this American mythos, renounces the cult of personality, and tries to submit to the other—to tradition, history, and God. But something inside the man—something perhaps unconsciously created by the mythos he consciously seeks to renounce—holds back and will not permit the necessary submission. The poet acknowledges the failure in *Ash Wednesday,* when he wonders if the veiled sister will pray for those who "cannot surrender" (CP, 66) and in "East Coker," when he laments the folly of old men and their "fear of possession/Of belonging to another, or to others, or to God" (CP, 125–26).

Eliot is also heir to a Puritan ancestry that emphasizes logos at the expense of eros. He uses French symbolist decadence as a device in his poetry, but it is filtered through a Puritan sensibility and becomes more the decadence of the moralist than that of the aesthete. In Eliot, the general humanism of the age is challenged by a fundamental Puritan morality; man always does the right thing for the wrong reason or the wrong thing for the right reason. Finally, although he strives to unify his sensibility, there is very little in his poetry that is erotic. If Eliot could find "the unimaginable/Zero summer" (CP, 138), would it not be one that freezes rather than scorches, one that effects a stasis of the mind's spirit rather than a frenzy of the spirit's body? Indeed, is there any doubt that it is Apollo rather than Dionysius who is the choreographer of the symbolic dance of the *Quartets?*

The American mythos, in the form of the tension between individuality and community, manifests itself in another inconsistency in Eliot's attempt to restore the right order. In the epigraph to "Sweeney Agonistes," Eliot quotes St. John of the Cross: "Hence, the soul cannot be possessed of divine union, until it has divested itself of the love of created things" (CP, 74). In "Choruses from *The Rock*," however, he writes, "There is no life that is not in community/And no community not lived in praise of GOD" (CP, 101). How are these pronouncements to be reconciled; how can one live—know human community, the love of creatures—if one renounces the love of created things? One answer is implicit in an American mythos that calls for the individual to reject the existing suppressive society in order to free himself and form a new, ideal community. In Eliot, one renounces the love of created things in order to attain the spiritual summit, from which one can then love created things more selflessly, more entirely, but, like Emily Dickinson, more distantly. What if, however, the intrusion of self circumvents the conversion to the other and the summit is not attained—then, what community, what communion? This is the great risk for those who opt for the *via negativa*, for the detachment of self from creation and the society of creatures.

Perhaps this last consideration explains why Eliot achieves great dramatic poetry and not great drama: the elements of human character and community are only minimally developed in the plays. Even Jesus—as man or as personified God—is, with the possible exception of an oblique reference in "Gerontion," noticeably absent from Eliot's Christian poetry. When one considers the inherent difficulty of restoring the right order and Eliot's inherited difficulty in surrendering the self to the other, one can understand why the later poetry of reparation does not consistently reach the poetic achievement of the earlier poetry of separation. Perhaps that is the lesson of the nursery rhyme and the explanation of Eliot's circumscribed greatness: all the king's men *alone* cannot put

Humpty Dumpty together again, and T. S. Eliot was most as-
suredly one of the king's men.

Wallace Stevens: All or Nothing at All

As one might suspect in the poetry of a modernist who rejects
the myths of tradition, variations of the mythopoeic pattern of
separation and reparation from the boundless are infrequent in the
canon of Wallace Stevens. Nevertheless, they are there, and they
significantly inform the major design of that canon. One of the
more concrete variations occurs in the imagery of "Esthétique de
Mal," where the big bird of imagination feeds on the yellow fruit
of reality out of an "incompleteness of its own."[20] That same incompleteness and desire for wholeness are evident in the single
candle light of "To an Old Philosopher in Rome," a light that tears
against its wick "to escape/From fire and be a part only of that
which/Fire is the symbol: the celestial possible" (CP, 509). Elsewhere, reparation takes the form of an anticipation of "the right
joining" of "the disparate halves/Of things" that is a "music of
ideas, the burning/And breeding and bearing birth of harmony"
(CP, 464–65).

The three images are variations on what J. Hillis Miller suggests
is the primary focus of Stevens's poetry, the attempt to reconcile
"subject and object, mind and matter, imagination and reality."
Sometimes reconcilement manifests itself in the submergence of
imagination in reality, sometimes in the transformation of reality in
the imagination, and sometimes in a marriage of both in
metaphor.[21] One such metaphor occurs in "An Ordinary Evening
in New Haven," where the dark giant of the imagination rises to
kill the bleak monster of the physical world, and the result is a
Platonic, androgynous union, "as if the crude collops came together as one,/A mythological form, a festival sphere,/A great
bosom, beard and being, alive with age" (CP, 466). It is a playful
use of Plato's symbol, in keeping with the hermeneutics implicit in
Stevens's poetry and explicit in his criticism.

As stated earlier, Paul Ricoeur suggests that hermeneutics, in
order to renew a dying tradition, must rescue from myth the symbol and its store of meaning.[22] Stevens is intent upon a similar
aesthetic; he, however, would take it a step further: "We shall have
gone behind the symbols/To that which they symbolize" (P, 391).
It is as though Stevens deliberately seeks a destruction of

mythopoeia in hopes of rescuing an abstracted, and therefore revived *poeia,* from a dated, and therefore dying, mythos. In that
effort, he ironically makes a contribution to the mythopoeic pattern of separation and reparation and its manifestation in American
literature.

In Stevens's work, separation is the given condition; in "Sunday
Morning," man lives "in an old chaos of the sun . . . Or island
solitude, unsponsored, free" (CP, 70). By "Notes Toward a Supreme Fiction," that solitude has been intensified by man's alienation from his dwelling place: "We live in a place/That is not our
own, and, much more, not ourselves/And hard it is in spite of
blazoned days" (CP, 383). Moreover, modern man, in a rejection
of a tradition no longer viable, is "disinherited in a storm of torn-
up testaments" (CP, 292), and, in his disinheritance, he is left to
"feast/On human heads" (CP, 228), on reflections of himself.

This sense of external separation and isolation is compounded
by internal division, for the salt-estranging sea "severs not only
our lands, but also ourselves" (CP, 30). More than the sea and the
"dividing and indifferent blue" (CP, 68) of the sky, it is the mind of
man that deals cleavage in the world of Stevens. Placid blue space is
changed by the mind asking questions: "To be blue/There must be
no questions" (CP, 429). For Stevens, however, there are always
questions: "It can never be satisfied, the mind, never" (CP, 247).
Consequently, there is always division. Thus, in "Auroras of Autumn," after a rare evocation of communion with both family and
place, when "we were Danes in Denmark all day long/And knew
each other well," Stevens questions of what disaster, of what separation *(dis)* from the stars *(aster),* of what fall into division, is "this
the imminence:/Bare limbs, bare trees and a wind as sharp as salt"
(CP, 419). He answers that question later in "An Ordinary Evening
in New Haven," when, responding to his query as to the origin of
division, he alludes to a primal separation wrought by an awakening mind, when the self "became divided," part holding "fast tena-
ciously to common earth," part searching out majesty "from central earth to central sky" and "in moonlight extensions of them in
the mind" (CP, 468–69). Thus, man is of three minds: one that
perceives the physical, common earth, one that conceives metaphysical worlds in and beyond the central sky, and one that tries to
join the other two.

For Stevens, intelligence destroys poetry (L, 305) or simply destroys (OP, 164), and it is the confusions of such intelligence that
the poet shares: thus, he "cannot tell apart/The idea and the

bearer-being of the idea" (CP, 466). Consequently, separation—"I am the poorest of all./I know that I cannot be mended" (CP, 201)—and the futile attempt at reparation—"I cannot bring a world quite round/Though I patch it as I can" (CP, 165)—are in Stevens two of the cries of the poem's occasions. Though it is true that intelligence severs man from nature and himself, the fall into knowledge is also a fall into imagination, into the music that can bring the parts of the world back into accord, into harmony: "The mind . . . is the only force that can defend us against itself. The modern world is based on this *pensee*" (OP, 173). Thus, in the imagination lies the possibility of integration.

In his quest for integration, Stevens orchestrates throughout his canon a point/counterpoint, the dominant point of which is a variation on the three major leitmotivs of oneness, centrality, and order. For Stevens, all things add up to one thing, to an Emersonian monism. One and one are one. The initial statement of this theme occurs in "Thirteen Ways of Looking at a Blackbird," in which a man and a woman (and a blackbird) are one; the final variation in the *Collected Poems* comes in "The Planet on the Table," in which Stevens symbolically resolves a lifetime ontological tension between the imagining self and the reality of matter, when he writes that "his self and the sun were one." Between these, Stevens varies the trope with the combination of creatures— "The deer and dachshund are one" (CP, 210), the integration of the aesthetic and divine—"poetry and apotheosis are one" (CP, 378), and the reconciliation of opposites—"The false and the true" (CP, 253), "as and is" (CP, 476), "real and unreal" (CP, 485) and "the end and this beginning" (CP, 506) are all one. The phrase rings like a refrain throughout the larger harmonium of Stevens's canon and reflects Stevens's endless attempt to make all things add up to one.

Reparation is not only a monistic arithmetic; it is also a geometry of process, in which completeness is a matter of finding and attaining the center. Whereas the poetic business of Emily Dickinson is circumference, that of Stevens is the center. In "The Ultimate Poem is Abstract," the speaker laments the fact that the essential blue of placid space has been diluted by interrogation; and the result is that he finds himself in a maze, with an intellect "of windings round and dodges to and fro,/Writhings in wrong obliques and distances," and he longs to be "not as now,/Helpless at the edge," but rather "just once, at the middle, fixed" in an order "to be/Complete."

Stevens links his association of order, oneness, and centrality with his idea of the poet as the one who unifies in "Asides on the Oboe." Having come to the end of the prologue of his poetic canon and having to make a final choice of fictions, he rejects the obsolete fiction, the man-made myth, that subjugates man to the dead gods and instead, in an imaginative extension of Emerson's metaphor of the poet as human eyeball, celebrates "the central man, the human globe, responsive/As a mirror with a voice, the man of glass/Who in a million diamonds sums us up." In addition, recognizing that the Whitman-like poet chants the war dead "buried in their blood," he sees a new kinship with the poet: "we and the diamond globe at last were one." Like Emerson and Whitman's poet, Stevens's man of glass is potentially any man of imagination; thus, in "The Final Soliloquy of the Interior Paramour," the "world imagined is the ultimate good," where "we collect ourselves/Out of all indifferences into . . . the obscurity of an order, a whole," where "God and the imagination are one" and where "out of a central mind," we "make a dwelling in the evening air." Thus, Stevens suggests that through the imagination man can reestablish a sense of belonging in the world.

Juxtaposed to the major point of order, centrality, and oneness is the equally important counterpoint of flux, poverty, and nothingness. Whereas Eliot searches out and celebrates the still point, Stevens celebrates the turning world,

> One of the vast repetitions final in
> Themselves and, therefore, good, the going round
>
> And round and round, the merely going round,
> Until merely going round is a final good,
> The way wine comes at a table in the wood.

[CP, 405]

In "Auroras of Autumn," the static white seascape is altered by the aurora borealis, which "is always enlarging the change/With its frigid brilliances, its blue-red sweeps/And gusts of great enkindlings, its polar green/The color of ice and fire and solitude" (CP, 412–13). Just as the "going round" passage inverts Eliot's trope of the still point, so these rich images invert Shelley's metaphor in "Adonais": here, the many-colored glass of the physical world is superior to the white light of the metaphysical world. That is why Stevens's man for all weathers is a global man of glass, a prismatic persona, who sums us up in a million diamond reflections. Paradoxically, that diamond-studded man of glass discovers that his "chiefest embracing of all wealth/Is poverty, whose jewel found/ At the exactest central of the earth/Is need" (P, 392).

This last passage suggests a kinship between Stevens and Thoreau in their quest for wholeness through a poetic *via negativa*. As we have seen, Thoreau equates order with a simplicity and poverty that "is radiant as gems on the weeds and stubble in a winter morning." Stevens's sense of order in the later poems is also one effected by a mind of winter, a search "for the fecund mini- mum" (CP, 35). In "Notes Towards a Supreme Fiction," in the third section stating the credo that the supreme fiction must give pleasure, Stevens ironically has the muselike sister of Canon Aspi- rin dress her daughters in "pauvred color paints . . . appropriate to/Their poverty" (CP, 402) and to the nature of Stevens's poet whose "poverty becomes his strong heart's core/ A forgetfulness of summer at the pole" (CP, 427). Thus, not unlike Eliot seeking the "unimaginable/Zero summer" in the midwinter spring of "Lit- tle Gidding," Stevens looks for centrality in a cauterized percep- tion of the poverty of "Credences of Summer":

> Let's see the very thing and nothing else.
> Let's see it with the hottest fire of sight.
> Burn everything not part of it to ash.
>
> Trace the gold sun about the whitened sky
> Without evasion by a single metaphor.
> Look at it in its essential barrenness
> And say this, this is the centre that I seek.
>
> [CP, 373]

This exploration for the center of being in poverty and barrenness is a major step in the *via negativa;* the final step is the encounter with nothingness.

In his incisive essay on Stevens's "Poetry of Being," J. Hillis Miller suggests that the idea and the word *nothing* come to domi- nate the later poetry of Stevens. He points out its earliest occur- rence in "The Snow Man," in which the winter mind, the man that is "nothing himself" and therefore free of the mind's fictions, can behold the "nothing that is not there and the nothing that is." He goes on to catalogue a list of passages manifesting the idea of nothingness, including the admonition that "if there must be a god in the house, let him be . . . a coolness,/A vermilioned noth- ingness" (CP, 328). He concludes that much of the late poetry is

"based on the presupposition that the center of reality is a nothingness that is 'a nakedness, a point,/Beyond which fact could not
progress as fact . . . Beyond which thought could not progress as
thought'" (CP, 402, 403).[23] Early in his poetry, Stevens points out
that "fluttering things have so distinct a shade" (CP, 18); in the
austere landscapes of "Auroras of Autumn," "An Ordinary Evening in New Haven," and "The Rock," it is as though "nothingness contained a métier" (CP, 526) that is the distinct shade of a
real being that is intimated only in the diffusion and annihilation of
the more palpable, but less real, world of things.

What occurs in this *esthétique du rien* is illustrated well in "A
Plain Sense of Things." The poem begins with the conventional
barrenness effected by the fall of autumnal leaves; with a series of
negatives and absences—"a minor house," "no turban walks,"
"lessened floors," "never so badly needed paint," "a fantastic effort has failed," "without reflections," "expressing silence,"
"waste of lilies"—it moves towards an even greater vacuity, "as if/
We had come to an end of the imagination." The end of the imagination has, however, a double meaning: not only is the plain sense
of things the cessation of summer imagination, but more importantly, the realization of a winter imagination that leads to the pure
being of no-thing-ness: "the absence of the imagination had/Itself
to be imagined." In other words, the nothingness that both Stevens
and Heidegger suggest is the ground of Being has itself to be
imagined, and it is such imagination that is the supreme fiction:
"Out of nothing to have come on major weather. . . . To find the
real,/To be stripped of every fiction except one,/The fiction of an
absolute" (CP, 404).

What Stevens suggests in his poetry, Kenneth Burke and Norman O. Brown state in their criticism. In a most provocative essay,
which he admits is "a kind of *tour de force*, locating the specific
nature of language in the ability to use the Negative," Burke con-
tends that, since there are no negatives in nature—when man says
the apple *is not* on the table, the natural phenomenon is that the
apple *is* on the tree or in the pie or in man—the negative is the
peculiarly human invention, the "marvel of language." Burke suggests that the negative and language itself probably originate in
signals of danger—warning sounds that become warning words—
and that the eventual "look out!" implies the negative, "stop what
you are doing and attend to the present and pressing danger."
Thus, for Burke, the claim, "there are no lions," really means "I
fear lions." In time, the tribal linguistic strategy of initiating and

directing positive behavior through negative commands takes the form of moral and ethical systems such as the Ten Commandments. Still later, the negative becomes the basis for theology and philosophy, as mystics seek God through the *via negativa* and existentialists such as Heidegger seek in nothingness the ground of pure Being. In short, for Burke, the negative is the supreme fiction of man.[24]

Brown, coming from the different direction of psychoanalysis and believing that "originally, everything was one, ONE BODY," arrives at a similar conclusion. For Brown, logic and discursive language is a fragmenting of the universe by a discovery of things through the discernment of boundaries. Symbolic language, particularly modern poetry, is the abolition of boundary and the fusion of images. Science, logic, and discursive language are the fall into thingness; symbolic language is the recovery of no-thing-ness, of the "ONE BODY."[25]

Looking at Stevens's poetry in terms of Brown and Burke's theories, one is tempted to conclude that Stevens's poetic arithmetic and geometry undergo a transformation: one and one are now none and being is a sphere whose center is nowhere. Such seems to be the drift of his winter mind, but even in that drift, Stevens tends to hold on to a sense of order that is still singular, perhaps because he intuits that the idea of the one is as much, if not more, the supreme fiction of man as the idea of nothing. Though Burke in his essay recognizes the kindredness of the *one* family of words and the *no* family of words, he does not pursue the relation and consequently overlooks another marvel of language that has no correlative in nature.[26]

Thingness is a matter of boundary; without boundary, without the ability to discern one thing from another thing, there is a no-thing-ness, a nothingness. Prior to his ability to make that distinction between things—between this and that, me and not-me—man can be said to experience a natural condition of plenitude that is a no-thing-ness. Contrary to what Burke posits, the negative in terms of nothingness is, as Brown suggests, a part of nature prior to consciousness and language. Indeed, it may be what Freud would call his uncanny, precognitive familiarity with the self-obliterating nothingness that triggers what Heidegger describes as the existential dread of nothingness.[27] In his progression from a precognitive state to a cognitive state, man leaps from no-thing-ness to at least two-thing-ness. If this is the case, if the rest of his evolution is a matter of greater cognitive division and multiplication, then man's supreme fiction—his linguistic invention for which there is no objective correlative in nature—is the one, whether it be the single phoenix of mythology, the singular androgynous creature in Plato's *Symposium*, the single God of monotheism, the single Being grounded in nothingness, or the single artificer who discloses being through the imagination of nothingness.

Burke points out that the negative is an idea for which there is no imagery. Even if no-thing-ness exists in precognitive nature, there could be no image for it, because all imagery requires boundary. Thus, man cannot think of nothing; the nearest he can come to it, according to Burke, "is to think of annihilating something, a feat which on closer inspection will be found to force upon us the thought of the annihilator."[28] Similarly, the poet, through stripping away, unlayering, deconstructing the positive world of nature, draws near the pure Being that is no thing but is within all things. Thus, the poet as creator paradoxically becomes the poet as de-creator, the artificer of de-creation.

Although his poetry shares much with Heidegger's beliefs about being and nothingness and with the philosophy of deconstruction engendered by those beliefs, Stevens is still very much in the main current of American romantic poetry.[29] He feels that it is necessary to smash up the old order so that it may be re-created. Consistent with the egocentricity of that romantic heritage, he believes that only "in the presence of a solitude of self" do we hear "the voice of union" (CP, 494), that "God is in me" (OP, 122), and that in the new world "all men are priests . . . in a land to be described" (CP, 254). This preoccupation of the solitary self with place has often been in American literature at the expense of a concern with persons. Stevens, not unlike Eliot, suffers from this deficiency and in the following passage implies a critique not just of himself and his poetry, but also of all those who try to achieve reparation through the *via negativa:* "Life is an affair of people, not of places, but for me, life is an affair of places and that is the trouble" (OP, 158).

So We Beat On: *All the King's Men* and *Invisible Man*

A culture is not a flow, nor even a confluence; the form of its existence is struggle, or at least debate—it is nothing if not a dialectic.

Lionel Trilling, *The Liberal Imagination*

When Wallace Stevens acknowledges that life is an affair of people, but that for him the trouble is that it has been an affair of places, he voices one more variation of the basic dialectic in the American experience—the tension between solitude and society, individuality and community—a vital tension in the symbolic pattern of separation and reparation in classic American literature. That pattern continues to inform, to give meaning and shape, to two important post-World War II novels—*All the King's Men* (1946) and *Invisible Man* (1952)—the central thesis of which is that the only viable reparation attainable in the modern world is not the harmonizing of individuality and communalism Orestes Brownson sought in the nineteenth century, but rather the delicate balance possible in the tension between both, between separation and union, extreme manifestations of which tend toward the fragmentation of society and the annihilation of the self.

Robert Penn Warren's novel concludes with an interesting and somewhat contradictory juxtaposition of truths, one of which the narrator Jack Burden has recently gleaned and the other reluctantly acknowledged. Burden concludes that Willie Stark and Adam Stanton (and by implication most of the major characters of the novel) are doomed to destroy or use or try to become the other, "because each was incomplete with the terrible division of their age." Shortly thereafter, Burden in his own way comes to accept Ellis Burden's testament that "separateness is identity" and that God could only truly create man by making man separate from himself. These two statements expressing the need for union and the necessity of separation, juxtaposed as they are at the end of the book, sum up the critical agon of the novel: how can man maintain a sense of identity, which requires separation, and yet ease the anxiety of incompleteness, which requires union? *All the King's Men* is Warren's attempt to resolve that crisis.

In a fictive gallery of incomplete men and women, Jack Burden is the central Humpty Dumpty character.[1] He has felt the pain of separation longer than anyone else in the novel, because he has felt disinherited since childhood. Jack has been deprived of his patrimony; his apparent father, Ellis Burden, walked out of his life when he was a child, leaving behind for Jack a sense of guilt, loneliness, and betrayal. He is also disinherited by his mother; for, believing as he does that she is incapable of love, because she drifts from lover to lover, Jack feels himself unloved and thereby motherless. Disinheritance is here, as it is in James's *Washington Square*, not so much the deprivation of money and property, but the deprivation of love and approval. In addition, Burden has been dispossessed of the only innocence he has known as a child and youth: of Anne Stanton, who is too much of a sister to become a lover; of Adam Stanton, who, because he is the friend of his youth, sees Burden not as he is, but as he was; and of Burden's Landing, a home to which he can never satisfactorily return, because, having lost the people there, he has lost the place.

Burden's disinheritance is furthered in his unsuccessful attempt to write his doctoral dissertation. Unable or unwilling to pursue the implications of the Cass Mastern papers, and, by interpreting them, give definition to himself, Burden puts the papers and history on the shelf and thereby further deprives himself of family, culture, and the past. His one attempt at union—his marriage to Lois—is aborted, as he withdraws into one of his Rip Van Winkle great sleeps, during which both things and himself change. Thus, Jack Burden and the reader become more and more conscious of a man divided from himself: the idealist from the realist, the graduate student of American history from the professional practitioner of *Realpolitik*, the vulnerable Jackie-Bird of Anne Stanton's Burden's Landing from the invulnerable public relations man of Willie Stark's state capitol.

Although the separation and incompleteness of the other characters are peculiar to each, they also serve as variations and reflections of Burden's condition. Adam and Anne Stanton are the Adam and Eve of Burden's Landing; although they are physically separated from the Garden earlier, it is not until Jack provides them with the truth of their father's complicity in Judge Irwin's acceptance of a bribe, that they, like Jack, are dispossessed of a father and the past. Warren even has Anne seduce Adam away from his uncompromising independence of Boss Willie, by proffering the knowledge of the evil that was a part of the good Governor Stanton. Moreover, just as Adam in his idealistic pursuit of good cuts himself off from everyone, including Anne, so does Burden, in his failure to compromise his vision of the Garden, also cut himself off from Anne.

Cass Mastern, who is, as Jack will discover, a little more kind than kin, is also a shadow figure of Burden. Like Jack, he is the one who is "never at home in any world." Just as Jack will initiate a series of tragic consequences with his investigation into Judge Irwin's past, so Mastern has by a "single act of sin and perfidy" initiated a "general disintegration" that splinters his world both within and without, "as the bough from the bole and the leaves from the bough." Mastern also comes to understand his participation in the terrible division of his age—the division between black and white, North and South, brother and brother.

The governor's men and women also suffer disintegration. Like Jack, Sadie Burke has lost her patrimony, because she survived the death of her youthful brother and has had to live with the recriminations of her drunken father and herself. Tom Stark on the other hand is killed more with kindness than with abandonment. His father indulges his excesses and uses his influence to reinstate him into a football game that ironically results in a destruction of Tom's nerve tissue, which the new governor's man—Adam Stanton—cannot knit back together again. Sugar-Boy, in his simple classification of people into the Boss and the bastards, becomes a grotesque version of Jack Burden, who from time to time seizes upon one truth—the great sleep, the big twitch—as the only truth.

Willie Stark is as much the center of the action of the novel as Burden, but as Warren writes, "the story of Willie Stark and the story of Jack Burden are, in one sense, one story." Willie, contrary to what Burden understands, is not only the man of fact, but also the man of idea. As a young man intent upon realizing the political myths of his country and helping the people, he is the naive, gullible, and dreaming Cousin Willy from the back country who is used by the political pros. After Sadie Burke awakens him from his drunken great sleep to the realities of state politics, he becomes the realist and pragmatist, who in his new identity as Boss Willie digs up the past and barters away the future in order to make things happen in the present. In the protean manner of the politician, he chooses from among his many voices the one appropriate to the particular constituency. Warren illustrates the division within Willie when he has Burden explain that the governor keeps Tiny Duffy around because "all the contempt and insult which Willie Stark was to heap on Tiny Duffy was nothing but what one self of Willie Stark did to the other self."

Burden discerns a similar relationship between Willie and Tom Stark: "the son was merely an extension of the father." Thus, when the self-indulgence of Tom forces Willie to compromise his plans for the hospital and give Gummie Larsen a contract, it is as though one part of Willie were undermining the goals of the other. Moreover, when Willie loses his future in losing Tom, he returns to the old idealism, reneges on his deal with Larsen and Duffy, and sets in motion the chain of events that culminate in his assassination by Adam Stanton. In trying to build the hospital as he had once tried to build a schoolhouse, free of political compromise and kickback, Willie Stark is destroyed by an absolute idealism that will not accommodate the realities of politics. He is also destroyed by three alter egos: Tom Stark, Tiny Duffy, and Adam Stanton. In effecting that chain of events, Willy recapitulates what Cass Mastern had foreshadowed—Jack Burden's single act of detective work that makes Anne, a mistress, Adam, an assassin, and himself, panderer and murderer.

The foreshadowing and recapitulation of Burden's act that has multiple consequences is but one variation of a major structural device that Warren uses throughout the novel to exemplify how past, present, and future and the lives of the major agonists interpenetrate and repeat one another.[2] For example, the novel begins with Willie's homecoming—a press agent's dream of the man in the Governor's Mansion returning to his grass roots on his father's farm—and ends with Jack's return to his father's home at Burden's Landing; in between, there are a series of homecomings in which Burden regards himself as "the thing that always came back." In other variations of another leitmotiv, the innocent triangle of love in that kingdom by the sea, where Jack in a sense betrays Adam by falling in love with Anne, is repeated with more overtly tragic consequences when Cass Mastern betrays his friend Duncan Trice by committing adultery with Annabelle and again in the same kingdom by the sea, with more covert tragic consequences, when Judge Irwin cuckolds his best friend, Ellis Burden. Another example of this structural device is the manner in which Governor Stanton's protection of the guilty Judge Irwin recapitulates Governor Stark's protection of the guilty Bryam White. By presenting Burden and the reader with the revelation of these parallel events in an anachronistic manner, Warren dramatizes what Burden finally awakens to—the chronic and human intercourse that is both life and love.

The key to Jack's understanding is his ability to finally comprehend what Cass Mastern meant when he wrote that "the world is all one piece . . . an enormous spider web and if you touch it, however, lightly, at any point, the vibration ripples to the remotest perimeter and the drowsy spider . . . springs out to fling the gossamer coils about you." Mastern had stirred the delicate network and came to realize his culpability in the death of his friend and the degradation of Annabelle's slave, Phebe. Jack, in his second research project, the fruits of which he shares with the Stantons and Judge Irwin, realizes his culpability in the deaths of Adam, Willie, and Irwin. The imagery of web and spider suggests that man is caught in a fatal labyrinth, the threads of which are spun by the blind spider. Indeed, one cannot help associate this woven net with the one that ensnares Oedipus and consequently Oedipus's case with Burden's. Both are investigators, one public, the other private; both uncover truths that kill their fathers and reveal their true identities; and both recover the love of their mothers. Both also discover that paradoxically their identities are not only inherent in their separations from their parents, but also bound up in their connections to their parents.

Just as tragedy purges the pity and terror evoked by the trauma of separation through the affirmation of order and justice in the universe, so the horror of the spider-god or spider-conscience in Warren's novel is compensated for by the full appreciation of the weblike world. Initially, the web would seem to be a Hawthornian community of sinners. As Willie points out in a Calvinist view of the world, man cannot inherit goodness, but only make it out of badness as nature makes out of common dirt, the green grass, the brilliant diamond, and even George Washington. It is an understanding not unlike Ellis Burden's and it would seem consistent with Jack Burden's new understanding of the dark side of the past. There is, however, more to the web.

Jack comes to understand that the web of life is like the parts of a puzzle, no single piece of which has meaning by itself, but all of which have meaning in relation to each other within the pattern. He begins somewhat to put Humpty Dumpty back together again, when his earlier observation that life "was a flux of things . . . and one thing had nothing to do, in the end, with anything else" gives way to his later observation that "reality is not a function of the event as event, but of relationship of that event to past and future events." He concludes that "only as we realize this do we live, for our identity is dependent upon this principle." In discovering the pattern of interrelationship, he discovers that each man is a "son of a million fathers."

It is this same discovery that deters Jack from informing Sugar-Boy of Duffy's complicity in Willie Stark's death and thereby effecting a perfect vengeance upon Duffy. Recalling Duffy's mysterious wink, Burden suddenly realizes that they "were bound together forever and I could never hate him without hating myself or love myself without loving him." Nor could he kill Duffy without killing himself. Jack comes to accept Hugh Miller's contention that although history may be blind, man is not; with that understanding and his refusal to duplicate Willie's assassination with Duffy's, Jack undertakes responsibility for redesigning the weblike world. He also begins to effect a balance in the tension of two ideas: he comes to understand that identity requires both separation and relation, that "you are not you except in terms of relation to other people." The acceptance of that same tension completes Jack's initiation into the rites of love.

Jack Burden dates his fall into self-consciousness on the day he began to distinguish Adam and Anne "as separate, individual people, whose ways of acting were special, mysterious." What prompts this distinction and self-identification is the image of Anne's face "lying in the water, very smooth, with the eyes closed, under the dark greenish purple sky, with the gulls passing over." When he and Anne fall in love, Burden realizes that in loving and being loved, "you . . . cease to be a part of the continuum of the uncreated clay and get the breath of life in you and rise up." In love, then, two people are created, the lover and the loved one: "The farther those two you's are apart the more the world grinds and grudges on its axis." The more perfect the love, he tells us, the less difference and distance between the two you's; they come together to "coincide perfectly . . . as when a spectroscope gets the twin images on the card into perfect adjustment."

Burden's metaphors suggest that his experience of young love is a narcissistic one in which the object of love is but an imagined projection of the lover. Indeed, first love, according to Burden, is very much like child-mother love, when the psyche also begins to separate itself from the continuum of clay and responds possessively to that from which it has been separated—the mother. This idea of love as narcissistic attachment is reinforced, when Warren describes Jack and Anne suspended and kissing in the water, wanting never to emerge. Burden fails at love initially, because he is unwilling to accept the separateness, unwilling to separate the image of Anne as innocent from that of Anne as woman; he could not touch her, because it were as though "she had been my little sister." It is only after he recovers his mother's love and accepts Anne's separateness that love becomes possible for Jack Burden.

To be in the world is to be a part of the uncreated continuum of clay, and to become conscious of self and the other is to become separate. To develop such consciousness in the modern world is to multiply the terrible division of the age and consequently yearn to repair to the continuum of clay. Warren's directive is that the only way to live meaningfully in the modern world is to accept one's separateness as a condition of identity, but also to acknowledge that one is not entirely separate, for one's identity also resides in relationship to another continuum—a network of personal and social relationship that extends backward into the past and forward into the future, a continuum of interpenetration that is forever shifting and thereby requiring a reinterpretation of a self and society that are in constant dialectical opposition. Though there is a different emphasis in its dialectic, Ralph Ellison's *Invisible Man* also suggests that authentic selfhood resides in a reinterpretation of one's heritage and in a tension between individuality and society.

In an essay entitled "Harlem is Nowhere," a study of the Lafargue Psychiatric Clinic of Harlem, written in 1948, but not published until 1964 in *Shadow and Act,* Ellison sums up the plight of the twentieth-century Negro who has been a part of a pilgrimage to the North in search of freedom: "One's identity drifts in a capricious reality in which even the most commonly held assumptions are questionable. One 'is' literally, but one is nowhere; one wanders dazed in a ghetto maze, a 'displaced person' of American democracy."[3] Thus, the black-American pilgrimage is ironically accomplished: seeking the more perfect, free society, the quester finds himself in utopia, the no place where the dream of autonomy is transformed into the nightmare of anonymity. Such is the central leitmotiv, or riff, in Ellison's poetic blues of invisibility, and the most important variation of that motif—and the turning point in the odyssey of the invisible man himself—occurs at the core of the novel, the central thirteenth chapter, when the narrator bears witness to the eviction of the elderly black couple in the heart of Harlem.

Before coming upon the street drama, the narrator suffers two prior encounters that psychologically prepare him for the subsequent shock of recognition. He is walking through Harlem in a snowstorm that seems to dissolve the district. Passing store windows, he sees in quick succession "a black statue of a nude Nubian slave" grinning out at him and a sales sign for an ointment that promises whiter skin and social success. He hurries away repulsed no doubt on an unconscious level by the symbol of the black person's flight from blackness, his own flight from self. Continuing on, he sees the candied-yam man, buys a sweet potato, indulges his taste buds in soul food and his reverie in a nostalgia for the past. He then concludes, "to hell with being ashamed of what you liked. No more of that for me. I am what I am. . . . They're my birthmark. . . . I yam what I am." Having had a glimpse of the identity from which he and his people are in flight, the invisible man is made ready for a most dramatic intimation of his invisibility.

Watching the eviction of the elderly Provo couple, the young narrator accidentally discovers the "FREE PAPERS" of former slave Primus Provo, and he turns away to the curb filled with a dry nausea. His thoughts turn to "remembered words, of linked verbal echoes, images" of his own past, and he suddenly feels "as though I myself was being dispossessed of some painful yet precious thing which I could not bear to lose." Among those recollected images is one of his mother's hanging wash on a cold windy day—an image that causes him discomfort beyond its intrinsic meaning and one that he sees *"as behind a veil that threatened to lift, stirred by the cold wind in the narrow street."*

The scream of the old Provo woman, declaring her intention to reenter her apartment to pray, however, breaks the spell of the narrator's reverie, and the veil does not lift. Events overtake the invisible man; recollection gives way to action, reverie to speechmaking, and he fails to follow the thread of memory. That is as it should be, for it is clear in Ellison's fiction—as it is in so many other fictive rites of passage in American literature—that the knowledge of self is more a matter of process than of moment and that it is a long time in unwinding. But the reader knows that the precious thing of which the narrator feels in danger of being dispossessed is an identity, a selfhood, that locates itself, among other places, in the landscape and ancestry of his Southern past, an identity that has been displaced in the maze that is a battle royal or a college education or a Northern city. Eviction is the concrete correlative of the loss of place, which is a disinheritance of the past and a consequent loss of self. Moreover, it is not just a black-American experience; it is the American experience, a fact that Ellison confirms in the epilogue, when the narrator encounters Mr. Norton, who in losing his sense of direction has also lost face and has become thereby invisible.

Ellison further reiterates the intimate connection of person and place in the epilogue, when he has Jack-the-Bear contemplate a return to the "heart of darkness across the Mason-Dixon line," to "the whole unhappy territory that is a part of me." Before that can happen or before the narrator can even begin to contemplate its happening, he must run the gamut not only of having no identity, but also, like Bliss Proteus Rinehart, of assuming several false identities in the maze of anonymity: "Not only could you travel upward toward success, but you could travel downward as well: up *and* down, in retreat as well as advance, crabways and crossways and around in a circle meeting your old selves coming and going and perhaps all at the same time."

The image of the maze—explicit in Ellison's description of the Negro's plight in "Harlem is Nowhere" and implicit in his description of the narrator's labyrinthine encounters with his several selves—is further evoked in the novel by Ellison's depiction of the process of vision. The invisible man begins consciously to understand his separation from his past and his past self and begins "for the first time" to accept both, when he learns "suddenly to look around corners" and discover that the "images of past humiliations . . . were more than separate experiences. They were me; they defined me." This image is repeated later, when, having decided to use the Brotherhood for his and his people's ends rather than be used by it, the invisible man senses that "incidents of my past, both recognized and ignored, sprang together in my mind in an ironic leap of consciousness that was like looking around a corner." The corner, of course, is not a very jolly one, and like James's Spencer Brydon and Eliot's Harry Monchensey, the narrator discovers around it the image of another and alien self.

Despite his glimpse around the corner, the invisible man continues to remain shortsighted; he does not see that he is still a pawn in the machinations of the Brotherhood and that it continues to use him in its orchestration of the Harlem riot. The narrator's mazelike world is, like Gerontion's, a bewildering wilderness of mirrors that reflect a bewildering number of selves, and consequently it makes the definition of self a series of visions and revisions. He finally escapes the labyrinthine world and its fractured vision, when he falls into a dark hole at the center of the maze, where he literally and figuratively collects himself and where in darkness he attains insight. In so doing, the narrator becomes an ironic Daedalus, plunging from and escaping the amazement of life through the atonement of art—through the telling of his own tale.[4]

The movement from amazement toward atonement manifests itself in one final, distinctive variation of the battle royal riff, as the invisible man, now alone in the labyrinth of self, moves through the dark maze, burning up his false identification papers in order to temporarily light his way before "whirling on in blackness knocking against the rough walls of the narrow passage." He finally sails headlong in a "dimensionless" room, where in utter exhaustion he, for the first time since he dreams of his grandfather's legacy, stops running and lies motionless. Having burned away his false identities in the boundless darkness, he must exorcise them psychologically. Thus, he dreams of his manipulators and oppressors tormenting him with the pain and emptiness of his disillusionments, but he counters in the dream with the recognition that such suffering has enabled him, like Strether and Burden before him, to "see that which I couldn't see."

What he sees is that his oppressors have betrayed his American dream of success by using that very dream to keep him running from himself. When Mr. Norton tells the youthful narrator in their outing on Founder's Day that "you are bound to a dream," he says more than either fully understands. To be *bound to* means not only to be committed to but also to be constricted by, and the invisible men in American literature—Rip Van Winkle, Lambert Strether, Jimmie Gatz, Jack Burden, and so many others—are to one degree or another so bound. The narrator comes to see that his dream of success as an educator in the South, in the mold of a Bledsoe or the Founder, and as a spokesman and organizer in the North, in the mold of Brother Jack, is the very stuff by which his oppressors use him. He becomes a cog in Bledsoe's educational machine, Brockway's paint machine, Liberty Paints' therapeutic renewal machine, Jack's political machine, and Norton's grandiose "first hand organizing of human life," all of which are programmed to keep invisible men in line. When he discovers that his efforts to organize others have, through the superior efforts of the Brotherhood, redounded upon himself—he is the one being organized—and that the "vast, seething, hot world of fluidity" is a "life [that] is to be lived, not controlled," the invisible man rejects the office of organizer and with it the conspiratorial Brotherhood.

Because of their recurrence in the lexicon of the American Black, because of their prominence in the ideology and mythos of democratic America, and because of their effective orchestration in Ellison's novel, the words and idea of *brother* and *brotherhood* are the basis of a most meaningful leitmotiv in *Invisible Man.* In many ways, the novel asks not only, who am I, but also who is my brother, what is my brotherhood? For Ellison, as for Warren, they are the same question insofar as true identity is a matter of relationship. It is easy to catalogue those brotherhoods that the narrator either joins or is associated with and ultimately repudiates: a college fraternity that has conspired to educate the black man into a sophisticated and therefore more nefarious Uncle Tom; the Harlem Men's House, some members of which are chained to their briefcases and consequently "still caught up in the illusions that had just boomeranged out of [the narrator's] head"; a Brotherhood that uses its white women to manipulate its black spokesman in order to manipulate his people into the local means of its international ends; and a nationalistic brotherhood, personified in Ras, the would-be Abyssinian chieftain, who would repudiate American identity in order to recover African identity. What is not nearly so clear, however, is the nature of the true brotherhood, if any, that the invisible man affirms and joins.

There is much in the novel—particularly in the veteran's advice to the undergraduate narrator to "be your own father" and in the seeming completeness of the invisible man's withdrawal from all society and therefore all community—to suggest a newly acquired autonomy that precludes brotherhood. It is as though the Emersonian hero commits himself to a self-reliance in the midst of a society that conspires against the manhood of each of its members. Such a reading is supported by those interpretations that posit that a heritage of black identity, personified in the trickster figures of the grandfather, the veteran, Tod Clifton, and Rinehart, is one never fully recognized nor accepted by the hero and consequently one from which the invisible man cannot infer his identity.[5] Such interpretations, however, seem a misreading, for these figures, together with the candied yam man, Peter Wheatstraw, and Mary Rambo, become an Eliotic "familiar compound ghost," with whom the narrator through his narration, through his putting down of his invisibility, recognizes both kinship and brotherhood.

In a way, the hero has always existed in the image of the tricksters mentioned above as well as in the image of the prototypical American trickster, Huck Finn, a seeming fool whose foolishness ironically undermines the systems of the satraps that seek to enslave him. Is it not in character that, during the battle royal speech, the narrator blunders out of "social responsibility" into "social inequality"; that in driving Mr. Norton to the Trueblood cabin, introducing him to the saga of Trueblood incest, and turning to the *Golden Day* for medicinal purposes, he demonstrates to Bledsoe that he knows how "to ruin an institution [of suppression] in half an hour that it took over a hundred years to build"; that in pouring the wrong black dope into the impure white paint he effects a greying of America? Against the main point of the invisible man's blindness to the oppressive system runs the counterpoint of the narrator's unwitting guile that unmasks the oppressor and the organizational conspiracy. Such a pattern of behavior connects the invisible man to those other tricksters; it also implies that beneath the surface series of false identities there lies a true, evolving self that is linked to others and to the past.

Indeed, the many rites of passage enacted and parodied throughout the novel tend finally to confirm once-bornness rather than twice-bornness. History may be a boomerang, but it is a continuous one of a continuous self. Jack-the-Bear is but the continuation and maturation of a young man whose roots are in the South, but whose branchings of the mind occur in the North. Like the archetypal American persona from Irving's Rip to the speaker in Eliot's *Quartets,* the invisible man has stepped out of time, between the beats, only to discover that his identity lies in time. It is a being that exists not only in the places and persons of time past, but also in those of time present and time future. The narrator's quest becomes the novelist's quest spelled out in *Shadow and Act:* "I was taken very early with a passion to link together all I loved within the Negro community and all those things I felt in the world which lay beyond."[6] Similarly, in trying to unravel the legacy of his grandfather's "yes," the invisible man recognizes the inevitability that "we through no fault of our own were linked to all the others in the loud clamoring semi-visible world. . . . weren't we *part of them* as well as apart from them and subject to die when they did?"

This discovery explains why the narrator stays his knife-wielding hand before the tall blond stranger who has, in his blindness, assaulted the invisible man with a word: because he recognizes what William Wilson discovers too late and what Jack Burden learns in time, that in killing the other he also kills himself.

The invisible man's narrative is a definition of character, because it is a viable evocation of the other—of the persons and places that form the linked community that is the hero's experience and consequently his self. It is one no longer disguised by dream or mask, nor committed to false brotherhood, nor consigned merely to what has been. Although the withdrawal from society into the underground world has sufficed for the collection and concentration of self, such separation will not serve for the evolution of self. Thus, Jack-the-Bear prepares to emerge from hibernation "like the Easter chick breaking from its shell," to face a future of possibility and uncertainty armed this time not only with love and hope, but also with the experience of persecution and invisibility. He will ironically approach reparation through division, seeking his and America's "fate to become one, and yet many," with the knowledge that such order must be sought against a background of chaos, and such love against a background of hate. Reparation will also be sought with the recognition of the greater brotherhood implied in his final query: "Who knows but that, on the lower frequencies, I speak for you?"

Thus, though *Invisible Man,* unlike *All the King's Men,* expresses the need for separation from oppressive societies, it too acknowledges that such separation must be balanced with the recognition that true identity is indeed an affair of people—an interrelation with others, with society, with both past and future. Like Warren, Ellison suggests that such interrelationship is continuously changing and thereby requiring a continual reinterpretation of a self and society that are in constant dialectical tension with each other. The novels of Warren and Ellison also clearly demonstrate that postmodern American writers continue to draw upon the mythopoeic pattern of separation and reparation; moreover, they do so in a manner that indicates a greater consciousness of the pattern and of its significance to their culture and their literature. Finally, Warren and Ellison reiterate the tendency of most classic American writers to reverse the emphasis given separation in the dialectic of American history and ideology, by voicing through their art a symbolic declaration of interdependence.

Notes

Chapter 1. A Great Fall

1. D. H. Lawrence, *Studies in Classic American Literature* (New York: Thomas Seltzer, 1923; reprint ed., Garden City, N.Y.: Doubleday Anchor Books, 1951), p. 64.

2. R. W. B. Lewis, *The American Adam: Innocence, Tragedy, and Tradition in the Nineteenth Century* (Chicago: University of Chicago Press, 1955; Phoenix Books, 1955), p. 7.

3. Ibid., pp. 7–8.

4. Leslie Fiedler, *An End to Innocence: Essays on Culture and Politics* (Boston: Beacon Press, 1955), p. 124; Kenneth Lynn, *The Dream of Success: A Study of the Modern American Imagination* (Boston: Little, Brown & Co., 1955), p. 7.

5. Frederic Carpenter, "The American Myth: Paradise (To Be) Regained," *PMLA* 74 (December 1959): 599.

6. Charles Sanford, *The Quest for Paradise: Europe and the American Moral Imagination* (Urbana: University of Illinois Press, 1961), p. 266.

7. *Sanford, Quest for Paradise*, p. 181; Roy Harvey Pearce, *The Continuity of American Poetry* (Princeton: Princeton University Press, 1961), p. 290.

8. A. N. Kaul, *The American Vision: Actual and Ideal Society in Nineteenth-Century Fiction* (New Haven and London: Yale University Press, 1963), p. 66; Leo Marx, *The Machine in the Garden: Technology and the Pastoral Ideal in America* (New York: Oxford University Press, 1964), p. 23.

9. Tony Tanner, *City of Words: American Fiction 1950–1970* (New York: Harper & Row, 1971), p. 29.

10. Sacvan Bercovitch, *The Puritan Origins of the American Self* (New Haven and London: Yale University Press, 1975), p. 13.

11. Orestes Brownson, quoted in Yehoshua Arieli, *Individualism and Nationalism in American Ideology* (Cambridge: Harvard University Press, 1964), p. 140.

12. Albert Friedman, "The Usable Myth: The Legends of Modern Mythmakers," in *America Folk Legend*, ed. Wayland Hand (Berkeley and Los Angeles: University of California Press, 1971), p. 43.

13. Paul Ricoeur, *The Conflict of Interpretation: Essays in Hermeneutics* (Evanston, Ill.: Northwestern University Press, 1974), p. 29.

14. Cf. John Vernon, *The Garden and the Map: Schizophrenia in Twentieth-Century Literature and Culture* (Urbana: University of Illinois Press, 1973). Though we start out with similar observations about separation, our studies vary in that my study is equally concerned with reparation and Vernon's concentrates on the schizophrenic in twentieth-century American literature.

15. See Erich Neumann, *The Origins and History of Consciousness,* trans. R. F. C. Hull (Princeton: Princeton University Press, 1954), pp. 307–12.

16. Nicolas Berdyaev, *The Destiny of Man,* trans. Natalie Duddington (London: G. Bles, Centenary Press, 1937), p. 251.

17. Giovanni Battista Vico, *The New Science,* trans. Thomas Goddard Bergin and Max Harold Fisch, (1725; 3d ed., 1744; Ithaca, N.Y.: Cornell University Press, 1948), p. 130; Claude Lévi-Strauss, *Totemism,* trans. Rodney Needham (Boston: Beacon Press, 1963), p. 101.

18. Paul Ricoeur, *The Symbolism of Evil,* trans. Emerson Buchanan (New York: Harper & Row, 1976; reprint ed., Boston: Beacon Press, 1969), p. 167.

19. See Edward Edinger, *Ego and Archetype: Individuation and the Religious Function of the Psyche* (New York: G. P. Putnam's Sons, 1972; reprint ed., Baltimore: Penguin Books, 1973), p. 163.

20. See Sigmund Freud, *Civilization and Its Discontents,* vol. 21 of *The Complete Works,* ed. James Strachey and trans. Joan Riviere (London: Hogarth Press, 1930), pp. 64–73; Sándor Ferenczi, "Thalassa: A Theory of Genitality," trans. Harry Alden Bunker, Jr., *Psychoanalytical Quarterly* 2 (1933): 20; Géza Róheim, *The Gates of the Dream* (New York: International Universities Press, 1952), p. 428.

21. Jane Harrison, *Epilegomena to the Study of Greek Religion and Themis: A Study of the Social Origins of Greek Religion* (Cambridge: Cambridge University Press, 1912, 1921; reprint ed., New Hyde Park, N.Y.: University Books, 1962), p. 485; Owen Barfield, "The Meaning of the Word 'Literal'," in *Metaphor and Symbol,* ed. L. C. Knight and Basil Cittle (London: Butterworth's Scientific Publications, 1960), p. 56.

22. See Marjorie Hope Nicholson, *The Breaking of the Circle: Studies in the Effect of the "New Science" upon Seventeenth-Century Poetry* (New York: Columbia University Press, 1960), p. 123. The John Donne quotations are from "Meditation 17" and "The First Anniversary"; the Matthew Arnold, "To Marguerite—Continued."

23. Philip Wheelwright, *Metaphor and Reality* (Bloomington: Indiana University Press, 1962), pp. 134–35.

24. Rollo May, *Love and Will* (New York: W. W. Norton & Co., 1969), p. 134.

25. William Butler Yeats, "The Second Coming"; Robert Frost, "Directive"; Wallace Stevens, "Anecdote of the Jar" and "The Idea of Order at Key West"; Dylan Thomas, "A Refusal to Mourn the Death by Fire of a Child in London"; T. S. Eliot, "Burnt Norton."

26. Pierre Teilhard de Chardin, *Christianity and Evolution,* trans. René Hague (New York: Harcourt Brace Jovanovich, 1971), p. 126; "What is Metaphysics?" *Martin Heidegger: Existence and Being,* ed. Werner Brock and trans. R. F. C. Hull and Alan Crick (Chicago: Henry Regnery Co., 1949; reprint ed., Gateway Edition, 1967), pp. 346–53.

Chapter 2. *Nomos* and the Genesis of America

1. *The Complete Works of Ralph Waldo Emerson,* ed. Edward Waldo Emerson, (New York: Houghton Mifflin & Co., 1903–04), 10:325–29.

2. Americo Castro, *The Spaniards: An Introduction to Their History,* trans. William F. King and Selma Margareiten (Berkeley and Los Angeles: University of California Press, 1971), p. 48; Edward Johnson, *Johnson's Wonder-Working Providence 1628–1651,* ed. J. Franklin Jameson (New York: Barnes & Noble, 1946),p. 53.

3. John Foxe, quoted in William Haller, *Foxe's Book of Martyrs and The Elect Nation* (London: Jonathan Cape, 1963), p. 110.

4. Bercovitch, *Puritan Origins of the American Self,* p. 18.

5. John Winthrop, "A Model of Christian Charity," *Winthrop Papers 1623–1630*, vol. 2 (N.p.: The Massachusetts Historical Society, 1931), p. 294, microfiche.

6. Winthrop, "Model of Christian Charity," p. 282; Max Weber, *The Protestant Ethic and the Spirit of Capitalism*, trans. Talcott Parsons (New York: Charles Scribner's Sons, 1958), pp. 121–22.

7. Edward Morgan, *Visible Saints: The History of a Puritan Idea* (Ithaca, N.Y.: Cornell University Press, 1965), p. 52; John Cotton, *The Way of Life* (London: L. Fawne and S. Gellibrand, 1641), p. 449 microfiche; Cotton Mather, *Bonifacius: An Essay . . . To Do Good*, ed. Josephine K. Piercy (Boston: Samuel Gerrish, 1710; reprint ed., Gainesville, Fla.: Scholars' Facsimiles & Reprints, 1967), p. 73.

8. Francis Higginson, quoted in Cotton Mather, *Magnalia Christi Americana*, ed. Thomas Robbins (1852; reprint ed., New York: Russell & Russell, 1967), 1:362; Johnson, *Wonder-Working Providence*, pp. 25–26.

9. Edward Morgan, *The Puritan Dilemma* (Boston: Little, Brown & Co., 1958), p. 199; Perry Miller, *The New England Mind: The Seventeenth Century* (New York: Macmillan Co., 1939; reprint ed., Boston: Beacon Press, 1961), pp. 415–16.

10. Anne Hutchinson, quoted in Bercovitch, *Puritan Origins of the American Self*, p. 93; Thomas Jefferson and Thomas Paine are quoted in Robert Bellah, *Beyond Belief: Essays on Religion in a Post-Traditional World* (New York: Harper & Row, 1970), p. 43; the final quotation is Philip Schaff, *America: A Sketch of the Political, Social, and Religious Character of the United States of America* (New York: Charles Scribner, 1855), p. 101.

11. *The Complete Writings of Roger Williams*, vol. 3 (Providence, R.I.: Narragansett Edition, 1886–1874; reprint ed., New York: Russell & Russell, 1963), pp. 13, 73.

12. James Madison, "Number 51," *The Federalist*, ed. Benjamin Fletcher Wright (Cambridge, Harvard University Press, Belknap Press, 1961), p. 358.

13. Richard Niebuhr, *The Social Sources of Denominationalism* (Cleveland: World Publishing Co., 1929; reprint ed., Hamden, Conn.: Shoe String Press, 1954); John Cotton, "A Reply to Mr. Williams his Examination, And Answer to the Letters Sent to him by John Cotton," in *The Complete Writings of Roger Williams*, 2:19; Alexis de Tocqueville, *Democracy in America*, ed. Phillips Bradley (New York: Alfred A. Knopf, 1945), 2:197.

14. Edward Shils, *Center and Periphery: Essays in Macrasociology* (Chicago: University of Chicago Press, 1975), p. 213; Bercovitch, *Puritan Origins of the American Self*, pp. 95–96.

15. Alan Simpson, *Puritanism in Old and New England* (Chicago: University of Chicago Press, 1955), p. 109.

16. J. Hector St. John de Crèvecoeur, *Letters from an American Farmer* (New York: Albert & Charles Boni, 1925), p. 66; Karl Marx, "On the Jewish Question," in *The Marx-Engels Reader*, ed. Robert C. Tucker and trans. T. B. Bottomore (New York: W. W. Norton & Co., 1972), p. 33.

17. See Robert Bellah, *The Broken Covenant: American Civil Religion in Time of Trial* (New York: Seabury Press, 1975) and "Civil Religion in America," *Beyond Belief*, pp. 168–89 and Sidney Mead, *The Lively Experiment: The Shaping of Christianity in America* (New York, Harper & Row, 1963); Mead, *Lively Experiment*, p. 65.

18. Samuel Johnson, *A Journey to the Western Islands of Scotland in 1773* (London: Paisley, A. Gardner, 1908), pp. 194–95.

19. *The Works of John Adams*, ed. Charles Francis Adams (Boston: Little, Brown & Co., 1856), 10:282.

20. Thomas Hutchinson, "The Address of the Governor," in *The Briefs of the American Revolution: Constitutional Arguments Between Thomas Hutchinson, Governor of Massachusetts Bay, and James Bowdoin for the Council and John Adams for the House of*

Representatives, ed. John Phillip Reid (New York and London: New York University Press, 1981), p. 20.

21. *The Life and Major Writings of Thomas Paine,* ed. Philip S. Foner (New York: Citadel Press, 1945), p. 23; Weber, *Protestant Ethic,* pp. 50–55.

22. Mather, *Magnalia Christi Americana,* 1:27.

23. See Leslie Fiedler, *Love and Death in the American Novel* (New York: Criterion Books, 1960; reprint ed., Cleveland, Ohio: World Publishing Co., 1962); and Norman O. Brown, *Life Against Death: The Psychoanalytical Meaning of History* (Middleton, Conn.: Weslyan University Press, 1959) and *Love's Body* (New York: Random House, 1966; New York: Vintage Books, 1966).

24. Madison, "Number 10," Federalist, 131; *The Works of Alexander Hamilton,* ed. John C. Hamilton (New York: S. Francis Charles & Co., 1851), 2:51; Madison, "Number 10," *Federalist,* p. 135; Adams, *Works,* 4:295.

25. Crevècoeur, *American Farmer,* p. 53; Paine, *Major Writings,* p. 19.

26. Cotton Mather, *The Wonders of the Invisible World: Being an Account of the Tryals of Several Witches Lately Executed in New-England,* (London: John Russell Smith, 1862), p. 14, microfiche.

27. Jonathan Edwards, "A Treatise Concerning Religious Affections," in *The Works of President Edwards* (New York: Jonathan Leavitt & John F. Trow; Boston: Crocker and Brewster; Philadelphia: Geo. S. Appleton, 1843), 3:18; Charles Chauncy, "Seasonable Thoughts on the State of Religion," in *The Great Awakening: Documents Illustrating the Crisis and Its Consequences,* ed. Alan Heimert and Perry Miller (Indianapolis and New York: Bobbs-Merrill Co., 1967), p. 298.

28. Emerson, "Nature," *Works,* 1:10.

29. Emerson, "Self-Reliance," *Works,* 2:49.

30. Emerson, "Nature," *Works,* 1:3; "Self-Reliance," *Works,* 2:73; "The Divinity School Address," *Works,* 1:145.

31. Bronson Alcott, quoted in David DeLeon, *The American as Anarchist: Reflections on Indigenous Radicalism* (Baltimore and London: Johns Hopkins University Press, 1978) p. 22; Tocqueville, *Democracy in America,* 2:98.

32. *The Convert, or Leaves from My Experience,* vol. 5 of *The Works of Orestes A. Brownson,* ed. Henry F. Brownson, (Detroit, Mich.: T. Nourse, 1882–87; reprint ed., New York: AMS Press, 1966), p. 75.

33. Emerson, "Society and Solitude," *Works,* 7:15; "The American Scholar," *Works,* 1:113; Josiah Warren is quoted in Arieli, *Individualism and Nationalism,* p. 293.

34. Tocqueville, *Democracy in America,* 2:318.

35. *The Works of John C. Calhoun,* ed. Richard K. Cralle, vol. 1 *A Disquisition on Government and a Discourse on the Constitution of the United States* (New York: D. Appleton & Co., 1883), p. 65; *The Papers of John C. Calhoun,* ed. Clyde N. Wilson, (Columbia: University of Southern Carolina Press, 1981), 14:107–8.

36. Abraham Lincoln, quoted in Richard Hofstadter, *American Political Tradition: And the Men Who Made It,* (New York: Alfred A. Knopf, 1948; New York: Vintage Books, 1948), p. 103.

37. Philip Slater, *The Pursuit of Loneliness: American Culture at the Breaking Point* (Boston: Beacon Press, 1970), p. 47; Emerson, "Ode," *Works,* 9:78; *The Education of Henry Adams,* ed. Ernest Samuels (1907; reprint ed., Boston: Houghton Mifflin & Co., 1973), pp. 5, 387.

38. Tocqueville, *Democracy in America,* 2:99; Emerson, "Society and Solitude," *Works,* 7:9.

39. See Raymond Williams, *Culture and Society 1780–1950* (New York: Columbia Uni-

versity Press; London: Chatto & Windus, 1958; reprint ed., New York: Harper & Row Torchbooks, 1966); Paul Ricoeur, "Hermeneutic of the Idea of Revelation" (Paper delivered at the Graduate Theological Seminary, February 1977, Berkeley, California.).

40. See Richard Chase, *The American Novel and Its Tradition* (Garden City, N.Y.: Doubleday Anchor Books, 1957), pp. 2–11; and Harry Levin, *The Power of Blackness: Hawthorne, Poe, Melville* (New York: Alfred A. Knopf, 1958; New York, Vintage Books, 1958), pp. 8–35.

Chapter 3. The Gothic Circle

1. See Neumann, *Origins and History*, pp. 8–9; Johann Jacob Bachofen, *Myth, Religion and Mother Right*, trans. Ralph Manheim (Princeton: Princeton University Press, 1967), pp. 24–25; Georges Poulet, *The Metamorphoses of the Circle*, trans. Carley Dawson and Elliott Coleman (Baltimore: Johns Hopkins University Press, 1966), pp. xi–xxvii.

2. See Mircea Eliade, *Images and Symbols: Studies in Religious Symbolism*, trans. Philip Mairet (New York: Sheed & Ward; London: Harvill Press, 1961; New York: Sheed and Ward, 1969), pp. 92–164; Octavio Paz, *The Labyrinth of Solitude: Life and Thought in Mexico*, trans. Lysander Kemp (New York: Grove Press; London: Evergreen Books, 1961), pp. 20, 64; Bettina L. Knapp, *Jean Racine: Myths and Renewal in Modern Theater* (University, Ala.: University of Alabama Press, 1971), p. 175.

3. See, for example, Aniela Jaffé, "Symbolism in the Visual Arts," in *Man and His Symbols*, ed. Carl G. Jung (London: Aldus Books, 1964; New York: Dell Publishing Co., 1964), pp. 266–84; Carl G. Jung, *The Portable Jung*, ed. Joseph Campbell and trans. R. F. C. Hull (New York: Viking Press, 1971), pp. 359–63; Carl G. Jung, *Psyche and Symbol: A Selection From the Writings of C. G. Jung*, ed. Violet S. de Laszlo and trans. R. F. C. Hull and Cary Baynes (Garden City, N.Y.: Doubleday, Anchor Books, 1958), pp. 318–22.

4. Walt Whitman, *Leaves of Grass: Authoritative Texts, Prefaces, Whitman on His Art, Criticism*, ed. Sculley Bradley and Harold W. D. Blodgett (New York: W. W. Norton & Co. Critical Editions, 1973), p. 35. All quotations from Whitman's poetry are from this edition and are cited in the text. When quotations are sufficiently identified by title, no citation is made.

5. David Halliburton, *Edgar Allan Poe: A Phenomenological View* (Princeton: Princeton University Press, 1973), p. 250.

6. Daniel Hoffman, *Poe Poe Poe Poe Poe Poe Poe* (New York: Doubleday & Co., 1972; Anchor Press, 1973), p. 256.

7. Halliburton, *Poe*, p. 209.

8. Maurice Beebe, "The Universe of Roderick Usher," and Richard Wilbur, "The House of Poe," in *Poe: A Collection of Critical Essays*, ed. Robert Reagan (Englewood Cliffs, N.J.: Prentice-Hall Spectrum Book, 1967), pp. 133, 110.

9. Allan Tate, "Our Cousin, Mr. Poe," in *Collected Essays* (Denver: Alan Swallow, 1959), p. 447.

10. Hoffman, *Poe Poe Poe*, p. 254.

11. Henry James, Sr., *Society: The Redeemed Form of Man, and The Earnest of God's Omnipotence in Human Nature, Affirmed in Letters to a Friend* (Boston: Houghton, Osgood & Co., 1879), pp. 485, 430.

12. Lawrence, *Studies*, p. 13.

13. See Emile Durkheim, *The Elementary Forms of the Religious Life*, trans. Joseph Ward Swain (London: George Allen & Unwin, 1915; reprint ed., New York: Macmillan Free Press, 1965), pp. 134–149 for a discussion of the concentration of mana in totem object.

14. Sigmund Freud, *Totem and Taboo and Other Works*, vol. 13 of *The Complete Works*, ed. James Strachey and trans. Joan Riviere (London: Hogarth Press, 1955), pp. 137–61.

15. The T. S. Eliot quotation is from "Little Gidding."

16. *A Wonder Book and Tanglewood Tales* in *The Centenary Edition of the Works of Nathaniel Hawthorne*, ed. William Charvat et al., (Columbus: Ohio State University Press, 1972), 7:207.

17. Lewis, *American Adam*, p. 114; Roy R. Male, *Hawthorne's Tragic Vision* (Austin: University of Texas Press, 1957), p. 117.

18. Jung, "Aion," *Psyche and Symbol*, pp. 1–60.

19. Ricoeur, *Symbolism of Evil*, p. 146; Rudolph Bultmann, *Primitive Christianity: In Its Contemporary Setting*, trans. R. H. Fuller (New York: World Publishing Co. Meridian Book, 1956), p. 54.

20. Michael Baxandall, *Painting and Experience in Fifteenth-Century Italy: A Primer in the Social History of Pictorial Style* (London, Clarendon Press, 1972), pp. 76, 80; see Weber, *Protestant Ethic*, pp. 168, 172; and Max Weber, *The Sociology of Religion*, trans. Ephraim Fischoff (Boston: Beacon Press, 1963), pp. 183, 245.

21. Ahab is identified with the following heroes: Prometheus, who is bound to the rock of ages for stealing fire from Zeus and giving it to man; Narcissus, who is atrophied by his consciousness of self; Oedipus, whose success as a detective redounds upon himself as self-blinding and self-exile; Lucifer, who is reduced to absolute darkness for aspiring to absolute light; and Adam, who is made to confront his mortality and is separated from the Garden for choosing the fruit of the tree of the knowledge of good and evil over that of the tree of life.

22. See John Halverson, "The Shadow in *Moby Dick*," *American Quarterly* 15 (Fall 1963): 441.

23. Eliade, *Images and Symbols*, pp. 114, 117.

24. Daniel Hoffman, *Form and Fable in American Fiction* (New York: Oxford University Press, 1961), pp. 33–39 comments generally on the significance of the Narcissus myth in *Moby Dick*.

25. Eliade, *Images and Symbols*, p. 51.

26. Halverson, "Shadow," pp. 436–46 refers to the mandala image of the vortex as a symbol of Ishmael's selfhood.

Chapter 4. Coming of Age in America

1. Ralph Ellison, *Invisible Man* (New York: Random House, 1952), p. 436; *Shadow and Act* (New York: Random House, 1964), p. 300.

2. See Otto Rank, *The Myth of the Birth of the Hero and Other Writings*, ed. Philip Freund and trans. F. Robbins and Smith Ely Jelliffe (New York: The Journal of Nervous and Mental Disease Publishing Co., 1914; reprint ed., New York: Vintage Books, 1959); Fitz Roy Somerset Raglan, *The Hero: A Study in Tradition, Myth and Drama* (London: Metheun & Co, 1936; reprint ed., New York: Vintage Books, 1956).

3. Lewis, *American Adam*, p. 115; Hassan, *Radical Innocence*, p. 35.

4. Henry James, Sr., *Society*, pp. 362, 430.

5. Kenneth S. Lynn, "Welcome Back from the Raft, Huck Honey!" *American Scholar* 46 (Summer 1977): 338–50 reaffirms this interpretation by concluding that Huck will be integrated into society.

6. Tocqueville, *Democracy in America*, 2:197.

7. Lionel Trilling, "Huckleberry Finn," in *The Liberal Imagination: Essays on Literature*

and Society (New York: Viking Press, 1950; reprint ed., Garden City, N.Y.: Doubleday Anchor Books, 1957), p. 104.

8. "Come Back to the Raft, Ag'in, Huck Honey," in *Collected Essays of Leslie Fiedler* (New York: Stein & Day, 1971), 1:142–51.

9. Philip Young, "Adventures of Huckleberry Finn," in *Ernest Hemingway: A Reconsideration* (University Park: Pennsylvania State University Press, 1966), pp. 211–41 concerns himself with Huck's fascination with death.

10. Harold Peter Simonson, *The Closed Frontier: Studies in American Literary Tragedy* (New York: Holt, Rinehart & Winston, 1970), p. 60.

11. T. S. Eliot, [An Introduction to *Huckleberry Finn*], in Samuel Langhorne Clemens, *Adventures of Huckleberry Finn: An Annotated Text, Backgrounds and Sources, Essays in Criticism,* ed. Sculley Bradley, Richmond Croom Beatty, E. Hudson Long (New York: W. W. Norton & Co. Critical Editions, 1961), p. 322.

12. Wright Morris, *The Territory Ahead* (New York: Atheneum, 1963) demonstrates the tendency of some critics to read *ahead* as a modifier of *territory.*

13. Eliot, "Introduction," p. 327; Fiedler, *Love and Death,* p. 584.

14. See Richard Palmer, *Hermeneutics* (Evanston, Ill.: Northwestern University Press, 1969), pp. 103, 108, 109, 186, 212; Ricoeur, *Conflict of Interpretations,* p. 16; Hans-Georg Gadamer, *Truth and Method,* ed. and trans. Garrett Barden and John Cumming (New York: Seabury Press, 1975), pp. 245, 341.

15. William James,*The Varieties of Religious Experience: A Study of Human Nature* (New York and London: Longmans, Green, 1902; reprint ed., New York: New American Library, 1958), p. 157. In distinguishing between healthy-mindedness and the sick soul, James implies that the sick soul requires a rejection of what he has been in order to be converted into a twice-born saint. Implicit also in his discussion is the idea that twice-bornness can lead to a multitude of rebirths and identities.

16. E. M. Forster, *Aspects of the Novel* (New York: Harcourt, Brace & Co., 1927; reprint ed., New York: Harcourt, Brace & World, 1954), p. 162.

17. T. S. Eliot, "A Prediction in Regard to Three English Authors," in *Henry James: A Collection of Critical Essays,* ed. Leon Edel (Englewood Cliffs, N.J.: Prentice-Hall, 1963), pp. 55–56; "Project of Novel by Henry James," in *The Notebooks of Henry James,* ed. F. O. Matthiessen and Kenneth B. Murdock (New York: George Braziller, 1947), p. 414.

18. Mark Twain, quoted in Henry Nash Smith, ed. "Introduction," *Adventures of Huckleberry Finn* (Boston: Houghton Mifflin Riverside Editions, 1958), p. xvi.

19. James, "Project," 415.

20. F. Scott Fitzgerald, *The Crack-up* (New York: New Directions, 1945; reprint ed., New York, New Directions, 1956), pp. 76, 70, 83, 310. The letter is from *The Letters of F. Scott Fitzgerald,* ed. Andrew Turnbull (New York: Charles Scribner's Sons, 1963), p. 32; the notebook entry is quoted in Arthur Mizener, *The Far Side of Paradise: A Biography of F. Scott Fitzgerald* (Boston: Houghton Mifflin Co., 1951; reprint ed., New York: Vintage Books, 1959), p. 180.

21. See Palmer, *Hermeneutics,* p. 28.

22. The William Butler Yeats line is from "Among School Children."

23. Sherwood Anderson, *Winesburg, Ohio* (New York: B. W. Heubsch, 1919; reprint ed., New York: Viking Press, 1966), pp. 24–25.

24. See Hugh Holman, "The Unity of Faulkner's *Light in August,*" PMLA 73 (March 1958): 155–66; and Richard Chase, "The Stone and the Crucifix in *Light in August,*" *Kenyon Review* 10 (Autumn 1948): 539–51.

25. T. S. Eliot, *Notes Towards the Definition of Culture* (New York: Harcourt, Brace & Co., 1949), p. 42.

Chapter 5: The *Via Negativa*

1. Emerson, "American Scholar," *Works*, 1:83.

2. Henry David Thoreau, *Journal*, ed. Branford Yorrey and Francis H. Allen (Boston: Houghton Mifflin Co., 1949), 4:246–47.

3. See Pseudo-Dionysius Areopagite, *The Divine Names and Mystical Theology*, ed. and trans. John D. Jones (Milwaukee: Marquette University Press, 1980); Clifton Wolters, ed., "Introduction," in *The Cloud of Unknowing* (Baltimore: Penguin Books, 1961, pp. 14–24.

4. See Wolters, *Cloud of Unknowing; Revelations of Divine Love Shewed to Mother Juliana of Norwich 1373* (London: Kegan Paul, Trench, Trubner & Co., 1902, microfiche); John Caputo, *The Mystical Element in Heidegger's Thought* (N. p., 1978); quotation is from Revelations of Divine Love, p. 51.

5. See "Introduction" and "What is Metaphysics?" in *Martin Heidegger: Existence and Being*, pp. 2–231, 325–61; quotation, p. 344.

6. *The Letters of Emily Dickinson*, ed. Thomas H. Johnson, 3 vols. (Cambridge: Harvard University Press, Belknap Press, 1958), 1:83. All references to Dickinson's letters shall be to this edition and shall be cited in the text by the letter *L*, volume, and page. Unless the text sufficiently identifies quotations by first line title, all quotations from Dickinson's poetry shall be to the following text and shall be cited by the poem number established therein: *The Complete Poems of Emily Dickinson*, ed. Thomas H. Johnson (Boston: Little, Brown & Co., 1960).

7. George Whicher, *This Was a Poet* (New York: Charles Scribner's Sons, 1935; reprint ed., Ann Arbor, Mich.: University of Michigan Press, Ann Arbor Paperbacks, 1957), pp. 244–45.

8. See Whicher, *A Poet*, pp. 153–69; and Thomas W. Ford, *Heaven Beguiles the Tired: Death in the Poetry of Emily Dickinson* (University, Ala.: University of Alabama Press, 1966), p. 178.

9. See poems 61, 160, 313, 370, 508, 633, 889, 1231.

10. T. S. Eliot, *The Complete Poems and Plays 1909–1950* (New York: Harcourt, Brace & World, 1952), p. 128. All quotations from this edition shall be cited in the text with letters *CP*. If the quotation is from a short poem and is sufficiently identified by title, there will be no citation. Quotations from *The Confidential Clerk* (New York: Harcourt, Brace & Co., 1954) and *The Elder Statesman* (London: Faber & Faber, 1959) shall be cited in the text by the letters *CC* and *ES* respectively; Gadamer, *Truth and Method*, p. 481.

11. See Eliot's reference to F. H. Bradley's *Appearance and Reality* in *Complete Poems*, p. 54.

12. T. S. Eliot, "Tradition and the Individual Talent," in *The Sacred Wood: Essays on Poetry and Criticism* (London: Metheun, 1920; reprint ed., London: Metheun; New York: Barnes & Noble, 1960), pp. 51, 53.

13. "*Ulysses*, Order and Myth," in *Selected Prose of T. S. Eliot*, (New York: Harcourt Brace Jovanovich, 1978), p. 177.

14. T. S. Eliot, *The Idea of a Christian Society* (New York: Harcourt, Brace & World, 1940), p. 19.

15. Eliot, *Notes Towards*, p. 59.

16. Ibid., p. 42.

17. *The Comedy of Dante Alighieri*, ed. and trans. Dorothy Sayers and Barbara Reynolds (Baltimore, Md.: Penguin Books, 1962), 3:345.

18. T. S. Eliot, *After Strange Gods: A Primer of Modern Heresy* (London: Faber & Faber, 1934), p. 47.

19. Pearce, *Continuity*, p. 291.

20. *The Collected Poems of Wallace Stevens* (New York: Alfred A. Knopf, 1954), p. 490. All quotations from this edition shall be cited in the text by the letters *CP;* if the quotation is from a short poem and is sufficiently identified by title, there will be no citation. Quotations from *Letters: Selected and Edited by Holly Stevens* (New York: Alfred A. Knopf, 1966); *Opus Posthumous: Poems, Plays, Prose,* ed. Samuel French Morse (New York: Alfred A. Knopf, 1957); and *The Palm at the End of the Mind: Selected Poems and a Play,* ed. Holly Stevens (New York: Alfred A. Knopf, 1971; New York: Vintage Books, 1972) will be cited in the text with the letters *L, OP* and *P* respectively.

21. J. Hillis Miller, "Wallace Stevens' Poetry of Being," in *Modern American Poetry: Essays in Criticism,* ed. Jerome Mazzaro (New York: David McKay Co., 1970), p. 96.

22. Ricoeur, *Conflict of Interpretations,* p. 29.

23. Miller, "Poetry of Being," pp. 107–10.

24. Kenneth Burke, *Language as Symbolic Action: Essays on Life, Literature and Method* (Berkeley, Los Angeles, and London: University of California Press, 1966), pp. 419–79.

25. Brown, *Love's Body,* pp. 141, 261.

26. Burke, *Symbolic Action,* pp. 422–23.

27. See Sigmund Freud, "The 'Uncanny'," in *Collected Papers,* ed. Ernest Jones and trans. Joan Riviere (London: Hogarth Press and The Institute of Psychoanalysis, 1924–50; reprint ed., New York: Basic Books, 1959), pp. 368–407; and *Martin Heidegger: Existence and Being,* pp. 337–38, in which Heidegger posits that nothingness is prior to the negative.

28. Burke, *Symbolic Action,* 437.

29. See Thomas J. Hines, *The Later Poetry of Wallace Stevens* (London: Associated Universities Presses, Lewisburg, Pa.: Bucknell University Press; 1976) for an explication of Stevens's poetry in terms of Heidegger's philosophy; Harold Bloom, *Wallace Stevens: The Poems of Our Climate* (Ithaca, N.Y.: Cornell University Press, 1977) for an analysis of Stevens as an American romantic poet.

Chapter 6. So We Beat On

1. See James Ruoff, "Humpty Dumpty and *All the King's Men:* A Note on Robert Penn Warren's Teleology," and Jonathan Baumbach, "The Meaning of Demagoguery: *All the King's Men* by Robert Penn Warren," in *Twentieth Century Interpretations of All the King's Men,* ed. Robert F. Chambers (Englewood Cliffs, N.J.: Prentice-Hall Spectrum Book, 1977), pp. 84–92, 126–42, for discussions of Jack Burden as the central figure in the dramatization of the disintegrated self.

2. See Jerome Meckier, "Burden's Complaint: The Disintegrated Personality as Theme and Style in Robert Penn Warren's *All the King's Men,*" in *Twentieth Century Interpretations,* pp. 57–72 for discussion of other stylistic reinforcements of the theme of the interpenetrations of the individual, society, and time.

3. Ellison, *Shadow and Act,* p. 300.

4. R. W. B. Lewis, "Days of Wrath and Laughter," in *Trials of the Word: Essays in American Literature and the Humanistic Tradition* (New Haven and London: Yale University Press, 1965), p. 220 suggests that the invisible man achieves atonement through his art of storytelling.

5. See Eleanor R. Wilner, "The Invisible Black Thread: Identity and Nonentity in *Invisible Man,*" *College Language Association Journal* 13 (March 1970): 242–57 for such a reading.

6. Ellison, *Shadow and Act,* p. 12.

Works Cited

Adams, Henry. *The Education of Henry Adams.* Edited by Ernest Samuels. 1907. Reprint. Boston: Houghton Mifflin Riverside Editions, 1973.

Adams, John. *The Works of John Adams.* Edited by Charles Francis Adams. 10 vols. Boston: Little, Brown & Co., 1856.

Alighieri, Dante. *The Comedy of Dante Alighieri.* 3 vols. Translated and edited by Dorothy Sayers and Barbara Reynolds. Baltimore: Penguin Books, Penguin Classics, 1962.

Anaximander. [A Fragment]. In *Love and Will,* by Rollo May, p. 341. New York: W. W. Norton & Co., 1969.

Anderson, Sherwood. *Winesburg, Ohio.* New York: B. W. Huebsch, 1919. Reprint. New York: Viking Press, 1966.

Arieli, Yehoshua. *Individualism and Nationalism in American Ideology.* Cambridge: Harvard University Press, 1964.

Bachofen, Johann Jacob. *Myth, Religion and Mother Right.* Translated by Ralph Manheim. Princeton: Princeton University Press, 1967.

Barfield, Owen. "The Meaning of the Word 'Literal'." In *Metaphor and Symbol,* edited by L. C. Knight and Basil Cittle, pp. 48–63. London: Butterworth's Scientific Publications, 1960.

Baumbach, Jonathan. "The Metaphysics of Demagoguery: *All the King's Men.*" In *Twentieth Century Interpretations of All the King's Men, A Collection of Critical Essays,* edited by Robert H. Chambers, pp. 57–72. Englewood Cliffs, N.J.: Prentice-Hall Spectrum Book, 1977.

Baxandall, Michael. *Painting and Experience in Fifteenth-Century Italy: A Primer in the Social History of Pictorial Style.* London: Clarendon Press, 1972.

Beebe, Maurice. "The Universe of Roderick Usher." In *Poe: A Collection of Critical Essays.* edited by Robert Regan, pp. 121–33. Englewood Cliffs, N.J.: Prentice-Hall Spectrum Book, 1967.

Bellah, Robert. *Beyond Belief: Essays on Religion in a Post-Traditional World.* New York: Harper & Row, 1970.

———. *The Broken Covenant: American Civil Religion in Time of Trial.* New York: Seabury Press, 1975.

Bercovitch, Sacvan. *The Puritan Origins of the American Self.* New Haven and London: Yale University Press, 1975.

Berdyaev, Nicolas. *The Destiny of Man.* Translated by Natalie Duddington. London: G. Bles, Centenary Press, 1937.

Bloom, Harold. *Wallace Stevens: The Poems of Our Climate.* Ithaca, N.Y.: Cornell University Press, 1977.

Brown, Norman O. *Life Against Death: The Psychoanalytical Meaning of History.* Middletown, Conn.: Wesleyan University Press, 1959.

———. *Love's Body.* New York: Random House, 1966; New York: Vintage Books, 1966.

Brownson, Orestes. *The Convert, or Leaves From My Experience.* Vol. 3 of *The Works of Orestes A. Brownson.* Edited by Henry F. Brownson. Detroit: T. Nourse, 1882–87. Reprint. New York: AMS Press, 1966.

Bultmann, Rudolph. *Primitive Christianity: In Its Contemporary Setting.* Translated by R. H. Fuller. New York: World Publishing Co. Meridian Book, 1956.

Burke, Kenneth. *Language as Symbolic Action: Essays on Life, Literature and Method.* Berkeley, Los Angeles, and London: University of California Press, 1966.

Calhoun, John C. *A Disquisition on Government and A Discourse on the Constitution and Government of the United States.* Vol. 1 of *The Works of John C. Calhoun.* Edited by Richard K. Cralle. New York: D. Appleton & Co., 1881.

———. *The Papers of John C. Calhoun.* Edited by Clyde N. Wilson. Vol. 14. Columbia: University of South Carolina Press, 1981.

Campbell, Joseph. *The Hero With a Thousand Faces.* Princeton: Princeton University Press, 1971.

Caputo, John D. *The Mystical Element in Heidegger's Thought.* N.p., 1978.

Carpenter, Frederic. *American Literature and the Dream.* New York: Philosophical Library, 1955.

———. "The American Myth: Paradise (To Be) Regained." *PMLA* 74 (December 1959): 599–606.

Castro, Americo. *The Spaniards: An Introduction to Their History.* Translated by William F. King and Selma Margareiten. Berkeley and Los Angeles: University of California Press, 1971.

Chase, Richard. *The American Novel and Its Tradition.* Garden City, N.Y.: Doubleday Anchor Books, 1957.

————. "The Stone and the Crucifixion in *Light in August.*" *Kenyon Review* 10 (Autumn 1948): 539–51.

Chauncy, Charles. "Seasonable Thoughts on the State of Religion (1743)." In *The Great Awakening: Documents Illustrating the Crisis and Its Consequences.* Edited by Alan Heimert and Perry Miller. Indianapolis and New York: Bobbs-Merrill Co., 1967.

Clemens, Samuel Langhorne. *Adventures of Huckleberry Finn: An Annotated Text: Backgrounds and Sources, Essays in Criticism.* Edited by Sculley Bradley, Richard Croom Beatty and E. Hudson Long. New York: W. W. Norton & Co. Critical Editions, 1961.

Cooper, James Fenimore, *Works of J. Fenimore Cooper.* 10 vols. New York: P. F. Collier, 1882. Reprint. New York: Greenwood Publishers, 1969.

Cotton, John. "A Reply to Mr. Williams his Examination; and Answer of the Letters Sent to him by John Cotton." Edited by B. J. Lewis Diman. In vol. 2 of *The Complete Writings of Roger Williams.* Providence, R.I.: Narragansett Edition, 1866–74. Reprint. New York: Russell & Russell, 1963.

————. *The Way of Life.* London: L. Fawne & S. Gellibrand, 1641. Microfiche.

de Chardin, Teilhard. *Christianity and Evolution.* Translated by René Hague. New York: Harcourt Brace Jovanovich, 1971.

Crèvecoeur, J. Hector St. John de. *Letters From an American Farmer.* New York: Albert & Charles Boni, 1925.

DeLeon, David. *The American as Anarchist: Reflections on Indigenous Radicalism.* Baltimore and London: Johns Hopkins University Press, 1978.

Dickinson, Emily. *The Complete Poems of Emily Dickinson.* Edited by Thomas H. Johnson. Boston and Toronto: Little, Brown & Co., 1960.

————. *The Letters of Emily Dickinson.* Edited by Thomas H. Johnson. 3 vols. Cambridge: Harvard University Press, Belknap Press, 1958.

Durkheim, Emile. *The Elementary Forms of the Religious Life.* Translated by Joseph Ward Swain. London: George Allen & Unwin, 1915. Reprint. New York: Macmillan, Free Press, 1965.

Ediger, Edward. *Ego and Archetype: Individuation and the Religious Function of the Psyche.* New York: G.P. Putnam's Sons, 1972. Reprint. Baltimore: Penguin Books, 1973.

Edwards, Jonathan. "A Treatise Concerning Religious Affections." In vol. 3 of *The Works of President Edwards.* New York: Jonathan Leavitt & John F. Trow; Boston: Crocker and Brewster; Philadelphia: Geo. S. Appleton, 1843.

Eliade, Mircea. *Images and Symbols: Studies in Religious Symbolism.* Translated by Philip Mairet. New York: Sheed & Ward and London: Harvill Press, 1961; New York: Sheed & Ward Search Book, 1969.

Eliot, T. S. *After Strange Gods: A Primer of Modern Heresy.* London: Faber & Faber, 1934.

————. *The Complete Poems and Plays 1909–1950.* New York: Harcourt, Brace & World, 1952.

————. *The Confidential Clerk.* New York: Harcourt, Brace & Co., 1954.

————. *The Elder Statesman.* London: Faber & Faber, 1959.

————. *The Idea of a Christian Society.* New York: Harcourt, Brace & World, 1940.

————. [An Introduction to *Huckleberry Finn*]. In Samuel Langhorne Clemens, *Adventures of Huckleberry Finn*, edited by Sculley Bradley, Richard Croom Beatty, and E. Hudson Long, pp. 320–27. New York: W. W. Norton Critical Editions, 1961.

————. *Notes Towards a Definition of Culture.* New York: Harcourt, Brace & Co., 1949.

————. "A Prediction in Regard to Three English Authors." In *Henry James: A Collection of Critical Essays.* Edited by Leon Edel, pp. 55–56. Englewood Cliffs, N.J.: Prentice-Hall Spectrum Book, 1963.

————. *The Sacred Wood: Essays on Poetry and Criticism.* London: Metheun & Co., 1920. Reprint. London: Metheun & Co.: New York: Barnes & Noble University Paperbacks, 1960.

————. *Selected Prose of T. S. Eliot.* Edited by Frank Kermode. New York: Harcourt Brace Jovanovich, 1978.

Ellison, Ralph. *Invisible Man.* New York: Random House, 1952.

————. *Shadow and Act.* New York: Random House, 1964.

Emerson, Ralph Waldo. *The Complete Works of Ralph Waldo Emerson.* Edited by Edward Waldo Emerson. 12 vols. Boston: Houghton Mifflin & Co., 1903–04.

Faulkner, William. *Light in August.* New York: H. Smith & R. Haas, 1932. Reprint. New York: Modern Library, 1950.

Ferenczi, Sándor. "Thalassa: A Theory of Genitality." Translated by Henry Alden Bunker, Jr. *The Psychoanalytical Quarterly* 2 (1933): 361–403; 3 (1934): 1–29, 200–22.

Fiedler, Leslie. *The Collected Essays of Leslie Fiedler.* Vol. 1. New York: Stein & Day, 1971.

————. *An End to Innocence: Essays on Culture and Politics.* Boston: Beacon Press, 1955.

———. *Love and Death in the American Novel.* New York: Criterion Books, 1960. Reprint. Cleveland: World Publishing Co. Meridian Books, 1962.

Fitzgerald, F. Scott. *The Crack-up.* Edited by Edmund Wilson. New York: New Directions, 1945. Reprint. New York: New Directions, Paperbook, 1956.

———. *The Great Gatsby.* New York: Charles Scribner's Sons, 1925. Reprint. New York: Charles Scribner's Sons, 1953.

———. *The Letters of F. Scott Fitzgerald.* Edited by Andrew Turnbull. New York: Charles Scribner's Sons, 1963.

Ford, Thomas W. *Heaven Beguiles the Tired: Death in the Poetry of Emily Dickinson.* University, Ala.: University of Alabama Press, 1966.

Forster, E. M. *Aspects of the Novel.* New York: Harcourt, Brace & Co., 1927. Reprint. New York: Harcourt, Brace & World, 1954.

Freud, Sigmund. *Civilization and Its Discontents.* Vol. 21 of *The Standard Edition of the Complete Psychological Works of Sigmund Freud,* edited by James Strachey and translated by Joan Riviere. London: Hogarth Press, 1930.

———. *Totem and Taboo and Other Works.* Vol. 13 of *The Standard Edition of the Complete Psychological Works of Sigmund Freud,* edited by James Strachey and translated by Joan Riviere. London: Hogarth Press, 1955.

———. "The 'Uncanny.' " In vol. 4 of *Collected Papers,* edited by Ernest Jones and translated by Joan Riviere. London: Hogarth Press and The Institute of Psychoanalysis, 1924–50. Reprint. New York: Basic Books, 1959.

Friedman, Albert. "The Usable Myth: The Legends of Modern Mythmakers." In *American Folk Legend,* edited by Wayland Hand, pp. 37–46. Berkeley and Los Angeles: University of California Press, 1971.

Gadamer, Hans-Georg. *Truth and Method.* Edited and translated by Garrett Barden and John Cumming. New York: Seabury Press, 1975.

Haller, William. *Foxe's Book of Martyrs and The Elect Nation.* London: Jonathan Cape, 1963.

Halliburton, David. *Edgar Allan Poe: A Phenomenological View.* Princeton: Princeton University Press, 1973.

Halverson, John. "The Shadow in *Moby Dick." American Quarterly* 15 (Fall 1963): 436–46.

Hamilton, Alexander. *The Works of Alexander Hamilton.* Edited by John C. Hamilton. Vol. 2. New York: Charles S. Francis & Co., 1851.

Harrison, Jane. *Epilegomena to the Study of Greek Religion and Themis: A Study of the Social Origins of Greek Religion.* Cambridge: Cambridge University Press, 1912, 1921. Reprint. New Hyde Park, N.Y.: Basic Books, 1962.

Hassan, Ihab. *Radical Innocence: Studies in the Contemporary American Novel.* Princeton: Princeton University Press, 1961.

Hawthorne, Nathaniel. *The Scarlet Letter and Other Tales of the Puritans.* Edited by Harry Levin. Boston: Houghton Mifflin Riverside Editions, 1960.

————. *A Wonder Book and Tanglewood Tales.* Vol. 7 of *The Centenary Edition of the Works of Nathaniel Hawthorne,* edited by William Charvat et. al. Columbus: Ohio State University Press, 1972.

Heidegger, Martin. "What is Metaphysics?" Translated by R. F. C. Hull and Alan Crick. *In Martin Heidegger: Existence and Being,* edited by Werner Brock, pp. 346–53. Chicago: Henry Regnery Co., 1949. Reprint. Gateway Edition, 1967.

Hines, Thomas J. *The Later Poetry of Wallace Stevens.* Lewisburg, Pa.: Bucknell University Press and London: Associated University Presses, 1976.

Hoffman, Daniel. *Form and Fable in American Fiction.* New York: Oxford University Press, 1961.

————. *Poe Poe Poe Poe Poe Poe Poe.* New York: Doubleday & Co., 1972; Anchor Press, 1973.

Hofstadter, Richard. *American Political Tradition: And the Men Who Made It.* New York: Alfred A. Knopf, 1948; New York: Vintage Books, 1948.

Holman, Hugh. "The Unity in Faulkner's *Light in August.*" *PMLA* 73 (March 1958): 155–66.

Hutchinson, Thomas. "The Address of the Governor." In *The Briefs of the American Revolution: Constitutional Arguments Between Thomas Hutchinson, Governor of Massachusetts Bay, and James Bowdoin for the Council and John Adams for the House of Representatives,* edited by John Phillip Reid. New York and London: New York University Press, 1981.

Irving, Washington. *The Complete Tales of Washington Irving.* Garden City, N.Y.: Doubleday & Co., 1975.

Jaffé, Aniela. "Symbolism in the Visual Arts." In *Man and His Symbols,* edited by Carl G. Jung, pp. 255–322. London: Aldus Books, 1964; New York: Dell Laurel Edition, 1968.

James, Henry. *The Ambassadors.* Edited by Leon Edel. Boston: Houghton Mifflin Riverside Editions, 1960.

————. *The Notebooks of Henry James.* Edited by F. O. Matthiessen and Kenneth E. Murdock. New York: George Braziller, 1947.

James, Henry, Sr. *Society: The Redeemed Form of Man, and The Earnest of God's Omnipotence in Human Nature: Affirmed in Letters to a Friend.* Boston: Houghton, Osgood & Co., 1879.

James, William. *The Varieties of Religious Experience: A Study in Human Nature.* New York and London: Longmans, Green & Co., 1902. Reprint. New York: New American Library, Mentor Book, 1958.

Johnson, Edward. *Johnson's Wonder-Working Providence 1628–1651.* Edited by J. Franklin Jameson. New York: Barnes & Noble, 1946.

Johnson, Samuel. *A Journey to the Western Islands of Scotland in 1773.* London: Paisley, A. Gardner, 1908.

Juliana of Norwich. *Revelations of Divine Love Shewed to Mother Juliana of Norwich 1373.* London: Kegan Paul, Trench, Trubner & Co., 1902. Microfiche.

Jung, Carl G. *The Portable Jung.* Edited by Joseph Campbell and translated by R. F. C. Hull. New York: Viking Press, 1971.

———. *Psyche and Symbol: A Selection From the Writings of C. G. Jung.* Edited by Violet S. deLaszlo and translated by R. F. C. Hull and Cary Baynes. Garden City, N.Y.: Doubleday Anchor Books, 1958.

Kaul, A. N. *The American Vision: Actual and Ideal Society in Nineteenth-Century Fiction.* New Haven and London: Yale University Press, 1963.

Knapp, Bettina A. *Jean Racine: Myths and Renewal in Modern Theater.* University, Ala.: Alabama University Press, 1971.

Lawrence, D. H. *Studies in Classic American Literature.* New York: Thomas Seltzer, 1923. Reprint. New York: Doubleday Anchor Books, 1951.

Levin, Harry. *The Power of Blackness: Hawthorne, Poe, Melville.* New York: Alfred A. Knopf, 1958; New York: Vintage Books, 1958.

Lévi-Strauss, Claude. *Totemism.* Translated by Rodney Needham. Boston: Beacon Press, 1963.

Lewis, R. W. B. *The American Adam: Innocence, Tragedy and Tradition in the Nineteenth Century.* Chicago: University of Chicago Press, 1955; Phoenix Books, 1955.

———. "Days of Wrath and Laughter." In *Trials of the Word: Essays in American Literature and the Humanistic Tradition,* pp. 184–236. New Haven and London: Yale University Press, 1965.

Lynn, Kenneth. *The Dream of Success: A Study of the Modern American Imagination.* Boston: Little, Brown & Co., 1955.

———. "Welcome Back from the Raft, Huck Honey!" *American Scholar* 46 (Summer 1977): 338–50.

Madison, James. "Number 10" and "Number 51." In *The Federalist,* edited by Benjamin Fletcher Wright, pp. 129–36, 355–59. Cambridge: Harvard University Press, Belknap Press, 1961.

Male, Roy R. *Hawthorne's Tragic Vision*. Austin: University of Texas Press, 1957.

Marx, Karl. "On the Jewish Question." In *The Marx-Engels Reader*, edited by Robert C. Tucker, pp. 24–51. New York: W. W. Norton & Co., 1972.

Marx, Leo. *The Machine in the Garden: Technology and the Pastoral Ideal in America*. New York: Oxford University Press, 1964.

Mather, Cotton. *Bonifacius . . . To Do Good*. Edited by Josphine K. Piercy. Boston: Samuel Gerrish, 1710. Reprint. Gainesville, Fla.: Scholars' Facsimiles & Reprints, 1967.

———. *Magnalia Christi Americana*. Edited by Thomas Robbins. 2 vols. 1852. Reprint. New York: Russell & Russell, 1967.

———. *The Wonders of the Invisible World: Being an Account of the Tryals of Several Witches Lately Executed in New-England*. London: John Russell Smith, 1862. Microfiche.

Matthiessen, F. O. *American Renaissance: Art and Expression in the Age of Emerson and Whitman*. New York: Oxford University Press, 1949.

May, Rollo. *Love and Will*. New York: W. W. Norton & Co., 1969.

Mead, Sidney. *The Lively Experiment: The Shaping of Christianity in America*. New York: Harper & Row, 1963.

Meckier, Jerome. "Burden's Complaint: The Disintegrated Personality as Theme and Style in Robert Penn Warren's *All the King's Men*." In *Twentieth Century Interpretations of All the King's Men: A Collection of Critical Essays*, edited by Robert H. Chambers, pp. 57–72. Englewood Cliffs, N.J.: Prentice-Hall Spectrum Book, 1977.

Melville, Herman. *Moby Dick or, The Whale*. Edited by Alfred Kazin. Boston: Houghton Mifflin Riverside Editions, 1956.

Miller, J. Hillis. "Wallace Stevens' Poetry of Being." In *Modern American Poetry: Essays in Criticism*, edited by Jerome Mazzaro, pp. 93–115. New York: David McKay Co., 1970.

Miller, Perry. *The New England Mind: The Seventeenth Century*. New York: Macmillan Co., 1939. Reprint. Boston: Beacon Press, 1961.

Mizener, Arthur. *The Far Side of Paradise: A Biography of F. Scott Fitzgerald*. Boston: Houghton Mifflin Co., 1951. Reprint. New York: Vintage Books, 1959.

Morgan, Edward. *The Puritan Dilemma*. Boston: Little, Brown & Co., 1958.

———. *Visible Saints: The History of a Puritan Idea*. Ithaca, N.Y.: Cornell University Press, 1965.

Morris, Wright. *The Territory Ahead.* New York: Atheneum, 1963.

Neumann, Erich. *The Origins and History of Consciousness.* Translated by R. F. C. Hull. Princeton: Princeton University Press, 1954.

Nicholson, Marjorie Hope. *The Breaking of the Circle: Studies in the Effect of the "New Science" upon Seventeenth-Century Poetry.* New York: Columbia University Press, 1960.

Niebuhr, Reinhold. *The Irony of American History.* New York: Charles Scribner's Sons, 1952.

Niebuhr, Richard. *The Social Sources of Denominationalism.* Cleveland: World Publishing Co., 1929. Reprint. Hamden, Conn.: Shoe String Press, 1954.

Paine, Thomas. *The Life and Major Writings of Thomas Paine.* Edited by Philip S. Foner. New York: Citadel Press, 1945.

Palmer, Richard. *Hermeneutics.* Evanston, Ill.: Northwestern University Press, 1969.

Paz, Octavio. *The Labyrinth of Solitude: Life and Thought in Mexico.* Translated by Lysander Kemp. New York: Grove Press and London: Evergreen Books, 1961.

Pearce, Roy Harvey. *The Continuity of American Poetry.* Princeton: Princeton University Press, 1961.

Poe, Edgar Allan. *The Complete Works of Edgar Allan Poe.* Edited by James A. Harrison. 17 vols. New York: Thomas Y. Crowell Co., 1902.

Poulet, Georges. *The Metamorphoses of the Circle.* Translated by Carley Dawson and Elliott Coleman. Baltimore: Johns Hopkins University Press, 1966.

Pseudo-Dionysius Areopagite. *The Divine Names and Mystical Theology.* Edited and translated by John D. Jones. Milwaukee: Marquette University Press, 1980.

Raglan, Fitz Roy Somerset. *The Hero: A Study in Tradition, Myth and Drama.* London: Metheun & Co., 1936. Reprint. New York: Vintage Books, 1956.

Rank, Otto. *The Myth of the Birth of the Hero and Other Writings.* Edited by Philip Freund and translated by F. Robbins and Smith Ely Jelliffe. New York: The Journal of Nervous and Mental Disease Publishing Co., 1914. Reprint. New York: Vintage Books, 1959.

Ricoeur, Paul. *The Conflict of Interpretations: Essays in Hermeneutics.* Evanston, Ill.: Northwestern University Press, 1974.

———. "Hermeneutic of the Idea of Revelation." Paper delivered at the Graduate Theological Seminary, February 1977, Berkeley, California.

———. *The Symbolism of Evil.* Translated by Emerson Buchanan. New York: Harper & Row, 1967. Reprint. Boston: Beacon Press, 1969.

Róheim, Géza. *The Gates of the Dream.* New York: International Universities Press, 1952.

Ruoff, James. "Humpty Dumpty and *All the King's Men*: A Note on Robert Penn Warren's Teleology." In *Twentieth Century Interpretations of All the King's Men: A Collection of Critical Essays,* edited by Robert H. Chambers, pp. 84–92. Englewood Cliffs, N.J.: Prentice-Hall Spectrum Book, 1977.

Sanford, Charles. *The Quest for Paradise: Europe and the American Moral Imagination.* Urbana: University of Illinois Press, 1961.

Schaff, Philip. *America: A Sketch of the Political, Social, and Religious Character of the United States of America.* New York: Charles Scribner, 1855.

Shils, Edward. *Center and Periphery: Essays in Macrasociology.* Chicago: University of Chicago Press, 1975.

Simonson, Harold Peter. *The Closed Frontier: Studies in Classic American Literary Tragedy.* New York: Holt, Rinehart & Winston, 1970.

Simpson, Alan. *Puritanism in Old and New England.* Chicago: University of Chicago Press, 1955.

Slater, Philip. *The Pursuit of Loneliness: American Culture at the Breaking Point.* Boston: Beacon Press, 1970.

Smith, Henry Nash. Introduction to *Adventures of Huckleberry Finn,* by Mark Twain. Boston: Houghton Mifflin Co. Riverside Editions, 1958.

———. *Virgin Land: The American West as Symbol and Myth.* Cambridge: Harvard University Press, 1950.

Stevens, Wallace. *The Collected Poems of Wallace Stevens.* New York: Alfred A. Knopf, 1954.

———. *Letters: Selected and Edited by Holly Stevens.* New York: Alfred A. Knopf, 1966.

———. *Opus Posthumous: Poems, Plays, Prose.* Edited by Samuel French Morse. New York: Alfred A. Knopf, 1957.

———. *The Palm at the End of the Mind: Selected Poems and a Play.* New York: Alfred A. Knopf, 1971; New York: Vintage Books, 1972.

Tanner, Tony. *City of Words: American Fiction 1950–1970.* New York: Harper & Row, 1971.

Tate, Allen. "Our Cousin, Mr. Poe." In *Collected Essays,* pp. 455–71. Denver: Alan Swallow, 1959.

Teilhard, Pierre de Chardin. *Christianity and Evolution.* Translated by René Hague. New York: Harcourt Brace Jovanovich, 1971.

Thoreau, Henry David. *Journal.* Edited by Branford and Francis H. Allen. Boston: Houghton Mifflin Co., 1949.

———. *Walden and Civil Disobedience: Authoritative Texts, Background, Reviews and Essays in Criticism.* Edited by Owen Thomas. New York: W. W. Norton & Co. Critical Editions, 1966.

Tocqueville, Alexis Charles de. *Democracy in America.* Edited by Phillips Bradley. 2 vols. New York: Alfred A. Knopf, 1945.

Trilling, Lionel. *The Liberal Imagination: Essays on Literature and Society.* New York: Viking Press, 1950. Reprint. Garden City, N.Y.: Doubleday Anchor Books, 1957.

Vernon, John. *The Garden and the Map: Schizophrenia in Twentieth-Century Literature and Culture.* Urbana: University of Illinois Press, 1973.

Vico, Giovanni Battista. *The New Science.* Translated from 3d edition (1744) by Thomas Goddard Bergin and Max Harold Fisch. Ithaca, N.Y.: Cornell University Press, 1948.

Warren, Robert Penn. *All the King's Men.* New York: Harcourt, Brace & Co., 1946.

Weber, Max. *The Protestant Ethic and the Spirit of Capitalism.* Translated by Talcott Parsons. New York: Charles Scribner's Sons, 1958.

———. *The Sociology of Religion.* Translated by Ephraim Fischoff. Boston: Beacon Press, 1963.

Wheelwright, Philip. *Metaphor and Reality.* Bloomington: Indiana University Press, 1962.

Whicher, George. *This Was a Poet: A Critical Biography of Emily Dickinson.* New York: Charles Scribner's Sons, 1938. Reprint. Ann Arbor, Mich.: University of Michigan Press Ann Arbor Paperbacks, 1957.

Whitman, Walt. *Leaves of Grass: Authoritative Texts, Prefaces, Whitman on His Art, Criticism.* Edited by Sculley Bradley and Harold W. Blodgett. New York: W. W. Norton & Co. Critical Editions, 1973.

Wilbur, Richard. "The House of Poe." In *Poe: A Collection of Critical Essays,* edited by Robert Regan, pp. 98–120. Englewood Cliffs, N.J.: Prentice-Hall Spectrum Book, 1967.

Williams, Raymond. *Culture and Society: 1780–1950.* New York: Columbia University Press; London: Chatto and Windus, 1958. Reprint. New York: Harper & Row Torchbooks, 1966.

Williams, Roger. *The Bloody Tenent of Persecution.* Vol. 3 of *The Complete Writings of Roger Williams.* Providence, R.I.: Narragansett Edition, 1866–74: Reprint. New York: Russell & Russell, 1963.

Wilner, Eleanor R. "The Invisible Black Thread: Identity and Nonentity in *Invisible Man.*" *College Language Association Journal* 13 (March 1979): 242–57.

Winthrop, John. "A Model of Christian Charity." In *Winthrop Papers*

1623–1630. Vol. 2. N.p.: Massachusetts Historical Society, 1931. Microfiche.

Wolters, Clifton, ed. *The Cloud of Unknowing.* Baltimore: Penguin Books, 1961.

Young, Philip. "Adventures of Huckleberry Finn." In *Ernest Hemingway: A Reconsideration.* University Park: Pennsylvania State University Press, 1966.

Index

Adam, 165 n.21
Adams, Henry, 50–51
Adams, John, 39, 43, 49
Agenbite of inwit: in Puritanism, 31; in Dickinson, 125, 127
Alcott, Bronson, 46
American dream: of democracy, 15; of success, 15, 157; of utopia, 15
American Gothic: in Dickinson, 122–23, 125; in *Light in August*, 112; in Poe, 60, 62, 64; reappropriation of symbolic language in, 52–54, 62; use of perverse in, 53–54
American Revolution: and antenomianism, 40–41; and Enlightenment, 39; Freudian interpretation of, 41; and separation and reparation, 38–44
American writer: and charter of belief, 52; heritage of separation for, 52; and reappropriation of Gothic, 53; style as means of autonomy for, 15–16
Anderson, Sherwood, 113
Antenomianism: and American Revolution, 40–41; defined, 40; and myth of paradise regained, 46; and Puritan conversion, 40
Antinomianism: in American ideology and culture, 29, 34–37; and American Revolution, 41; of Anne Hutchinson, 34; effect of, on American writer, 52; in *Huckleberry Finn*, 97; and myth of paradise regained, 46; and outlaw, 36; in *The Scarlet Letter*, 75
Apollo, 24, 108, 138
Ariadne, 72, 100, 104
Arnold, Matthew, 24
Atomism of American society, 48

Attenuation of charisma, 36; and Calvin, 36; and Congregationalism, 36; U.S. Constitution as, 43; and genesis of American, 36–38, 47; and Luther, 36; romantic reaction to, 44–45
Auto-machia, 31; in Dickinson, 125; and Puritanism, 31; in *The Scarlet Letter*, 74
Autonomianism: in American ideology and culture, 29; defined, 29; effect of, on American writer, 52; of Jefferson, 34; in myth of paradise regained, 46; of Paine, 34; and Puritanism, 39; and transcendentalism, 46
Autonomy: dream of, become nightmare of anonymity in *Invisible Man*, 153–59; of self and commitment to other in *The Ambassadors*, 104; style as a manifestation of, 15–16

Bachofen, Johann Jacob, 164 n.1
Baumbach, Jonathan, 168 n.1
Baxandall, Michael, 76
Beebe, Maurice, 63–64
Bellah, Robert, 37
Bercovitch, Sacvan, 18, 31
Berdyaev, Nicolas, 21
Blake, William, 24
Bloom, Harold, 168 n.29
Bradley, F. H., 167 n.11
Brown, Norman O., 144–45, 163 n.23
Brownson, Orestes, 18, 46–47, 147
Bultmann, Rudolph, 76, 107
Burke, Kenneth, 144–46

Calhoun, John, 48
Calvin, John, 36
Campbell, Joseph, 86

181

Ptolomey, 23
Puritanism: and agenbite of inwit, 31;
and attenuation of charisma, 36; and
auto-machia, 31; and autonomianism, 39; and call to community, 31; as
community of crisis, 31; and covenant, 34; and Dickinson, 123–24,
129; and Eliot, 137–38; in *Moby
Dick*, 83–84; and narcissism, 18, 31;
and *The Scarlet Letter*, 71, 75–76; and
separation and reparation, 29–37

Raglan, Lord, 86
Rank, Otto, 86
Reformation: and discovery of America, 40; and dissociation of sensibility, 24; and evolution of consciousness, 29
Reparation: as becoming in Eliot, 137;
and effect of U.S. Constitution, 43;
death as, in *Moby Dick*, 83; Judaic-
Christian myth as, 20; Puritan theocracy as, 34; ritual and myth as, 22;
social sanction as, 75–76; for unlived
life in *The Ambassadors*, 98, 103
Ricoeur, Paul: hermeneutics, 166 n.14;
isolation and guilty conscience, 75;
myth as recovery of oneness, 21;
reappropriation of symbol from
myth, 139; symbolic language as restoration of participation in things, 51
Rite of passage: aborted, in *The Scarlet
Letter*, 70–71; in *The Ambassadors*,
98–106; and denitiation, 86; existentialist and private, 24–25; as flight
from self, 85–88; in *The Great
Gatsby*, 106–11; in *Huckleberry Finn*,
88–97; in *Light in August*, 111–18; in
Moby Dick, 87; in *The Pioneers* and
The Prairie, 87; as process in *Invisible
Man*, 154; as resolution of dialectic of
innocence and memory, 15; as return
to womb, 22; in *The Scarlet Letter*,
68–69, 72, 75, 87; as symbol of separation and reparation, 27, 85–88; in
Walden, 87
Róheim, Geza, 161 n.20
Romanticism: and dissociation of sensibility, 24; and Enlightenment, 45;
and evolution of consciousness, 29;

reaction of, to attenuation of charisma, 44; and symbolic language,
53–54; and transcendentalism, 45–48
Rousseau, Jean Jacques, 41
Ruoff, James, 168 n.1

Sacred: in Eliot, 134–37; medieval ca-
thedral as center of, 23; in *The Scarlet
Letter*, 68–69, 71; still point in *Moby
Dick*, 80
Saint-Gaudens, Augustus, 50
Sanford, Charles, 16
Separation: concluding note in *The
Ambassadors*, 106; as determination
of nationhood, 30; effect of, on
American writer, 52; of individual
from community, 46; intrinsic to
American experience, 28–30, 43, 133;
knife of, 48; necessary for individual
identity, 148; resolution of colonies'
conflict with Parliament, 40; of self
from society, 51
Separation and reparation, symbolic
pattern of: in American history and
ideology, 28–51; in American Puritanism, 29–37; in American Revolution, 38–44; in Civil War, 48–49;
defined, 19–26; and existentialism,
24; and individuation, 22; and Industrial Revolution, 49–51; and myth of
the Fall, 19–20; and ontogeny of
man, 20–21; and phylogeny of mankind, 21–23; and Protestantism, 32;
and reconstruction, 49–51; and rite of
passage, 85–88; and romanticism,
44–49; summarized, 25- 26; in Western civilization, 23–26. *See also* initial
entries under Clemens; Dickin-
son, E.; Eliot, T. S.; Ellison; Faulkner; Fitzgerald; Hawthorne; James,
H.; Melville; Poe; Stevens; Thoreau;
Warren, R. P.; Whitman
Separatists, 29, 33
Sewall, Samuel, 50
Shakespeare, William, 97, 132
Shelley, Percy Bysshe, 142
Shils, Edward, 36
Simonson, Harold, 95
Slater, Philip, 50
Smith, Henry Nash, 14, 16